W9-ARI-018
01/2021

PALM BEACH COUNTY
LIBRARY SYSTEM
3650 Summit Boulevard
West Palm Beach, FL 33406-4198

TARGET RICH ENVIRONMENT

**VOLUME
2**

To purchase any of these titles in e-book form, please go to www.baen.com.

TARGET RICH ENVIRONMENT

VOLUME 2

A Collection by
LARRY CORREIA

BAEN

TARGET RICH ENVIRONMENT: VOLUME 2

This is a work of fiction. All the characters and events portrayed in this book are fictional, and any resemblance to real people or incidents is purely coincidental.

Copyright © 2019 by Larry Correia

A Baen Books Original

Baen Publishing Enterprises
P.O. Box 1403
Riverdale, NY 10471
www.baen.com

ISBN 13: 978-1-9821-2422-9

Cover art by Kurt Miller

First printing, December 2019

Distributed by Simon & Schuster
1230 Avenue of the Americas
New York, NY 10020

Library of Congress Control Number: 2018023358

Printed in the United States of America

10 9 8 7 6 5 4 3 2 1

Additional Copyright Acknowledgements:

"Tokyo Raider" by Larry Correia. Copyright © 2014 by Larry Correia.
First appeared in *The Baen Big Book of Monsters*, published by Baen Books.

"Testimony of the Traitor Ratul" by Larry Correia. Copyright © 2019 by Larry
Correia. First appeared on www.baen.com.

"Shooter Ready" by Larry Correia. Copyright © 2016 by Larry Correia.
First appeared in *Galactic Games*, published by Baen Books.

"Three Sparks" by Larry Correia. Copyright © 2017 Twentieth Century Fox
Film Corporation. All Rights Reserved. Reprinted by permission of Twentieth
Century Fox Film Corporation. First appeared in *Predator: If It Bleeds*.

"Reckoning Day" by Larry Correia. Copyright © 2013 by Larry Correia.
First appeared in *The Monster Hunter International Employee's Handbook
and Roleplaying Game*, published by Hero Games.

"Weaponized Hell" by Larry Correia & Jonathan Maberry. Copyright © 2016
by Larry Correia and Jonathan Maberry. First appeared in *Urban Allies: Ten
Brand-New Collaborative Stories*.

"Son of Fire, Son of Thunder" by Larry Correia & Steve Diamond. Copyright
© 2011 by Larry Correia and Steve Diamond. First appeared in *The Crimson
Pact: Volume 2*.

"Episode 22" by Larry Correia. Copyright © 2017 Twentieth Century Fox
Film Corporation. All Rights Reserved. Reprinted by permission of Twentieth
Century Fox Film Corporation. First appeared in *Aliens: Bug Hunt*.

"Absence of Light" by Larry Correia. Copyright © 2016 by Larry Correia.
First appeared in *V Wars: Night Terrors*.

"Psych Eval" by Larry Correia. Copyright © 2017 by Larry Correia and
Jonathan Maberry. First appeared in *Joe Ledger: Unstoppable*.

"Musings of a Hermit" by Larry Correia. Copyright © 2017 by Larry Correia.
First appeared in *Forged in Blood*, published by Baen Books.

"Instruments of War" by Larry Correia. Copyright © 2013 by Larry Correia.
First appeared in *Instruments of War*, published by Skull Island Expeditions.

"Murder of Manatees" by Larry Correia. Copyright © 2018 by Larry Correia.
First appeared as an audiobook produced by Audible Studios.

ACKKNOWLEGEMENTS

We had a contest on my blog, Monster Hunter Nation, to come up with a name for this collection. I want to thank Logan Guthmiller for suggesting *Target Rich Environment*. It was a great idea, and it hearkened back to the opening quote used in my first novel.

I also want to acknowledge all of the editors from the various anthologies these stories were originally published in. Gathering a bunch of authors together for an anthology is like herding cats, and editors often have a thankless job.

CONTENTS

TARGET RICH ENVIRONMENT

VOLUME
2

TOKYO RAIDER

"Tokyo Raider" originally appeared in The Baen Big Book of Monsters, *edited by Hank Davis, published by Baen Books in 2014. This story is set in my Grimnoir universe, where magic appeared in the 1850s and our timeline diverged from there. "Tokyo Raider" takes place about twenty years after the novel* Warbound, *so if you've not read that trilogy yet you might want to skip this one because there are a few spoilers . . . and a whole lot of giant robot fights.*

Adak, Alaska
1954

"YOU WANTED TO SEE ME, sir?"

The colonel of the 2nd Raider Battalion was pouring himself a cup of coffee and looking a bit more surly than usual. He returned the salute and gestured at the chair on the other side of his desk. "Take a seat, Lieutenant."

The building was quiet. The office walls around them were covered in maps of the Imperium. If—or more likely, *when*—there was war with the Japanese, this place was going to be hopping, but until then the Marines on the island of Adak had to watch and wait, train, freeze, and shoo caribou out of the barracks. The colonel was normally in a rotten mood before he had his coffee, so Joe got ready for another ass-chewing. He was the new guy, and he didn't fit in. Those made for a bad combination.

Luckily, the colonel got right down to business. "We got a priority magical transmission. Since everybody forgets about us stationed out here on the ass end of nowhere, the commo boys get excited when their window actually starts talking to them. They woke me up, telling me that the Commander in Chief of the Pacific Fleet himself had special orders for one of my butter bars."

So much for keeping his head down.

"Turns out my new junior platoon leader is some big shot back in the states. I knew you were a Heavy. File says you're really good at manipulating gravity, and you're qualified on a Heavy Suit, but nobody told me you were supposed to be some sort of genius wizard."

"I wouldn't say genius. It's all in my file. I have a degree in magical engineering from MIT and a master's from the Otis Institute."

"You went to college at what, twelve?"

"I graduated when I was nineteen, then I joined the Marine Corps, sir."

"Why the hell you ended up . . . Never mind. Whatever you've done impressed somebody. Congratulations, Lieutenant, you're going to Japan."

That was certainly unexpected. "Japan, sir?"

"Tokyo, to be exact. You'll be leaving immediately. An airship is being prepped now."

Joe took a deep breath. The ceasefire had held for a few years. There'd been some skirmishes and the usual saber rattling, but the Japanese had been too busy fighting the Soviets to cause any trouble for the American forces in the Pacific. The peace process must have broken down. If they were sending Raiders to Tokyo, that meant a full-blown war. A Marine Raider's job was to be dropped behind enemy lines to cause as much chaos as possible. Tokyo wasn't just behind their lines: it was the enemy heart. Joe wasn't sure if he was scared, eager, or a combination of both, but he'd signed up, so he'd do whatever needed to be done. "Are we jumping in?"

"I believe you'll just be landing at the air station."

Now he was really confused, but Raiders were trained to be flexible. "My platoon is ready for anything."

"No, Lieutenant, they're not. Your platoon is made up of Marines who are still trying to decide if they trust their newly assigned half-Jap officer to fight the Japanese. Frankly, I'm not sure if they'd follow you or frag you. Can you blame them? You speak the enemy's language, know their culture, and you even kind of look like one of them. I've heard of black Irish, but never yellow Irish."

"The men don't know if they should stick with rice or potato jokes, sir, but I carry on."

"Don't be a wiseass. Hell, I've been told you've got kanji brands on your body like one of their Iron Guards."

"No, sir. Those spells are a family recipe. They were inspected and approved by the War Department when I joined."

"I've been trying to decide what to do with you."

Joe appreciated the colonel's honesty. "My mother was born in the Imperium, but she was a *slave*. I may have been too young to make the last war, but I hate the Imperium as much as any man who's fought them, and I'll be here for the next."

The colonel sighed. "I believe you, but I'm not some dumb private who's going to be tempted to roll a grenade into your tent while you're sleeping because he's thinking he's doing his country a favor. I've no doubt you'll prove yourself to them eventually, but luckily, this assignment is just you."

There were limits to a Raider's flexibility, and Joe wasn't feeling up to invading the Imperium by himself. "I'm kind of hazy on the nature of my orders."

"Me, too. Per the peace treaty, you're to be a military observer. I neglected to mention that the radio man was mistaken. Turns out it wasn't the Commander in Chief of the Pacific Fleet calling, but *the* Commander in Chief."

"The president?"

"Yeah. I even voted for the man. I'll tell you, that was an unexpected way to start my day. I was a little concerned about being told to send one of my junior officers off by himself to the Imperium capital with orders to *help* those bastards, but the president spoke rather highly of your aptitude. How come you never told anybody you're buddies with President Stuyvesant?"

"Our families are acquainted."

"He said that you would be too humble, but that you were the best man for the job. That sounds fairly acquainted to me."

"Well, the First Lady does insist I call her Aunt Faye."

"Uh-huh . . ." The colonel took a drink of his coffee. "He said your presence as an observer was requested by the high commander of the entire Imperium military, General Toru Tokugawa. You know, the man in charge of our enemies, who rules over an evil empire with an iron fist. You're supposed to do him a favor for diplomacy's sake. I take it you're acquainted with him, too?"

He shrugged. "He and my father once worked together. It's complicated."

"Well, then, I can't imagine why your men don't have complete faith in you. Good luck in Japan, Lieutenant Sullivan."

Tokyo, Japan

IMMEDIATELY AFTER LANDING, Joe Sullivan had been met with a lot of ceremony by the Imperium Diplomatic Corps and then picked up by an armored car and some Iron Guard who didn't seem nearly so big on polite conversation. The Imperium elites had driven him directly to an ancient palace surrounded by cherry trees. The trip confirmed that Japan really was as pretty as Mom had made it out to be. They'd escorted him through the castle, to an ultramodern military command bunker beneath it. Then he'd stood there, waiting in his dress uniform, being eyeballed by a bunch of Japanese soldiers as they talked all sorts of shit about the *gaijin*, until somebody who'd been briefed told those idiots that he spoke Japanese, and they'd shut up.

The Imperium didn't seem to be hiding anything. The red markings on the wall maps told him that the Russians were pushing back against the Imperium in Asia. The unit markers were either true, or it was an elaborate setup for his benefit. Either way he memorized every unit and location so he could put it all in his report when he got home and let the intel types decide.

There was only one marker he didn't understand. It was shaped like a dragon, was red like the rest of the communist forces, and it had to represent something naval because it was tracking up the east coast of the island, heading for Tokyo Bay, and several Japanese naval units had been destroyed along its path, including an entire carrier battle group. Several submarines were marked as missing. The kanji on the marker identified it with the code name: *Gorilla Whale.*

The Imperium were big on treating guests with respect, so the lack of respect had to be meant as an insult. After half an hour of waiting, without being offered so much as a chair, there was some shouting in the hall. Several military aides fled as a big, stocky, thickset Japanese man stomped into the bunker. He'd heard a lot about Toru Tokugawa growing up. Even though they'd been opponents, his dad had held more respect for this Imperium warrior than he did for most of the men supposedly on their side. The recent war had proven him to be one of best tacticians in the world, and in his youth he'd been one of the strongest Brutes to ever live.

Toru Tokugawa didn't disappoint in person.

"Damn those wretched Soviet pig dogs!" the general shouted as he stormed across the command center. The rest of the Imperium army staff remained quiet and polite as expected, as Tokugawa, on the other hand, was not. "Stalin has no honor!" He punched one of the bunker's walls, cracking the concrete. Tokugawa may have been in his fifties, but he still possessed an impressive connection to burn Power like that. "They fight like cowards!"

As their supreme commander flipped over a map table, the Japanese officers exchanged nervous glances. Having a visitor witness their leader acting in such a passionate manner was a loss of face. Tokugawa stood there, seething and glowering at the shower of falling papers, until one of the staffers broke the awkward silence. "Pardon me, General, the American observer you requested has arrived."

"Already? That was fast . . ." He composed himself, adjusted his uniform, then turned around and switched to English. "Present our guest."

"Second Lieutenant Joseph Sullivan of the United States Marine Corps," announced one of the Iron Guard.

"General Tokugawa." Sullivan bowed, careful to keep the gesture to the appropriate respectful level of a visiting dignitary of *equal* stature.

Tokugawa snorted. "You look more like your father than I expected. American Heavies are all so blocky and . . . corn fed . . . You're not quite so doughy as most of your fat countrymen. You could almost pass for a proper Imperium soldier, if you'd been lucky and taken a bit more after your mother, that is."

"I'd suggest leaving my parents out of this," Joe stated.

"Why would I do that? Your parents are the reason I asked for you. If I were to inadvertently insult them, what would you do about it?"

"I know you changed a lot of the Imperium's laws after the Chairman died, especially the ones about torture, slavery, and experimenting on prisoners, which all reasonable men can appreciate, but you've still got that thing where you can duel over insults, right?"

The Iron Guards shared nervous glances, but Tokugawa smiled. "Ha! Excellent. That is the defiant attitude I was hoping for. You will do. I was hoping you'd inherited your father's fearlessness, not to mention his sense of diplomacy. This will save time." Toru glanced at the assembled command staff. "All of you, leave us." They complied, rapidly shuffling out the door. The two Iron Guard escorts remained standing behind Sullivan. "You may leave as well."

"Our Finder believes he bears seven kanji, General. The Grimnoir knight is dangerous."

"They're not kanji," Joe said, as if he'd stoop to copying the spells of Imperium butchers. "And I'm not Grimnoir."

"I'm not worried," Toru stated. "Go." The Iron Guards bowed and left without another word. Toru waited for the bunker's door to be closed. "Not Grimnoir . . . Curious. You do not wish to follow in your father's footsteps?"

He'd had a bit of a disagreement with the Society, but that was none of Tokugawa's business.

"Interesting . . . An American who has barely lived there, who chose to join a military where he will never be accepted because of his half-breed race, refuses to join the one organization that must surely want him. Where do you *belong*, Sullivan?"

He was still working on that question himself. "My orders say I'm supposed to help. What do you want?"

"It pains me to admit it, but I require your assistance. In a show of mutual cooperation, your president has seen fit to grant my request. Apparently, your old friend Francis sees the Soviets as the greater threat at this time. This agreement should be beneficial to both of our nations. America and Imperium have been enemies in the past, but today we are . . . temporarily on the same side."

"Why in the world would he want me to help you? Once the

Imperium finishes off the Russians, you'll go back to trying to conquer the rest of the world."

"I prefer the term *liberate*, but if you do not help, then we will be forced to use Tesla weapons to stop this threat, which will cause the deaths of hundreds of thousands of innocent civilians . . . Ah, your face betrays your emotions, young Sullivan. You'll need to work on that if you expect to make it long in this world. You might not wear the ring, but it appears you still have a Grimnoir knight's morals. I need an Active of your particular skills."

"I'm only a Gravity Spiker. We're a dime a dozen."

Tokugawa chuckled. "I believe I've heard that line before. Yet, according to my sources, despite your youth, your ability to manipulate gravity is unmatched."

"I learned from the best."

"Of course. We all stand upon the shoulders of those who came before us. Your father was self-taught. You benefit from his discoveries. We are alike in that way. I understand what is required to be the son of a great man. It is a burden, but also an incredible honor." Considering who Toru's father had been, that was probably one hell of a compliment around these parts. "There are many of your kind among the Iron Guard, some of whom are incredibly strong, far stronger than you, no doubt, but strength alone does not make a warrior great. That also requires awareness and will."

"Most folks chosen by the Power to control gravity aren't the sharpest knives in the drawer."

"I intended to be polite and say they lack nuance, but yes, most of them are stupid oxen good only for lifting things or throwing their bodies at the enemy. I've yet to find one among my army capable of the subtle manipulations of gravity your father was. Are you up to the task?"

Joe didn't actually know the answer to that. Those were some big shoes to fill. "What's the mission?"

Toru walked to the biggest wall map and pointed at the red dragon symbol. "Trust me, the monster is far more impressive in person."

As the Iron Guard moved their general and his guest across Tokyo in a convoy of armored vehicles, Toru Tokugawa had continued his briefing. "They have sent giant demons against us before, but nothing like this. The Soviets have been experimenting with increasing the abilities of their Summoners ever since they saw what happened to Washington D.C. in 1933."

"If I recall correctly, you were there for that," Joe said.

"The god of demons swatted me as if I were an annoying insect. We were only able to stop it because it was new and not yet fully formed. Luckily for all of mankind, even Stalin is not foolish enough to Summon anything that mighty. It would be too dangerous, too uncontrollable. However, they have made great strides over the last twenty years. This one is extremely resilient, far more armored than the last. The fact that they are still able to direct a demon this powerful is astounding."

"It's already destroyed a chunk of your navy."

"Correct."

"So that part was real, but I'm guessing everything else on those maps was probably wrong so I'd provide bad intel?"

"You are a perceptive man, Sullivan." Which didn't confirm or deny anything. Joe figured the temper tantrum earlier had been some sort of test as well. "The Summoned is approximately fifty meters tall and apparently still growing. Its capabilities are a mystery. It is amphibious and has been walking along the sea bed, only emerging every few days to attack. It has already damaged several cities along the coast."

"Civilian casualties?"

"I'm surprised you care."

"They didn't ask to be born under tyranny," Joe answered.

"Perhaps you may get that duel after all . . ."

Joe figured he would lose, but he wasn't in the mood to put up with nonsense. "I control gravity, so when we pick weapons, I vote telephone poles."

"As your people say, the apple does not fall far from the tree. Twenty years ago I would have taken you up on that duel. I'd enjoy knocking the smug off your face, but we do not have time for that. There are over one hundred thousand dead so far, but we are still pulling bodies from the rubble."

Joe gave a low whistle.

"Intelligence predicts the demon will be here within the week.

Iron Guard have been unable to defeat it. Our own greater Summoned have been stepped on. Conventional weapons harm it, but then once sufficiently wounded it retreats back out to sea to hide and heal for a few days before striking again. Depth charges have done nothing. My forces have been unable to track it in the sea. Every submarine I have sent after it has been lost. Aerial bombing has stung it, but has caused more harm to the city it was attacking than the beast itself."

"Have you tried Tesla weapons?"

"Once. A low powered firing to minimize collateral damage, but it did not work as expected. The demon's hide does not react like human flesh. I destroyed an entire town only to chase it back into hiding." The Imperium was far more casual about sacrificing its people than the West, but unlike his predecessor, it seemed this Tokugawa actually cared.

The general was staring out the narrow slit of the window at his capital city. They drove into a tunnel and Tokyo disappeared. "Our defense force is prepared to intercept it. We have moved the emperor somewhere safe. Anyone who is not vital to the war effort is being evacuated from the city. The *Yamamoto* is our newest airship and carries our most powerful Tesla weapon. It is on station above us and its Peace Ray is charged. If the demon cannot be stopped I will have no choice but to fire upon it at full power."

That would obliterate a good chunk of Tokyo in the process. "So what's the plan?"

The general didn't answer. The armored car came to a stop. The doors were opened, revealing that they'd parked inside some sort of vast hangar. Tokugawa climbed out, and Joe followed. His first thought was *Why are they building a skyscraper underground?* Then he realized they weren't actually underground, as much as they'd hollowed out an entire hill and covered the top to protect the interior from spy planes. The place was crowded with soldiers and engineers, and they began to panic when they saw who their distinguished visitor was. The Iron Guards snapped at them to get back to work. Hundreds of men were scrambling about on this level, and in the several floors of scaffolding overhead.

"There is my plan, Lieutenant Sullivan."

Directly in front of them was an armored metal rectangle,

painted olive drab. His first thought was that it was a train car missing its wheels. Then he realized it was a *foot*.

"Behold, the Nishimura Super *Gakutensoku*. It has taken over a decade to build. It is the most daring feat of magical engineering ever attempted by Cog science."

He looked up, and up, and *up*. It was hard to wrap his brain around the size of the thing. "That's one *big* robot."

"Forty-six meters tall and nearly two thousand tons, it would destroy itself if it tried to move . . ."

"Galileo called it. That square cube law is a real stickler," Joe agreed.

"Which is why it must be piloted by someone who can break the rules."

"I'm good, but I'm not that good."

"The spells bound upon it will increase an Active's connection to the Power by an order of magnitude. It has a crew of seventy Actives, and the Turing machines inside control all of the minor systems. In theory, it should be as easy to drive as a suit of Nishimura combat armor. *If* the *Gakutensoku* works as projected, we should be able to defeat the demon and send Stalin a message."

He couldn't figure out what kind of spells they'd carved onto that thing to get it to work. Even powered down he could feel it pulling magic from the air around him. It was hard to tell through all the scaffolding, but it was shaped like a broad-shouldered man, with two arms that were too long and two legs that were too short. He couldn't even imagine this thing moving.

Then he realized that there were craters on the concrete floor from where the thing had fallen. He glanced around the vast hangar. There were a lot of craters.

"I will speak plainly. As you can see from the dents on my giant robot, every other Heavy has lacked the will necessary to control it. We are still repairing the damage from yesterday's test. I had hope for the last test pilot, since he was very intelligent for a Heavy. Sadly Captain Nakamura lacked finesse, tripped over his own feet within two hundred meters, and the Super *Gakutensoku* fell on its head."

"I imagine it takes practice."

"Feedback from the spell caused him to have an aneurism and die."

"Great." Helping his sworn enemies work the bugs out of a super weapon sure as hell wasn't what he'd joined the Marines for. "So now that you're running out of time, you asked for me."

"Deciding between asking for American help or blowing up our capital with a Tesla weapon was a very difficult decision."

Considering the fact that Joe had less than a week to learn how to drive a mechanical man the size of a 12-story building . . . "Keep that Peace Ray warmed up, General, because I'm not making any promises."

"If it is any consolation, Lieutenant Sullivan, the Super *Gakutensoku* is purely a defensive weapon system," Hikaru told him. "Since you are helping us—as you Americans say—*work out the kinks,* there is no way we could bring this magnificent device to America to lay waste to your cities and crush your armies beneath its massive steel feet. How would we get it there?"

"Good point," Joe muttered, resisting the urge to drop a few extra gravities on the annoyingly helpful Cog's head. It turned out that the Japanese Actives capable of magical bursts of intellectual brilliance were just as squirrely as their Western counterparts.

Hikaru continued talking while fastening electrodes to Joe's freshly shaved head. "There is no airship that could carry it. Moving a machine of this size via sea would be too dangerous. Not to mention we've not solved the deep-water pressure problems of walking it across the ocean floor yet."

"Yet?"

"Uh . . . I . . . Never mind." The Cog spoke English better than Joe spoke Japanese, and he knew the Super *Gakutensoku* inside and out, so he'd been appointed Joe's assistant. Hikaru taped down the last wire. "There you go. The Turing machines are now monitoring your brain. The spells have been activated. The crew is ready. We are ready to test."

Joe glanced across the control center. He knew how to fly an airplane. This was way worse. He'd spent the last twenty hours memorizing every control, and they'd skipped all the *unimportant* ones. There were four pedals beneath each foot, friction sticks directly in front of him, and half a dozen levers for each arm. Cables and pulleys were attached to bands around his abdomen, chest, biceps, and wrists. It was bad enough that he needed to tell each "muscle group" what to do physically; he had to simultaneously tell gravity what to do magically.

"It looks more complicated than it is. This should be no worse than controlling a Heavy Suit."

"Have you ever driven a Heavy Suit, Hikaru?"

"No, Lieutenant. I have not personally, but that is what it says in the manual."

"Then do me a favor and shut up." Joe looked out the armored portholes. Cranes were lifting away the scaffolding to the front, and the workers were taking cover. The row of gauges told him that all twenty of their diesel engines were running. The indicator board was all green lights. There were Fixers on board making sure everything was working, Torches for damage control and weapons systems, Iceboxes making sure nothing overheated and taking care of the ridiculous amount of friction generated by their movement, Brutes to manhandle shells and guns, and other Gravity Spikers just to help channel enough magic into the machine's spells to keep them balanced.

Joe checked his own connection to the Power. The magic was gathered up in his chest, waiting to be directed. He used a bit of it to test the world around him. Spells had been carved all over the interior of the Super *Gakutensoku*. They magnified his connection but also distorted it. It was like looking through a microscope that was just a little bit out of focus. Maybe it was because he was running on coffee and determination at this point, but it was already starting to give him a headache. No wonder the last guy had a stroke.

He put his right foot down on a pedal while simultaneously pushing forward with the right friction stick. At the same time he called upon his magic, imagining the pull of the earth against his own leg, and easing that *just* enough. He'd never tried to change gravity over such a gigantic space. It was like magic was being ripped from the Power and channeled through his body out into the great machine. Joe ground his teeth and held on.

A hundred tons of foot scraped along the concrete before rising a few dozen feet and then slamming back down with an impact that shook the whole world.

There were ten other men in the *Gakutensoku*'s head. They began rattling off readings and stats from their CRTs and gauges. This was requiring such focus that Joe only barely heard them. He pushed down with his left foot and repeated the process. The robot lurched forward, but stayed balanced and upright. The crew let up a cheer. They'd gone *two* whole steps.

"How are you feeling, Lieutenant?" Hikaru asked.

In actuality he felt like he'd just been mule-kicked in the head. The Power draw made his teeth hurt, and he wanted to vomit. "Are you asking because you've bought into that propaganda about how soft Westerners are?"

"Quite the contrary. On our first test, at this point blood shot from the test pilot's ears. I just wanted to make sure I had the spells calibrated correctly."

It was taking effort simply to keep from sinking into the floor. Joe lifted one hand to wipe the sweat that had instantly formed on his brow. The unconscious movement caused one giant robot arm to rise up and crash through the scaffolding, tearing it all to pieces. Luckily he froze before swatting the cockpit and decapitating them. The noise of cascading, crashing metal could barely be heard through their thick armor, but it still went on for several painful seconds. Joe slowly lowered the arm, then pushed the disconnect button so he could turn enough to look out the side porthole. Yep. The scaffolding was just gone. Hopefully they'd had the sense to get everybody off of it before starting the test.

"Perhaps that is enough for your first day?" Hikaru asked hesitantly. "The physical and magical strain is considerable."

Iron Guard weren't the only ones around here taught to never show weakness. "I'm just getting warmed up." Joe looked up at the bank of CRT screens. Since the robot couldn't turn its head and their footprint took up a city block, those cameras were as close as he was going to get to peripheral vision. He found the exit out of the hillside. "Buckle up, Hikaru. Let's see what this baby can do."

Five days later, the second biggest demon to ever walk the earth attacked Tokyo.

General Toru Tokugawa stood on the observation deck of the tallest building in the city, watching out the window with his hands folded behind his back. He'd moved his command center here temporarily for this very view. It was a beautiful, clear day. Twenty miles to the southwest he could see buildings falling and smoke rising.

One of his aides entered the room in a hurry. "General, the demon is crossing Yokohama."

"I am aware," Toru stated.

"We have begun the mass evacuation as instructed. The coastal defense cannons were engaging before we lost contact with them. The Iron Guard are moving into position now. The air force is scrambling. The *Yamamoto* is awaiting your orders."

Nearly ten million people lived in the wards that would be directly affected by the Peace Ray. Those who would be instantly incinerated were the lucky ones. The burns and radiation sickness were far more painful ways to die. "And the Super *Gakutensoku*?"

"It is in the hills to the west. A message has been sent." From his aide's tone, Toru could tell the officer had very little faith in that option working.

He'd understated the danger to the American, Sullivan. This demon's presence and constant raids were crippling his country and endangering the entire war effort. Demons could be banished from this world, but they were not as easy to kill as a mortal being. Their bodies were artificial magical constructs. They had no internal organs to wound or bones to break. They were filled with magical substances that best resembled ink and smoke, and the only way to end one this powerful was to bleed it dry. That took time.

"Tell the *Yamamoto* to hold its fire for now. The Iron Guard must fall back. Draw it in, farther onto land, and then we will strike. Wait for the demon to be distracted by the *Gakutensoku*, then we will hit it with every conventional weapon at our disposal. If we cannot fell it, only then will we fire the Peace Ray. Better to raze the greatest city in the world than to endanger the whole Imperium." It would either be a scalpel or a *tetsubo*, but one way or the other, Stalin's demon died today.

"We should get you to the *Yamamoto* immediately, General."

"No." Toru looked back toward the growing pillars of black smoke. If this city died, then he deserved to die with it. "I believe that I'd like to watch the fight from here."

❖ ❖ ❖

They were making excellent time. The robot's legs were too short to call it a run, but when you covered this much ground with each stride, a shuffling jog still got them to fifty miles an hour. The fact that there wasn't much they had to go around meant they could travel in a straight line. Joe had gotten good enough that he even managed to step *over* individual houses. Mostly.

Hikaru was giving him directions based upon roads, power lines, and compass directions. They'd quickly discovered that when you were twelve stories up you couldn't give directions based on street signs, and local landmarks meant nothing when your pilot had never been here before. Joe's entire knowledge of Japan's geography came from stories his mother had told him and maps he'd studied in the off chance the Marines got to invade the place.

"The demon is tracking north. To the east is an orchard, after you cross it there is a railway. Follow that toward the city," Hikaru told him.

"Got it." He couldn't see the Cog or the rest of the crew sitting behind him. Joe had learned the hard way not to turn his head enough to look back over his shoulder because the Turing machines read that the wrong way. The first time he'd done it they'd face-planted in a field. On the bright side, that had been a few days ago, and it had taught him how to stand this thing back up without waiting for multiple construction cranes to come save them.

Moving was fairly instinctive at this point. There was a rhythm to it. *Clomp. Clomp. Clomp.* It made sense that the cockpit was where the robot's head should have been, since that was how the human body's control center was wired, and once you were magically connected, he was the brain and it was all a matter of scale. He'd spent the last few days learning to move about with a modicum of grace, and slugging boulders, and it really wasn't that much different than working a punching bag with his own fists . . . except for the part where he could punch through mountains.

The buildings were getting taller and the neighborhoods more populated. Joe had to step carefully to keep from landing on any moving cars. He was burning a lot of magic trying to keep a light step, but they still weighed so much that each footstep left an impact crater, so he wasn't sure how many of those automobiles unwittingly drove into the suddenly created holes they'd left in the roads.

One armored foot clipped the edge of a warehouse, but it was enough to rip one wall off. "I wish you people would've built wider streets!"

"I'll have you know Tokyo is the most advanced city in the world," Hikaru snapped.

"Horseshit. We've got an interstate highway system in America you could drive an aircraft carrier down. Hang on, I see smoke." The buildings here were already smashed flat or knocked over. A giant lizard-shaped footprint was clear as day in the middle of a park. "I've got the demon's trail." Joe guided the robot toward the path of carnage. Since everything here was already destroyed, he might as well take it up a notch. Joe pushed both friction sticks forward. "Hang on!"

ClompClompClomp!

The trail was easy to follow, what with all the spreading fires and collapsed buildings. Hundreds of civilians were down there. He could lie to himself and say they looked like bugs from up here, but they still looked like people, and he tried his best not to land on any of them. They might have just had a war, but that was no excuse to be an asshole.

Following in the demon's wake gave him a good glimpse into how the creature thought. If he'd been down there at ground level, he would have missed it. The scene would have just been too damned big to take in, but from up here, from the perspective of somebody twelve stories tall and nearly indestructible, he could tell that the demon was angry. It was heading toward the capital, but it was meandering about, swatting down anything that stood out along the way. A temple had been kicked over. Ornate wooden arches had been stepped on. It had gone three blocks out of its way to chase down a bus. It had picked up a passenger train and tossed it out into the ocean. The miles went by, showing an ever-increasing amount of spite. This Summoned was an engine of destruction.

It was enjoying itself.

"I can't believe this," Hikaru whispered as he looked out over the devastation. "This is nearly as bad as when the Americans firebombed the city."

"That was different," Joe snapped.

"How?"

"You started it. Now zip your lip. I'm concentrating."

An alarm horn sounded. There was some shouting in Japanese. Joe had thought he was fairly fluent, but polite Japanese was different than the profanity-laced military exclamations you got when one of the techs spotted a giant demon. Joe eased back on the sticks to slow them down.

They were in an open campus of large, ornate buildings, probably a university. The opposite end of the space was covered in black smoke, and through it, something truly *vast* moved. Long spines appeared, cutting ripples through the smoke, and there was a tremendous crash as a clock tower was knocked off its foundations to topple to the ground. The spines froze, then swiftly turned and disappeared, as the demon sensed the approaching footfalls.

Four brilliant beams of red light appeared in the smoke, about even with the *Gakutensoku*'s cockpit. Those were its *eyes*. It was watching them.

"All weapons, prepare to fire," Joe said with far more calm than he actually felt. Hikaru relayed the order. The gravitational magic lurched as a dozen other forms of Power were channeled through the spells carved on the great machine. "Let's hit this son of a bitch with everything we've got."

The wind shifted. The smoke parted and the Summoned revealed itself. It was reptilian, with a dark, glistening hide perforated by random shards of black bone. It was thick-set, muscular, with a long spiked tail, two squat, powerful legs, and arms that ended in claws that looked like they could do a number on even the *Gakutensoku*'s armor. The demon stepped full into view, lowered its dragon-shaped head, and roared. It was so loud that it vibrated through their hull. Humans on the ground probably had their eardrums ruptured from the blast. The screech dragged on until it threatened to blot out the world. Then it snapped its razor jaws closed, spread its arms, and raised itself to its full height to meet this new challenge.

It was *far* bigger than they were.

"I believe that the greater Summoned may be significantly taller than the specified fifty meters," Hikaru stated.

It didn't matter what country you were in, military intelligence was always wrong.

"Put that record I gave you on the player, Hikaru. I want it blasting at full volume over the PA system."

"Lieutenant, despite your intentions, I truly do not believe that music really soothes the savage beast. That is just a colloquialism."

"Put my record on the player or I'm getting out of this chair." He waited until he heard the scratch of the record and the whine of the intercom. "That's better." Joe flipped open the safety cover and put his finger on the trigger. "Fire on my command."

Toru watched as the two titans faced each other. To the north was the Summoned, a horrible alien creature, its spirit torn from another realm and given form here. On the bony plates of its chest the Soviet Cogs had engraved a hammer and sickle, and then filled it in with molten bronze so that it would never heal. To the south was the Super *Gakutensoku*. It was rather impressive, though not nearly as intimidating as the demon. Though it made no sense to camouflage a walking mountain, they'd painted it brown and olive drab, except for the glorious rising sun painted on its shoulder plates. Both sides of this duel were proud to claim their champions, each one representing their mighty nation. There was a certain dignity to this event.

A deadly silence covered the city after the demon's roar. It had been loud enough to break windows a mile away, and Toru could smell the smoke through the open wound in the building's side. There was a new sound, tinny, and much quieter than the demon's bellow. It was coming from the Super *Gakutensoku*. The machine had been equipped with a bank of loudspeakers for psychological warfare purposes. Now it was playing a song.

"What is that noise?" asked one of his aides.

So much for dignity. Toru sighed. "I believe that is the American National Anthem."

Magical energy was building in the air. A bolt of lightning erupted from the clear blue sky and struck the *Gakutensoku*. Thunder rolled across the city. The mighty robot lifted one arm. Brilliant orange fire danced along that hand. Then the other arm came up, shimmering with reflected light as ice formed along that limb. Hatches opened on the giant robot's torso as cannon barrels extended outward.

Toru stuck his fingers in his ears. This was going to be very loud.

❖ ❖ ❖

"Open fire!" Joe shouted. A dozen 120mm anti-tank cannons went off simultaneously. Expanding gray clouds appeared across the demon's body.

"Spells are charged," Hikaru said.

"Magic up!" The Actives released their magic, and Joe hurled it at the enemy. He slammed the far right stick forward. Normally a Torch could direct a stream of magical fire or cause small objects to combust, but, magically augmented by the *Gakutensoku*'s spells, that same magic now caused a super-heated ball of plasma the size of an automobile to shoot across the campus, melting everything beneath it, before crashing into the demon in a shower of sparks and smoking demon flesh.

The demon charged. He'd been expecting that. That's what an aggressive beast would do when confronted by a seeming equal rather than being stung by hundreds of ants.

Joe cranked on the left stick. A wave of magical cold shot forth. It was absolute zero at the release point, and not a whole lot warmer when the wave struck the demon's hide. It shuddered as molecules slowed, tissues became inflexible and cracked. Then Joe activated one of the right sticks to throw a punch. The *Gakutensoku* responded a second later by slamming its steel knuckles into the monster's side. The frozen layers of hide shattered. Flaming ink ruptured from the hole.

There was an impact that shook the entire *Gakutensoku*. The shift in gravity told him that they'd been hit low, in the legs. *The tail!* Joe directed gravity to pull them back from tripping while he worked the foot pedals. They slid across the campus, through a four-story building and out the other side, but they didn't fall.

"Damage to the secondary servos and the port accumulator," Hikaru reported.

"I don't even know what those things are," Joe said, trying to concentrate on not killing them all while the Power surging through him felt like it was going to yank his heart out of his chest.

The forest of spines was visible through the portholes, and then it was gone. The demon was circling to the side faster than they could turn. One of the CRTs had gone black, the camera lens covered in demon sludge. The others told him that it was about to grab hold of them. There was a lot to keep track of, especially on a system this complex that he hadn't had time to properly learn, but Joe was a Sullivan, and Sullivans didn't get rattled.

"Cracklers. Release on my signal," Joe ordered, and Hikaru repeated it to their Actives who could direct electricity. The *Gakutensoku* shuddered and metal groaned as the demon collided with them. "Now!"

The stored energy leapt between the two huge bodies, and a billion volts blasted the demon off of them. It flew back, across the street, through several apartments, and disappeared in a cloud of dust at the base of a large office building.

There was a terrible burning smell inside the cockpit. Smoke drifted in front of his face.

"That's horrible!" Then Hikaru began to gag. "One of our electricians is on fire. The augmented spell was too much."

Joe couldn't turn to see right now, he was trying to turn the robot to keep track of the demon. "Have one of the Torches put him out. I'm busy," Joe snarled. The magical strain was really getting to him. "Get another Crackler in that chair. Charge our magic. Get those guns reloaded. I want them to fire every time they've got a shot. Pour it on!"

The demon lifted itself off the ground. The *Gakutensoku* covered the distance in a few strides and caught it on the way up. As the big fist came down, Joe threw as much extra gravity as possible to haul it down faster. The blow hit so hard that it blew demon ink out of one of the demon's eye sockets.

It hit them around the midsection, wrapping its arms around their center of mass and squeezing. Cannon shells fired at point-blank range. A few floors below, one of their Brutes died screaming as flaming demon ink poured through the gun hatch, and then the noise stopped as it washed him away.

Joe acted on instinct, the robot an extension of his own body, as he pummeled the demon. There was an awful grinding noise, and the stick wouldn't pull back. That arm wouldn't retract; it was stuck. It took a moment to find the right CRT screen to see that their wrist was stuck on a horn. So Joe reached across with their other hand, grabbed that horn, and squeezed. The diesels powering those hydraulics redlined and it still wouldn't break, so Joe changed gravity's direction to the side and basically hung tons of extra weight on that horn. It tore free with a sick crack that they probably heard back in China.

The Summoned lurched away, spraying flaming blood everywhere. Joe still had the horn, and it was pretty stout, so he went about beating the beast about the head with it. Their movements were powerful, but slow. The demon was organic, fluid, and far faster. It caught the descending horn with one hand, turned it aside, and then bit down on their shoulder.

It was distant and down a floor, but he could heard the grinding of metal, breaking of welds, and the scream of men as they were torn from their seats and flung to their deaths. More smoke filled the air, and this time it smelled like burning wires. More CRTs had gone black. Half the lights on the warning panel had gone red. He tried to hit it with the horn again, but couldn't tell if it worked. Feedback through the electrodes told him that hand was now empty.

"Torch magic is charged," Hikaru said.

Joe drove their right fist deep into the monster's side. "Fire!"

The contact point between them was briefly hotter than the surface of the sun. The explosion rocked them. A wave of heat flashed through the robot.

"Right arm is not responding," Hikaru warned. "Repeat, right arm down!"

Joe could have told him that by the way the control had frozen up. "Get the Fixers on it, now." The demon lurched away, so Joe lowered their uninjured shoulder and pushed both of the friction sticks all the way forward.

ClompClompClompClomp!

They collided, a wall of steel meeting a wall of meat. One of the armored portholes shattered. A thick chunk of glass spun over and hit Joe in the jaw. It hurt; he could feel the cut leaking blood, but he sure as hell didn't have time to check it. He jerked back on both sticks, stomped on the pedals to plant their feet, and even let gravity return to normal for an instant to drag them down into the ground to stop their forward momentum. Their feet dug a hundred-foot-long trench through the road, tearing up water mains, but they came to a full stop.

The demon wasn't so lucky. It hit the next building, a big

twenty-story affair, and went *through* it, to crash across the next street, trip on a bridge, and then roll over to shatter a canal.

Joe drove them around the collapsing building. The demon was already getting up. Cannon shells were falling around it like rain. "Where's my ice magic? Come on!"

"Still charging. Two of our Iceboxes were in the shoulder. They are not responding."

There were more explosions around the demon than could be accounted for with just the *Gakutensoku*'s 120mms. Tanks were rolling down the street. Several fast-moving aircraft buzzed by just overhead, strafing cannon shells into the monster before veering off. Tokugawa had sent in the cavalry.

Black demon ink was pouring from its wounds, down the gutters, pooling on top of the canals to shimmer like oil, but it charged them anyway. It leapt across the distance, and the only thing he could see through the portholes was a forest of spines. "Brace for impac—"

BOOM!

No amount of gravity manipulation was going to keep them on their feet this time.

They hit a building, and then another building, and another. Joe couldn't tell what was going on. They were changing direction too fast. The demon had ahold of them, and was swinging them back and forth. It was hitting them over and over again. Magical energy was flowing back through the electrodes, and each impact was like getting hit directly in the brain with a hammer. Every warning light on the panel was red, and then the panel disappeared entirely as the demon ripped the *Gakutensoku*'s face off.

The black, slimy claw, big as a bulldozer blade, was thrashing back and forth, only a foot in front of him. It should have been terrifying, but all Joe could think of at the time was that it smelled like the ocean. And then the claw vanished as fast as it had come, and they were falling forward.

The view through the hole was of rapidly approaching ground. Joe slammed the main left arm stick forward and mashed the button to open their hand. He called upon all his magic at once, reversing gravity, trying to pull them upwards, but even the spells on this thing couldn't reverse two thousand tons once it was in motion.

Their hand hit, and that took most of the impact. They froze in place for a moment, leaving Joe hanging by the straps on his chair, staring down into a pile of debris and squirting pipes. Somebody had unbuckled their harness and fell past him, screaming, to disappear out the face hole. He hoped that hadn't been Hikaru, because he needed the little guy to relay orders.

Then a big hydraulic cylinder in the arm burst, and they were falling. Joe stomped on the pedals to kick out, pushing them so they'd land on their shoulder rather than flat. Facedown—assuming he didn't just get impaled on some rebar or smashed like a mouse beneath a boot heel—they wouldn't be able to get back up as easily, especially with one working arm. Besides, everybody in that shoulder was probably already dead.

On the upside, they landed like he'd hoped. On the downside, he smashed his head against the controls hard enough to knock himself stupid. Joe came back to reality a moment later dangling sideways about thirty feet over a ruined street. The moisture on his face was from a broken fire hydrant spraying upward.

It hurt to think. Talking was worse. "Hikaru, you still alive?"

"Yes, Lieutenant."

"Good, because we're not done yet." His voice was ragged. He didn't know if it was because he was breathing in clouds of dust, or if all the magic he was burning had damaged his vocal cords somehow. They were at a really awkward angle and looking out a jagged hole, but from the noise and shadows, it appeared the demon was trying to get away. If Tokugawa thought it was going to make it back to the ocean to heal, he'd light it up with the Peace Ray. "Get those Fixers to work. I want my arm and my ice magic, and I want them now."

"I'll do my best."

"If you don't, we're going to get flash-fried." Joe very gently tested the pedals. He'd gotten this thing stood up before, but he'd had both arms and a whole bunch of monitors to keep him informed then. This was going to take some finesse and a whole lot of screwing with gravity. "On that thought, get me a radio. This might take a minute."

"The *Gakutensoku* appears to be disabled, General. The beast is severely wounded, but it is merely fleeing back toward the bay. They have failed to stop it." The aide presented him with a radio. "The *Yamamoto* awaits your orders."

Toru took the radio with a heavy heart. He grieved for his nation, and gave no thought to his own life. The greater Summoned had to be stopped. If not now, then it would simply heal in the depths and then return to finish the job, even stronger than before. "This is General Tokugawa granting permission to fire the Peace Ray. Authorization code one five three tw—"

"General!" Another staff officer rushed forward. "Please wait."

Normally Toru was very unforgiving of rude interruptions, but since he was about to obliterate them all, he was allowed to hope for a bit of good news. "Hold on that authorization . . . What is it?" He was handed another radio.

"It is the Super *Gakutensoku*!"

"*—hear me, Tokugawa, you son of a bitch! Don't you dare touch that thing off. I can still do this.*"

Toru keyed the radio. "This is General Tokugawa."

The young Sullivan sounded exhausted. "*We're not out of the fight yet. We're getting back up. I can still stop it before it gets back to the ocean.*"

One of his aides warned, "Time is of the essence, sir. It will be at Minato soon. Once it is out to sea, we will lose it."

"What is your status, Sullivan?"

"*Just peachy.*" There was something that sounded like a groan of metal and a loud clang. "*Couldn't be better.*"

"There! The *Gakutensoku* rises." A spotter was pointing at the financial district.

Broken glass crunching underfoot, he moved over to see. In the distance the mighty mechanical man was swaying, badly charred on one side, and missing an arm . . . but *standing*. The men began to cheer.

"There is no time, General!" the aide shouted.

"*Give us one more shot.*"

Toru had once trusted this man's father and he'd not been disappointed. He keyed the radio. "Sullivan, go southeast as fast as possible. You can cut it off at the port."

"*Got it. Sullivan out.*"

The *Gakutensoku* began an awkward limping jog through the city.

"That is our only chance. Do everything we can to slow the

monster down. When it reaches the ocean, we will have no choice."
He handed back the radio that offered hope and took up the one that
could only dispense doom. "*Yamamoto,* await my signal."

Joe didn't worry about the landscape now. It was better to bounce
off a building to keep up speed than to move carefully if the whole
place was minutes from being vaporized anyway. Since the robot
was missing half of its head, wind was blowing freely through the
cockpit. He'd not thought he'd need to wear goggles. On the bright
side, now that they had a convertible, they all had a lot better view.

"Demon sighted!" Hikaru shouted.

The forest of spines was visible on the other side of some
buildings to their left. It had gotten turned around and slowed down
while being harassed by the Imperium military and not taken the
most direct route to the bay. So they'd caught up before reaching the
ocean, and judging by the numerous cargo cranes in front of them,
just in the nick of time.

"Radio your air force to back off for a minute." With them all
hanging in the breeze, one unlucky hit and shrapnel would kill them
all. Then what good was their fancy robot? Joe had both friction sticks
all the way forward and was running the foot pedals as fast as he could.
He veered them to the side and tracked directly toward the demon.

The magic draw was intense. His personal Power had long since
been exhausted. He was only a conduit now, a circuit between the
Power itself and the hungry spells on this machine. The other
Gravity Spikers aboard had either been killed or incapacitated,
because it felt like he was on his own. He knew he was probably
going to die here, but that just made him want to make sure this
thing didn't get away even more.

The demon heard them coming. It had to be severely weakened,
because rather than turn to meet them, it kept on moving toward the
ocean. The demon was stumbling as bombs kept going off around it,
leaving a smoking trail of lost tissue. They were almost on top of it.

"Cold magic ready." Hikaru had to shout to be heard over the
wind.

"About damned time. I've got an idea. Hold on."

They were both in the open, smashing their way through stacks
of cargo containers and trucks. He realized what was really slowing

down the demon. The horn that he'd ripped off earlier had wound
up impaled through one of its legs, causing it to limp. *So I did stick
it. Nice.* Joe pulled back on the friction sticks, slowing them just a
bit, allowing the demon to reach the water first.

"What're you doing?" Hikaru probably thought Joe had decided
to throw in the towel.

"Trust me."

The demon reached a moored freighter and began clambering
over it. Waves crashed as the ship capsized and the beast hit the
water. Joe lifted their remaining arm. The crosshairs used for aiming
earlier were long gone, but he wasn't shooting at the monster: he
was shooting at the ocean around it. "Release the ice magic now!"

He'd not realized how well insulated they'd been before. The cold
that blasted through the cockpit was a shock to the system, but it
was far, far worse on the receiving end. The ocean around the
monster turned solid instantly. Partially submerged, the creature
could no longer move its legs or tail, and fell forward. Its snout
smashed into the suddenly hard surface, and it flailed about through
the slush and breaking ice.

Joe plowed ahead, only there was no longer ground ahead of him,
only man-made dock facilities, and those came apart beneath their
weight. It took all of his skill and concentration to keep them from
falling over in the mud, but below that was bedrock, and that was
solid enough to get some gravity-assisted purchase on. Waist deep,
they slogged forward as water came rushing through the fresh holes
in their robot.

The demon was sliding, trying to gain purchase. The loss of
smoke and ink was shrinking it. The thing was no longer so massive
and imposing, and Joe drove straight into the monster, crushing it
back into another ship. Once he was sure they were partially on top
of it, and there was solid rock beneath, Joe cut his Power and let
gravity return to normal.

There was an unholy screech as the giant monster's legs were
crushed, but demons didn't have bones to break, so there was still
work to be done.

Its head was far beneath them, jaws snapping, so Joe lifted their
remaining arm, pushed the button to form a fist, and then let the
thing have it right in the teeth. He kept hitting it, arm rising and

falling like a jackhammer. Each blow caused the head to deform further, spraying burning ink in every direction. The second of its four eyes went out, and then a third, and Joe just kept on hitting it.

The monster was shrieking and thrashing, A claw caught the rest of their cockpit and tore that away, but the controls were still connected, so Joe just kept on plugging away. There was so much black floating on the waves that it looked like the ship they'd rolled over had been an oil tanker, but that was just demon ink.

There was a gleam of bronze through the churning salt water. It was the giant hammer and sickle embedded on the demon's chest. Joe opened the palm and reached down, plunging the robot's fingers through the thick hide until they were around the symbol. Then he hit the button to make a fist. Satisfied that the crunch meant he'd caught it, he yanked back on the controls, ripping it from the demon's body.

The demon opened its mouth to screech one last time, and this time Joe slammed the hammer and sickle right down its throat and through the back of its head.

The vast Summoned body began to dissolve, but so did Joe's consciousness. The pain was making it hard to think. He was leaning forward, and as he lost it, so did the robot.

The dark ocean rushed up to meet him.

Joe woke up in a hospital bed. General Tokugawa was sitting in a chair next to him.

"You know, if I ran this Imperium the same way my father did, I would simply notify your president that you perished in the battle and your body was lost in the harbor. Even his best spies would not be able to discern the truth. I have thousands of witnesses who saw the ruined Super *Gakutensoku* sink into the bay. Then you would be experimented upon, your will broken, and your impressive Power utilized for the greater good."

"Lucky for me you're not like your father," Joe croaked.

"And lucky for my city, you are very much like yours . . . I have named you an honorary Iron Guard and awarded you the Order of the Golden Kite. Wear the medal with pride."

"The Marine Corps is gonna *love* that."

"You may stay here if you wish, and I will gladly change that from honorary to official . . . From your expression I shall take that as a no? Oh well . . . My Healers have repaired your wounds. All that remains is the exhaustion. Soon, you will be returned to your country, whether to a hero's welcome or to the shame of having aided an enemy, I do not know. Your people are fickle and unpredictable."

"Yep, but they're *my* people."

"Indeed." Tokugawa smiled. "It is good for a warrior to know where he belongs."

One of my favorite things about short story collections are the little extra bits the author puts in explaining how the story came to be and the process behind it.

*In this case, "Tokyo Raider" was kind of an experiment. The original Grimnoir trilogy (*Hard Magic, Spellbound, *and* Warbound*) began in 1932, in a world that diverged from ours when magical abilities started appearing among the populace in the 1850s. It was inspired by noir, pulp, and hardboiled detective stories. It often gets labeled as "diesel punk."*

But for the second trilogy I thought it would be fun to jump ahead a bit so I could get more into the golden age of sci-fi—basically I wanted to write wizards in space—and since technology is moving faster in the Grimnoir universe than our own, that meant the 1950s. So I jumped ahead a couple of decades to take a look at the son of two of the previous trilogy's heroes doing a favor for one of the previous trilogy's antagonists.

Plus, I'm a sucker for giant robots.

One fun thing about this series that fans of old monster movies will catch, in Spellbound *I had a giant monster climb a building swatting biplanes in the same year King Kong came out in real life, and "Tokyo Raider" is set the same year as the original Godzilla. That's where the code name Gorilla Whale came from.*

That 1950s Grimnoir trilogy is currently in the works.

THE TESTIMONY
OF THE TRAITOR RATUL

"The Testimony of the Traitor Ratul" first appeared on Baen.com in 2019. It is set in my epic fantasy Saga of the Forgotten Warrior universe. The first book in this series is Son of the Black Sword, *which was nominated for the David Gemmell Award, and won the 2016 Dragon Award for Best Fantasy.*

I HAVE BEEN CALLED MANY THINGS, like Ratul the Swift, or Ratul Without Mercy, and much later I was known as Ratul the Mad, or Ratul the Traitor. I have held many offices, most notably the rank of Master within the Protector Order, a title reserved for only the fiercest defenders of the Law. Yet that mighty office paled in importance to my illicit calling, when the Forgotten appointed me the Keeper of Names. I gave up one of the mightiest stations in the land to become a fugitive, and did so gladly, for I truly believe the gods are real.

Some say I am a fool, and all say that I am a criminal. Religion is illegal; preaching, as I have done, is punishable by death. My time will come. I embrace my fate, for they are the fools, not I. It is the world which has forgotten the truth. Soon they will be forced to remember, and it will be a most painful event.

Yes, I have been called a great many things, from heroic leader and master swordsman to fanatical rebel and despicable murderer, but young Ratul Memon dar Sarnobat was a kind-hearted child, nothing at all like the jaded killer I would become.

Those years are long distant now. I was born on the moors south of Warun, second son of a vassal house, and second sons of the first caste are commonly obligated to serve the Capitol for a period of time. It is said the houses keep their eldest close to prepare them to inherit and rule, but offer the rest of their children to the Capitol to demonstrate their total commitment to the Law. In truth, it is in the hope we can secure offices of importance within the various orders to siphon wealth and favors back to our families, but I was naÔve then, and did not yet understand the hypocrisy and rot within our system.

Young Ratul dreamed of being obligated to the Historians Order to maintain the relics in the Capitol Museum, or perhaps the Archivists Order, to spend my days organizing the stacks of the Great Library, for young Ratul loved stories and books. I also had a great talent for music and dance, as did all in my house, but I was the most graceful child. Perhaps I would be best obligated to an artisan's school, and go on to compose great plays? Maybe I would be an Architect, raising mighty monuments to the Law, or something odd and secretive like the Astronomer, tracking the moons and cataloging the sky? Regardless of where I was obligated, I looked forward to living in the magnificent Capitol, where it was said all the women were beautiful, the food was rich, and the waters pure and free of demons.

As a gangly boy with thin arms, a narrow chest, and a sensitive disposition, it never even entered my mind that I might be obligated to one of the militant orders. Only upon the flag of Great House Sarnobat is the wolf, and such a cunning predator is a fitting symbol for the family which mine was vassal to. I shall not delve into the petty house politics which resulted in my obligation going to the Protector Order, but basically, my father had given some inadvertent insult to our Thakoor. Thus it amused our leader to give me to the most infamous order of all, the brutal enforcers of the Law, where it was common for their young obligations to die in their unforgiving training program.

I recall my mother sobbing as I left our house, because she knew in her heart that her soft summer-born child would fail and die miserably.

At fourteen years old—which, by the way, is a little old to become a Protector acolyte—I traveled, not to the glorious and wealthy

Capitol, but to the austere and miserable Hall of the Protectors, near the top of the world, high in the unforgiving mountains of Devakula, in the distant frozen south. I was despondent the entire journey there. All I knew of the Protectors were that they did nothing but pursue and execute lawbreakers. . . . That, and they were one of the few orders whose members were not allowed to wed until their obligation was fulfilled, so they lived a life of stoic solitude. At that age I was a silly romantic, so the idea of being bereft of female companionship until my obligation was done filled me with dread. My service was to last for a period of no less than ten years. And let us be honest, the odds of me surviving ten years of murderous village-burning butchery were slim as my waist.

We crossed a great many narrow bridges over deep chasms on the way to the Hall in Devakula, and I contemplated hurling myself off of every single one. Those I travelled with would surely tell my family it was an accident, for slipping on ice and falling to your doom—though ignominious—was a more honorable end than suicide. Hitting the sharp rocks would've been a much faster end . . .

Except it was during this journey that I found I possessed a great stubbornness, for I would not give my Thakoor the satisfaction of expiring so quickly. To the ocean with him.

Though he was the focus of my great hate at the time, honestly, I can no longer even remember my Thakoor's face—he is as forgotten by me as the gods are to man—but that initial spark of defiance which flickered into being on a swaying bridge high in those mountains has remained with me ever since.

Decades later, that tiny spark would grow into a great roaring fire.

Later that fire would help ignite a conflagration which would threaten to burn the entire world . . . but I get ahead of myself. Gather close my children. I must tell you how I believed in those days, for I still had much to learn.

The Law required there to be three great divisions within our society: the caste that rules, the caste that wars, and the caste that works. Every man has a place. Some said that there was a fourth division, meaning those without caste, but such speech could be considered subversive, for the Law declares that the casteless are not really people at all.

The first caste is the smallest, yet obviously the most important of all whole men. They are the judges and the arbiters of the Law, the members of the various Orders of the Capitol, and the Great House families.

Each Great House has an army to defend its interests. These are the warrior caste. They are more numerous than the first, yet far fewer than the third. I thought of them as a bloodthirsty, boisterous lot, with their own odd customs and a peculiar code of honor, but they were kept in check by the Law and the will of their Great House.

The worker caste was the greatest in number, yet the simplest in direction. They exist to labor. The structure provided by the Law and the wisdom of my caste had shaped Lok into a land of industry and wealth. It was the worker who dug the coal, weaved the cloth, and grew the crops. They paid taxes to the first caste, and paid again for the warriors to defend them, but in turn they required payment for their toil and their goods, for the callous worker is often more motivated by greed than allegiance to the Law.

The castes are the great division, but there are many—perhaps innumerable—lesser divisions beyond that, for each caste had a multitude of offices and ranks, and only members of that particular caste could hope to decipher where they all stood in relation to each other. Every duty or achievement bestowed status upon the individual who held it, and status determined everything else. A miner and a banker were of the same caste, only one could sleep in a mansion and the other in a hovel, yet both would bow their head in deference to the lowliest vassal house arbiter, for he was closer to the Law.

Usually caste was determined by birth, but on rare occasions the Law might require a man to be assigned to a new caste. I'd heard of a particular worker who'd shown great strength, who the warriors had claimed, and in the opposite direction, of an inept and cowardly warrior who'd been ordered to trade his sword for a shovel. A particularly brilliant man could be promoted into the first, but a member of the first would cut his wrists in shame rather than accept the humiliation of leaving his caste.

It turned out my new Order was one such place where warriors could become members of the first, albeit temporarily, for when their obligations ended they would return to their place. It was during my induction ceremony that I stood among children of the warrior caste for the first time. Every one of them, even the ones who were two or more years younger, were far bigger and stronger than I. To the Protectors, the new acolytes were all equally nothing. For the first time in my life, the status I had been born with had become utterly meaningless.

Our training began. Previously I had thought that I understood what hardship was. That had been a delusion. The Hall was as grey and stark as my house was bright and colorful. I'd lived in a land of song, but our only song in the Hall was groans of weariness and cries of sudden pain. Our instruments were wooden swords. Our drums were our sparring partners' helms.

Over and over we were broken, physically and mentally, and constantly remade, not just with muscle and brain, but also with magic. It is said Protectors are more than man. This is true. I shall speak no further about this, for there are some vows which even the vilest traitor still holds dear.

I know now that the program is a thing of beauty. It is so cruel not because the Protectors hate their acolytes, but because we love them. Great suffering prepared us to overcome any obstacle, to face any challenge without flinching, even unto death.

The Order is not so different from the gods in that respect.

As I'd been warned, many of the acolytes perished. However, I would not be among them. For despite being the weakest of the acolytes, I was also the angriest, and in my heart was a great capacity for hate. Hate fueled me. It kept me warm through the cold nights, and every night in Devakula is cold.

At first my hate was directed at that now forgotten Thakoor, who had robbed me of my dreams of idle comfort. Then my hate shifted to the few acolytes who saw in my frail form a victim to be bullied. Tormenting me provided them a temporary distraction from their own torment. But the stupid and morally weak do not last long in the program, so after I outlived those, I needed a new outlet for my hate.

Thus I began to hate the enemies of the Law.

It was the reasoning of a bitter young man. If criminals did not exist, then there would be no need for the Protector Order. If every man kept to his assigned place and did as he was told, then those of us obligated to the militant orders would be free. When it came time for the acolytes to be given lessons in the application of the Law, I excelled, as I always pronounced unhesitating condemnation upon every infraction, and I unfailingly recommended the harshest sentence allowed.

My teachers thought it was because I was smart enough to grasp the nuances of the Law, that I was impartial and calculating as a Protector should be. This was not the case. I was filled with hate. Luckily for me, so was the Law.

It is curious that it is the softest ore which can be forged into the hardest steel. After three years of training my long limbs had turned wiry strong and my already quick mind became sharper. Most beneficially I discovered that the unconscious rhythm and grace of the dancer was not so different from the timing and agility required to master the sword.

Upon obtaining the rank of Senior Protector I went forth into the world to dispense cruel justice.

It turned out that I was rather good at it.

This was the era in which I became widely known as Ratul Without Mercy. None were as devoted as I. Wherever I was assigned, criminals became afraid. From the jungles of Gujara to the plains of Akershan, I spilled blood. I shall spare you the litany of the many sins I committed in the name of the Law. It is a long list, and we have not the hours left before dawn.

Upon my tenth year, my mandatory obligation expired. I had the choice: retire and return to the house where my service had brought them great honor, to do any of the many artistic or intellectual things I had once aspired to, have a marriage arranged for me, create my own house, and raise my heirs . . . or voluntarily continue as a Protector.

Strangely enough, this was not a difficult decision, and I remained with the Order. I'd never have a wife to love me. I would make do with the loveless company of vapid pleasure women whose names and faces were forgotten the next day. I would never have heirs. There would be no sons to carry my name. I would never have a house of my own. The only symphonies I composed were the sounds of battle and my instrument was my sword. I had forgotten how to dream, but I had not forgotten how to hate. I knew that for every criminal I'd executed there was another still in hiding, and I would not be able to rest until every last lawbreaker was dead.

For a righteous hate can be addictive as the poppy.

It was as Protector of the Law, Eleventh Year Senior, that I Ratul encountered the lawbreaker who would start me on my path of rebellion. Of the many types of criminals Protectors hunted—rebels, rapists, murderers, unlicensed wizards, smugglers of bone and black steel, and so forth—none were more hated than religious fanatics, for it was those who practiced illegal religions who were the most nefarious. The others were motivated by things most of us could understand because we'd felt glimmerings of them in our weakest moments, like greed, lust, or jealousy. But the fanatic was motivated by something inscrutable, a belief in invisible forces and imaginary beings. Such foolishness was infuriating to the Law-abiding man.

For many weeks I had searched for this particular fanatic in the hill country of Harban. There had been reports of a nameless man— probably of the worker caste—going about and preaching of gods and prophecies, trying to rouse the people to rebel. As was usual with these types he'd found some success among the casteless. I thought of the non-people as gullible, and a few of them had risen up and struck down their overseer, proclaiming their actions as "the will of the Forgotten" even as the hangman's noose had been put around their necks.

I'd killed many such fanatics. I expected this one to be cut from the same cloth. A raving lunatic, bug-eyed and foaming at the mouth, filthy and unkempt, leaping about and cursing me with the wrath of his unseen gods, but when I finally tracked down my prey, I found a calm, soft-spoken scholar instead. Not of the worker caste as alleged, but like me, born of the first. He didn't live in a muddy cave, or a hollowed-out tree. He lived in a small but sturdy cottage, on a hill overlooking the city of Lahkshan.

Unlike most—guilty or innocent—who answer a knock at their door and discover a Protector waiting, this man showed no fear. If anything, he seemed resigned, as if weary from his labor. He was just old enough to be a grandfather, no more. There was a sadness in his eyes. I remember this clearly.

"Come in, Protector," said he without preamble.

I had no time for foolishness or a fanatic's tricks. The cottage was humble, but big enough to conceal several enemies. He made no comment upon my drawing my sword as I followed him inside.

There was no rebel ambush waiting therein, just a cot, a pair of comfortable-looking chairs, a kettle warming on the small stove, and a shelf *full* of actual books. That, I marveled at, because it would still be another year before the Order of Technology and Innovation approved the sale of printing presses. Only men of the wealth and status could obtain such a library in those days, and those were usually prominently displayed in a Great House, not a one-room abode in the hills.

I had not even declared the charges against him, when the fanatic declared, "I am guilty of all the crimes you suspect, and probably more. I will not resist, and I accept my punishment without protest."

"The penalty for proselytizing is death."

He simply nodded. Even though I was about to slay him, this fanatic was so polite that I almost felt bad for not taking off my shoes before entering his home.

Curious, I went to the shelf and started checking the books. Some of them were new, approved volumes purchased from the Great Library of the Capitol, but others appeared to be ancient. I opened one of those, gently, for its binding felt as if it might crumble to dust. I skimmed a few pages, at first thinking it was a history of some kind, and instead discovered the most heinous of crimes. These were religious tomes.

They were *scriptures*. There was nothing more illegal in the world.

I dropped the book as if it had burned my fingers. "Saltwater!"

"Though still forbidden, these are not originals, Protector. Those rotted away long ago. These are copies of copies, handed down in secret."

"Why would you keep such terrible things?"

"To learn about our past and our nature. The people of Lok had many different religions before the demons fell from the sky, each believing different things. I have gathered the holy books of several of those over my travels. The books disagree on more things than they agree, but all are fascinating in their own way."

I'd seen the various rough-hewn idols of the fanatics scattered about Lok; the four-armed man, the elephant-headed man and his mouse, the smiling fat man, and I'd broken each one I'd found, but I'd never before seen one of their books, because the Order of Inquisition had burned most of them long ago.

"I am curious, Protector. You've not yet set my home to the torch."

"Oh, I will."

"I know, but you hesitate. I have a feeling that you are a student of history."

He had guessed well. "As much as the Law allows."

"Then that is why you wait. May I ask of what house you were before joining your Order?"

I do not know why I answered truthfully, but I had never before engaged a madman in a conversation. "Sarnobat. Of the vassal house Memon."

"Ah!" The fanatic went to the shelf and picked out a particular book. "Your people were a rare minority in old Lok. This was the holy book your ancestors used." Upon its cover was a crescent moon and a star. I'd seen such a symbol before, in my childhood, when a farmer had unearthed an old stone, and the Inquisitors had come and smashed it to dust with hammers. He held the book out to me, like he was offering a gift, but I did not take it. Seemingly disappointed, he put the illegal tome back on the shelf. "Of course, you would not want that one anyway, Protector. That is not why you are here."

"I'm here to execute you for violations of the Law."

"You are here because the Forgotten wanted you to be. There were many religions before, but only one that mattered after the demons came." He picked out a different book, bound in grey, narrower than the others. I did not accept it either, but he left it standing alone. "This one is a copy of a book written during the Age of Kings, from after the demons were driven back into the sea. The Forgotten wants you to have it."

Genuinely baffled, I asked, "All these gods are forgotten now, so why speak of this one as if it's special?"

"I did not choose him. He chose me. And now he has chosen you."

I grew tired of this talk. The time had come. He did not so much as cringe as I raised my sword.

I could not help but ask, "Why are you not afraid?"

"Because in a dream the Forgotten showed me the man who would claim my burden and my life. Farewell, Ratul."

I had never told the fanatic my name.

Strangely enough, I did not hate this man. I stabbed him in the heart because it was expected of me, but I did not hate him.

I would have returned quickly to my duties, but the hour was late, and a cold rain had begun to fall, so I decided to spend the night in the fanatic's cottage and return to Lahkshan in the morning. I ate the fanatic's dinner of curried goat, and sat in his comfortable chair, as he lay dead on his floor.

My sleep was plagued with strange dreams. I awoke with a great unease.

My eyes kept drifting back to the shelf, and that book. Not the one of my ancestors, but the strange grey one which had come after. A sick curiosity gnawed at the back of my mind. Part of me desired to read this lurid tale from the Age of Kings, an era whose records were declared mostly off limits to us. The Law was clear that I should not so much as let my eyes touch those pages, but I have already established that I was not a being of Law, but rather a being of hate.

I'd dealt with fanatics before, but I had never once been tempted to understand their superstitions beyond what I needed to know to better kill them. The Law said I should not, but my defiance said I should. I've fought many battles, but none were more difficult than the one I faced that night as I tried to decide between looking inside and placing it in the stove. Eventually I decided I would look briefly, and *then* I would burn it, so it could tempt me no more.

I lit an oil lamp and retrieved the book.

The brief glance I allowed myself stretched into hours as I read all through the night.

It was the forbidden history of our people, and all that came before. It did not read like the ramblings of madmen, or the lies of charlatans. I was pulled along, seemingly against my will, as I read of things strange, yet somehow familiar.

It struck me as true, and that was troublesome.

The book told of what had been, what was, and what would be. How we would rise, and fall, and rise, and fall again. It was in that last section, filled with dire prophecies, that I stopped, suddenly afraid, as I realized that centuries ago, this writer had been *writing about me.*

I speak not of generalities, or vague mumbling that could be about anyone if you squinted hard enough, but of a man without mercy, enforcer of an unjust code, who would stab a faithful servant in the heart and then read this very book while sitting next to his cooling corpse.

Suddenly furious, I threw the book on the floor. Then I dashed the oil lamp against the wall, setting the cottage ablaze. I stormed outside . . . only to be tempted to rush back in to try and save that damnable book. But I did not, and instead watched the cottage burn to the ground. Once I was satisfied all was ash, I walked back to Lahkshan in the dark and rain.

In the days that followed I devoted myself to the Law, and did my best to forget all that I had read. Ratul Without Mercy was the scourge of criminals everywhere. Rebels and fanatics fell to my sword.

Yet no matter how hard I worked, or how many criminals I killed, I could not shake the feeling that book had imparted to me. My dreams were haunted. If they were visions from forgotten gods, or figments of my imagination, I could not tell. I told no one, not even my closest friends in the Order, about what was troubling me.

As the years went on, I saw more distressing things, events which could be taken as signs of dire prophecies, indicators of a looming apocalypse. *If* the book was true, and *if* the prophecies were true, then drastic action had to be taken soon or man was doomed.

I had been taught that before the Law, there was only madness. That it had been created by the first judges to save Lok from the chaos that was the Age of Kings. The Law was all-encompassing. All things are subject to the Law. Even the demons of hell must obey. They remain in the sea and man stays upon the land. Those who violate are guilty of trespass and will be punished.

But the Law could give me no answer. Merely voicing my concerns would have resulted in me being hung upon the Inquisitor's Dome to cook to death beneath the sun, my flesh devoured by vultures, and my bones swept into a hole. Though my faith in the Law was shaken, my loyalty to my Order remained strong, for I loved my brothers. There is a kinship that can only be found in hardship. Yet even among them, there was none whom I could confide in. To do so was to condemn them as I was condemned.

I began to question my assumptions and everything I believed. I required knowledge. Using my status as a Protector I was able to access parts of the Museum and the Great Library which were off limits to all but a select few. In secret I studied the black steel artifacts which had survived the Age of Kings. I consulted with the Historians. I learned what the Astronomers were really watching for. My desperate search across the Capitol was a grotesque version of the dreams once held by Young Ratul.

My sustaining hatred did not die, but once again shifted its aim. My fixation became the judges who had kept us from the truth for hundreds of years. I began to despise the Capitol for the things it had me and my brothers do. As I lost respect for those who wrote and interpreted the Laws, I began to delve into more forbidden areas of research.

It was in a cavern, deep beneath the world, that I met a giant. I speak not of a large man, like Protector Karno who stands a head above most, but of a true giant. Ten feet tall, with skin blue as a Dasa, who'd slept through the centuries, but had been born when kings still ruled.

The giant told me of a place in the steaming jungles of Gujara. There I sought out a legendary temple with carvings upon the wall where the last oracle of the Forgotten had prophesied of those who would be gathered to once again lead the Sons of Ramrowan in the final battle against the demons. There were three old symbols—the Priest, the Voice, and the General—representing those who must be found. Then more symbols, vague warning of some of those who would stand against the Forgotten's chosen, such as the Crown, and the Mask, and then the Demon, the last of which surely represented the entire host of hell.

In the distant south, in the coldest winter, I waited until the ice froze enough for me to walk across the ocean without being eaten by sea demons, so that I could knock upon the impenetrable gates of Fortress. They tried to blast me to pieces with their terrible magic before I convinced them that I too was a seeker of truth. I spoke with the guru and discovered that I was not alone in preparing for the end.

Yet, doubts remained.

Despite all my quests for forbidden wisdom into the darkest corners of Lok, the truth was finally revealed to me, not by a wall in a distant jungle temple or a fantastical being, but by one of my fellow Protectors. For it was I, Ratul, twenty-five-year Master of the Protector Order, who discovered the secret identify of one of our acolytes. A secret which would shake the very foundations of our society should it be revealed, for a lowly casteless had been chosen to bear the most powerful magic in the world.

It took this clear fulfillment of prophecy to finally convince me, and through conviction at last came my conversion.

The prophecies were real. *The gods were real.*

It took more research before I was certain that this boy was meant to be the Forgotten's warrior. I could never tell him who he really was. To do so would be to destroy him. And selfishly, in the meantime, I did not wish to deprive the Protectors of this powerful weapon which had revitalized and strengthened our waning order.

As I tell you that tonight, I know it seems senseless that even after being converted I would still try to help the very Order which has done so much harm to the faithful. They may be misguided by the Law, but the Protectors are the best of men. They do more good than harm. Though they despise me now, and they will surely take my life soon, they remain my brothers.

After that, I lived two lives simultaneously, Lord Protector beneath the eyes of the Law, and rebellious criminal in the shadows. While I still have faith the gods would show the General his path, it was my duty to search for the Voice and the Priest. I carefully checked every report from my Protectors involving religious fanatics. I did everything I could short of revealing my treachery to save what worshippers I could, ordering my men elsewhere, giving faulty intelligence, or even sneaking messages to the faithful to run.

That was how I found the genealogy and secretly became the Keeper of Names.

It was twelve long years after my conversion before I found the Voice in Makao. Yes, children, a true prophet walks amongst us once again. For their safety, I will not speak here of this person's identity, but the Voice lives, and I give you my word that the Voice is real.

The Forgotten speaks to us, and he requires great things of us before we may have our reward.

Unfortunately there were witnesses to my discovery. Word of that event spread to my Order. I was required to explain my actions. Why had Ratul Without Mercy spared the life of an illegal wizard? I told the closest friend I've ever had the truth.

He turned his back on me.

My treachery was at last revealed, and I had to flee.

My name is worth saltwater. I am the most hated man in the history of the Protectors . . . for now.

I have hidden among the casteless and continued my search. It is here, in the borders of Great House Uttara, that I believe I have finally found the Forgotten's High Priest. He is clever, but driven by anger and bitterness, like I once was. Yet it is his ambition which will finally free our people.

We are out of time.

Ratul had suddenly looked to the south, eyes narrowed dangerously. She knew that Ratul's senses—augmented by the magic of the Protector Order—were far superior to anyone else present. Maybe he had smelled the smoke of the burning barracks, or the blood of warriors being shed. Perhaps he heard the screams of the dying as the casteless attacked the warriors.

"That damned fool," Ratul muttered, sounding now like the tired old man that he was. "I must go and save his life. Farewell."

He said that not to the mob of dirty casteless who had been clustered around him, listening intently to his story, but to her. His testimony was really intended for her alone. These casteless did not know it yet, but they would probably all be dead by morning, caught up in the bloody purge which would follow Keta's inevitably failed rebellion.

She would live, as she always did.

Ratul rushed out the door of the shack. She got up and followed. There was a faint orange glow in the distance as the arson fires spread.

"There is a Protector there," she warned him.

"I know. I can sense the magic in his blood."

"Does it tell you which one?"

"No, but I suspect who it will be . . ." Ratul turned back to face her, grim. "Since my treachery was revealed, each night as I have dreamed, the Forgotten has shown me the same vision. I am wading through waist deep snow, in the mountains of Devakula, and I know that I am being pursued by a mighty predator. It is one of the great southern bears, white as the snow, powerful and proud. In the dream, there is no escape. And every night, the bear gets closer and closer. Last night, it was so near I could feel the hot breath upon my neck, and when I looked up, it had a bloody scar across its face."

"Devedas." She knew of him, but she knew a great many things, more even than Ratul. "Then if you go, you will surely die."

"There was one thing I did not speak of tonight. The last prophecy in that book I read in that dead man's cottage all those years ago, that enraged me so. It foretold my death, cut down by a man I'd love as a son, who would love me more than his own father . . . That knowledge . . . comforts me." The condemned man smiled. "I have no hate left."

"May the gods lift you, Ratul of many names."

"Thank you for all of your help, Mother Dawn."

Then Ratul went to seal his testimony with his blood.

This story was released to come out about the same time as the second book in the series, House of Assassins, *and it was a chance for me to write about a character who had not shown up very much in the books, yet who had been extremely important in the lives of a few of the main characters.*

With "The Testimony of the Traitor Ratul," I used a style that was different than the main series. In this case I wanted Ratul to just tell his story in his own way. I had been listening to a few different Robert E. Howard collections on Audible at the time, and he used that tough guy sitting by the fire telling his tale method really well. I'm a big Howard fan, so I thought it would be fun to try that here.

The third novel in this series, Destroyer of Worlds, *will be out in 2020.*

SHOOTER READY

This story originally appeared in Galactic Games, *an anthology of science fiction stories with a sports theme, edited by Bryan Thomas Schmidt, and published by Baen Books in 2016.*

A GOOD SHOOTER *does all his thinking before stepping into the box. Survey the course, plan your strategy, check your gear one last time, get that out of the way while you're on deck, because if you take the time to think after that, you lose. Shooting needs to come as natural as breathing. When it's your turn and you're there, waiting for that buzzer, hands raised to the surrender position, pistol in your holster, you don't think.*

You just act.

Clear your head and shoot. It isn't draw stroke, move to the firing position, target, front sight focus, trigger squeeze, repeat a few hundred times until the course is done and you collect your trophy and your prize money and head to the after party to bang the hot groupies. That works for local circuits on your home world, but there's nothing normal about this level of competition. When the difference between the first-place winner and hundredth-place loser is separated by a grand total of a second over eight or ten stages, there's no time for this step A, step B, step C bullshit. That's too slow.

I'm the last pure flesh-and-blood human practical shooting champion for a reason. I'm beating cyborgs with laser range finders in their eyeballs, and vat babies literally born to shoot. I'm beating robots that were designed to be one-man SWAT teams.

You know why I win? It's because in my head I go to this place where I see everything, time means nothing. It's Zen, man. I'm just shooting, five, six aimed shots a second, moving and manipulating as efficiently as I can, but never thinking about what I'm doing. Stimulus, response. After the match me and my coaches can watch the videos and see what I could have done better for next time, but I never think during the stage.

Pure action, time ceases to exist. It feels slow, but it's really fucking fast. I'm talking some Miyamoto Musashi-state-of-being shit here, you get me?

Of course you don't get it. If you got it, you'd have my job and I'd be the sports reporter.

The Zen state . . . Well, your body knows what to do because you've already trained it. Millions of rounds over thousands of hours, shooting and shooting and shooting until your hands bleed. I've loaded so many mags that there are dead spots where my fingers can't feel anything. I spent so much time at the range that my wife left me and I didn't notice she was gone for a week. I've shot so many rounds that my sinuses are permanently filled with carbon. No, seriously, flowers and perfume smell like smoke. I fired six hundred rounds this morning before coming to this interview.

By the time you get to this level, you've performed so damned many repetitions that the actions are burned into the pathways of your brain. It knows what to do to win, even if you consciously don't.

If you waver for even a fraction of a second, you're too slow. That's how the robots beat most of us. People blame it on them being so much faster and stronger. Robots don't get tired. Robots don't have muscle tremors. They don't have a heart that's pounding too hard to make that two-thousand-yard shot after running up Puke Hill at the Ironman. That's bullshit. That's a cop-out.

The robots win because they're programmed to win.

See this? This was the body I was born with. I'm not genetically engineered. I'm not augmented. I'm not on stims. There's no Hampson device plugged into my brain downloading techniques right into my memory. I'm just a man with a gun.

I win because I've programmed myself to win.

That's why I'm the last human champion, and that's why I'm the best there has ever been.

❖ ❖ ❖

As he watched the old interview play, it made him smile. *I sure was a cocky little bastard.* He'd been so confident and full of himself back then, but nothing taught humility quite like a decade of getting your ass kicked.

"Could I get your autograph, Mr. Blackburn?" the fan held out the projector. "You were a legend. On New Hebron we've got these nasty carnivorous whistle spiders. I watched your lesson on snap shooting, and it's saved my ass a few times."

"Glad to hear it, kid." He used his fingertip to sign the hologram. That made the fan happy. There weren't as many fans as there used to be, but he was still enough of a draw that gun companies kept hiring him to sit in their booths during arms expos. "Why don't you grab some swag?" He looked around for the marketing guy. "Hey, Frank, hook this young man up with a T-shirt. Here you go. Keep practicing, and don't forget to check out the"—he had to look at the logo on the T-shirt in his hands to remember which minor company he was shilling for today—"Krasnov. When you think directed energy weapons, think Krasnov."

The crowd moved on. People played with disabled guns, shouldering them, flipping switches, and looking through sights. Most of them were polite enough to keep them pointed in a safe direction. Salesmen cut deals, money was exchanged, and purchase orders placed. The off-world dealers just bought the schematics so they could pay royalties to print the guns in their own shops, which was way cheaper than shipping them across space. There were a lot of big money types wandering around, buyers from different militaries, government agencies, and large corporations, but most of the crowd were regular gun nuts who just wanted to play with cool new things and score free stuff. Arms expos always felt the same, even on backwater colony planets.

Since being a minor celebrity at this sort of thing paid his bills now, he knew them very well.

The next man to enter the booth was obviously one of the big fish. He didn't bother to look at the merchandise. He was wearing a gold VIP badge and one of those super-expensive suits with the light-transmitting fibers that made the wearer seem to glow. The man didn't care about the free pens, buttons, and probably wasn't a T-shirt type. Passing the salesmen, he went right to the minor celebrity guest. "Are you Scott Blackburn?"

"Yes, sir." He tried to read the man's badge, but the name and company weren't lit. "How can I help you?"

Now that he was closer, it was obvious the man was Human 2.1, maybe even higher. He towered over everyone else in the booth, and was just too obnoxiously ageless and perfect. It was like looking up to a god. "Are you the Scott Blackburn who won the tri-systems practical shooting championship from '78 to '81?"

"That's me." But the post-human already knew that. Their brains were wired with facial recognition programs.

"You were the best competitor?"

He couldn't tell if that was a question or a statement. "Briefly?"

"Forgive me if I am unclear. I only downloaded English a few minutes ago. I am Mr. Lee. May I buy you lunch?"

"Well, I'm working . . ." but apparently the Krasnov marketing manager knew who Mr. Lee was, and was making shooing motions to get Scott out of the booth. This Mr. Lee must have been in position to buy a shitload of guns. "What's this about?"

"It is about being the best, Mr. Blackburn. Ultimately, everything is about that."

This is it, folks. We're here at the first stage of the Grand Halifax Open Class Invitational. As you can see, our reigning champ, Scott Blackburn, is stepping into the box. There's been a lot of talk on the circuit this year about the threat posed by the new Diomedes 5 competition robots. After last year's narrow victory over the Diomedes 4, which the Diomedes Corporation blamed on a last-minute programming error, the pressure is on Blackburn. They claim that this new generation is significantly faster than last year's model. The question on everyone's mind, can the human champ hold on one more year? What do you think, Jess?

My money is on Blackburn still, Javier. The kid's got heart. This stage will follow the highlighted route, with the shooter engaging holographic moving targets from five to five hundred meters. They'll be starting with pistols, and then switching to long guns once they clear the obstacles. Grand Halifax scoring is brutal, anything other than an X-zone hit adds half a second to your overall time. A miss adds a whopping two whole seconds. To put that in perspective, the X-zone on a Grand Halifax hologram is ten centimeters wide, and the whole hologram is only thirty centimeters across.

Pure accuracy will go to the machine, but it remains to be seen if it's got the programming to pay the bills . . . They're ready. We're switching live now to Blackburn.

"Shooter ready?"

"Shooter ready."

BEEP.

And he's off.

Damn, that's fast. Blackburn is already at the first array. I don't think I've ever seen anybody clear a star that quick. He's in top form today.

You can see him dodging through the obstacles. He's not even slowing down as he shoots on the move. Blackburn's running a 6mm 3011 set on three-round burst. As you're watching, keep in mind he's still experiencing some recoil there. That's no energy weapon, and the 6mm loads still make major power factor . . . Did you see that, Jess?

Holy moly, that was quick!

Blackburn's reloading on the move. Remember, the Diomedes has an autoloader in its wrist and performs half-second mag changes.

Transitioning to the long gun, now Blackburn's got to slow down enough to nail the longer-range targets.

He's not slowing down much.

Grand Halifax is at .7 standard gravity and has zero wind, so all that training on Mars is probably coming in handy for Blackburn right now.

Remarkably, he's still down zero points. Not a single miss. He's switching to the shotgun barrel for the final speed run. And . . . the stop plate is down.

55.64 seconds clean! Down zero points. That is the fastest that anyone has ever run this stage at Grand Halifax. He burned it down.

Starting the day by setting a new stage record? Team Blackburn has got to be feeling pretty good about keeping the championship in human hands for one more year. We're going to the pit to try and catch a word with Scott Blackburn. He's unloading and showing clear to the safety officer, and it looks like Tom has caught up with our champ for a word—

Hang on. Switch back. Diomedes has already started its run.

Transcript note: Period of stunned silence. Transmission resumes.

Jesus . . .
Diomedes 4 just ran the course in 38.08.
I've never seen anything like it.
I think we've just witnessed the end of an era, Javier.
Or maybe the beginning of a new one, Jess.

From the team of security guards surrounding them, and the way every local vendor in the place bowed nearly to the floor as they passed, Mr. Lee was a big fucking deal. Despite that, they just went to the convention center food court to eat.

The glowing post-human man-god ordered chicken fingers. "Let me begin by saying the history of your sport fascinates me. To succeed requires a combination of grace, fine motor coordination, and skill. It is not about pure accuracy, like some other sports, but accurate enough, while going extremely fast. Engaging multiple targets from different positions and on the move, from conversational distance to long range, switching between different weapon systems as you go, it is all very exhilarating to watch. It is no wonder it has become one of the most popular sports on many planets."

Mr. Lee just sounded so damned earnest about it that Scott had to chuckle. "Yeah, we used to say that it was the most fun you could have with your pants on."

"Tell me about why you got into competitive shooting, Mr. Blackburn."

"Are you a sports reporter or something?"

"I am not, but I own several sports reporters."

"Oh . . ." Scott wasn't sure which system Mr. Lee was from, so he wasn't sure if that was the language download glitching or if he actually owned slaves. "Well, my grandfather started long-range shooting competitions on Mars, and my father was the champ for years. Hell, my great-grandfather shot USPSA back when there was still a United States. So I guess you can say it's in my blood."

"But you have said yourself that good competitors are not born, they are made. Raw talent and physical gifts are no match for a developed mindset." Mr. Lee tapped the side of his head for dramatic effect. "I have downloaded all your interviews."

"If you already know my answers, why ask the question?"

Mr. Lee shrugged. It was a remarkably human gesture from

someone who was beyond humanity. "I have spoken with many washed-up athletes. I've found that answers provided in interviews are often different than the truth."

"I'm not *washed up*. I still shoot and I still win."

"My apologies. That was a poor choice of phrase. I meant to say that you are no longer at the top of your game. You still win, but in front of a much smaller audience, and only against other unaugmented humans in Limited Class."

The box containing Scott's lunch slid out of the dispenser chute. At least he was getting a free meal out of this bullshit. "What do you want?"

"I am what you would call a *sports fan*."

It's been a hell of a ride for former champ Scott Blackburn. From the height of the sport to several losing seasons in a row, we caught up with him after his humiliating defeat at Garnier Station.

Scott, what happened out there?

Shooting in zero g is always a challenge. When you're using projectile weapons, every shot is going to propel you along. You've got to be not just aware of where you are, but where you're going to be after you start spinning and plan your angles accordingly. It's the toughest environment to shoot in. I made a bad call and misjudged the ranges going in.

But, Scott, the winner had four arms and clung to the walls with a prehensile tail. He was bred to live in space. How could you possibly hope to beat him?

I know the winner. Grez is a hell of a nice guy. He's a good competitor and a good shooter. This is a big win for him.

But wouldn't you say his genetic modification gave him an unfair advantage?

Are you looking to get me to spout off some pure human supremacy nonsense? No. Grez is a good dude. I lost, he won. That's competition. End of story. Open Class means anything goes.

Some are saying that it is time for you to get out of Open and move down to Limited Class.

I know I've lost some sponsors this year, but that's how these things go. I'll train hard during the off season and come back and try again next year.

But, Scott, some say that you've hit a physical plateau. You're as good as a normal human can ever hope to be. Have you thought about getting yourself modified?

This interview is over.

As their conversation had gone on, Scott had realized that Mr. Lee wasn't just a fan, he was one of those dreaded *super fans*, a geeky walking encyclopedia of sports trivia. Memorizing stats wasn't particularly impressive when you'd been genetically engineered to have a super brain, but it was obvious Mr. Lee was passionate about this stuff.

"I'm betting you've got one hell of a collection of sports memorabilia."

"Yes. It is impressive. The centerpiece is Madison Square Garden. I had it dismantled brick by brick, and reassembled on my home planet."

Scott didn't know what a Madison Square Garden was. "That's nice."

"History fascinates me. Did you know that though practical shooting has been around for centuries, it has only been in the last hundred years your sport has become huge? It was held back from going mainstream on Earth due to logistical, cultural, and political reasons."

Scott ticked off reasons on his fingers. "Some politicians hated people having access to guns. You needed a big area to fling lead around. Some cultures were scared of regular folks with weapons."

"Indeed. The proliferation of 3D printing destroyed the concept of gun control forever. And as mankind rapidly spread across the stars, many habitable colonies had to deal with primitive aliens."

Nothing put the practical into practical shooting like having the local life forms constantly trying to kill you. You were hard pressed nowadays to find a colony world where people weren't armed to the teeth. Scott took a drink of his soda, thankful that at least he was way past the point of his career where he needed to hire out as *pest control*.

"Shooting clubs proliferated. The introduction of holographic and robot targets added a new element of spectator enjoyment." Mr. Lee seemed really pleased about that. "As they say, the rest is history."

"Which would make me a historical footnote."

"Exactly!" Mr. Lee laughed, only Scott hadn't been trying to be funny. "You know, they made a movie about the first robot that took your championship. Diomedes was portrayed as a modern day Jackie Robinson. You were the villain."

"I haven't seen it," Scott lied.

"I love sports movies. It is all about narrative." He said it like he was savoring the word. "Practical shooting is a throwback, the rare Olympic sport celebrating combative skills, which are now obsolete, like wrestling, or throwing the javelin. Did you know that shooting was the second-to-last sport where unassisted humans reigned supreme?"

"What was the last holdout? Golf?"

"Surprisingly enough, bowling."

He wouldn't have guessed that, but then again, he hadn't bowled in fifty years, and most of that had been futilely chucking balls down the gutter. "Go figure."

"It was easy for science to make men stronger, but it took longer to replace pure humans in games that required more finesse."

"Makes sense." Scott picked at his food with his chopsticks but wasn't feeling particularly hungry. Talking with super fans always ended up depressing.

On the other hand, Mr. Lee seemed to be having a grand time talking about his love. "Do you remember football, Mr. Scott? The American style football? The one you throw. Not the kind you kick."

"Sure." Scott had even watched it as a kid. He'd been born on Mars, but his ancestors had come from Texas, so granddad had declared their compound to be Cowboys fans. "It's still popular on some worlds."

"It was once the biggest sport on Earth. The National Football League held an event called the Super Bowl, which for many years was the most lucrative sporting event on the planet. It was a celebration of the greatest athletes, and most of humanity tuned in to watch the struggle. Have you ever watched a Super Bowl, Mr. Blackburn?"

The last one of those had been long before he'd been born. "Can't say that I have."

"There is a reason it went away. When scientists invented performance-enhancing drugs, the NFL banned them, because that would be *cheating*. They would create an *unfair* advantage." Mr. Lee banged one fist on the plastic table for emphasis. "Can you imagine such backwards thinking?"

Several of the security guards glanced his way. Scott just gave them an apologetic look. It was the rich post-human who was getting spun up, not him.

"When the first true cyborg limbs were invented, they were also banned. When drastically improved organs were grown in vats, banned. Genetic modification and splicing, banned. Every scientific improvement for the betterment and improvement of mankind, all banned." This really seemed to bother Mr. Lee, and as a post-human himself, it made sense why. "They said this was for fairness, for equality, to level the playing field. Do you know what killed the NFL, Mr. Blackburn?"

"No."

"Boredom. People do not watch sports for *equality*. It is the quest for excellence. It is to celebrate the best, and to *be* the best. Other leagues were created which were not burdened by such racist, old-fashioned rules, or blocked by arbitrary and capricious laws. Until one day most viewers realized that instead of watching the same old limited humans playing the same limited old game, they could watch a defense made up of eight-foot-tall, six-hundred-pound titans, trying to stop a running back with a cybernetic lower body sprinting at sixty miles an hour."

"That isn't sport anymore. That's just seeing who is willing to graft more crap onto their body, replacing skill with software and muscles with hardware." Scott shook his head. "Some of us weren't in it for the spectacle."

"Too bad your audience was. Limited Class has a tiny fraction of the viewership of Open Class now. Your division has slightly higher ratings than the one where people dress up as cowboys and compete with old-timey six-shooters."

"You're right. Nobody wants to watch us boring, limited humans anymore." Scott was tired and annoyed. "Look, I might just be some washed-up nobody now, working here one step up from a booth babe, but I was pretty damned good once." Scott put his chopsticks on the table and quickly stood up. The guards tensed. "Now if you'll excuse me, I'm going to go back to degrading myself for money."

"Please wait, Mr. Blackburn."

"No." He made it another five feet before his temper got the better of him and he turned back. "You wait. I was the best. I trained my ass off. Back in my day it was about your heart and your work ethic, not your DNA or your CPU. I won because I earned it."

"I know. That's why I sought you out."

He hesitated. "What exactly is it that you want then, Mr. Lee?"

"To give you another shot at the title."

Matt,

I'm really sorry, but I'm not going to be able to see you this month. I got a slot in the Manzanita System division championship match. It was a last-minute thing. One of the Open shooters dropped out and the network needed a replacement. I've not gotten an Open slot for years. By the time you watch this recording, I'll be through the wormhole.

You're probably sick of explanations and excuses. I know, you're thinking "Oh great, Dad's missing another birthday because he's off losing again. He must care more about his game than he does about me." But it isn't like that. When I was your age, my dad was always gone, too. When he came home he was distracted and bored, just killing time until the next match. He had the bug. So I know how you feel. I really do.

I didn't get him then, but I get him now. If you're not competing you're not living, you're just existing. I wish I could explain it better, but I can't. I couldn't explain it to your mom, which is probably why she left me. And I really can't blame her.

I've only ever been good at one thing, but the universe kept progressing and left me behind. Now I'm a joke to them. The only reason I got this slot was because watching me fail amuses the audience. They get to feel smug and say, wow, look how far we've come in so little time. Isn't technology wonderful?

Sorry, Matt, it's never been about beating the other guys, or entertaining the crowds, it's been about beating myself. There's a feeling you get when you achieve something nobody else can do. It makes you feel alive. It's about one last chance at being the best.

I know I can't be the best anymore. But I still have to try.
Be good for your mom. I love you, son.

"Please, sit down." Mr. Lee gestured at the abandoned chair.

Scott reluctantly returned to the table.

"I know everything about you, Mr. Blackburn. I know that your body chemistry won't accept cybernetic enhancements because you've already tried repeatedly. You're too old to try manipulating your genetic code, but you paid a fortune to black market biohackers to try anyway and nearly died in the process."

"It hurt like you can't imagine," he muttered.

"Oh, I can. One of my many companies designed most of the drugs involved. I've seen the pain involved break the will of the strongest specimens. Yet you still tried *four* times. That is dedication. You were willing to destroy your body in an attempt to be a little better. To what lengths will someone like you go to win?"

Scott had no answer.

"Even if you'd succeeded, it wouldn't have mattered very long anyway." Mr. Lee opened his hand and a hologram appeared over his palm. "This is Diomedes 7. It is predicted to run the first stage at Grand Halifax under thirty seconds next season. It has an AI which would have been worthy of a starship ten years ago, and a thorium reactor meant for a hover tank. Every limb is a different, maximized weapon system, projectile, beam, plasma, and nano. In a tenth of a second, it sees every target on the course and paints them with a laser that analyzes the movement of every air molecule in its path. And after it annihilates its competition, it will put on a very realistic flesh mask and provide compelling interviews."

"I'm sure its sponsors will love that."

"No. We won't. It lacks *heart*. Test audiences like it when their heroes have to struggle." Mr. Lee moved his fingers slightly and the hologram of the robot changed to a machine even more advanced. "Which is why I want to put your brain inside of this."

Scott read the stats flashing past. It was a monster.

"Those are conservative estimates based upon our existing test subjects. Using you as the biological core, I think we can make it even faster."

"My brain would only slow that thing down."

"On the contrary, the decisions are processed in advance based on hypothetical scenarios and extrapolations, then stored. When the decision is triggered, there is only instantaneous action." Mr. Lee said patiently.

"That's how I shoot . . ."

"Exactly. Which is why you were chosen for this project. You would be surprised what the human brain can accomplish when freed from its fleshy tethers."

He spoke like he'd removed a lot of brains. "What do you do for a living anyway?"

"I own several planets, Mr. Blackburn. It is easier to ask what do I not do."

"But why are you doing *this*?"

Mr. Lee gave him a benevolent, godlike smile. "I believe sports to be about the quest for excellence. It is about pushing the boundaries of achievement. You were willing to die for this game. Instead, I ask you to live for it." He changed the hologram again, this time to a contract. "I have just sent a copy of this to your agent and your attorney."

The contract was for more money than Scott had ever imagined, but that wasn't what mattered.

"As I said before, a good sports story is all about narrative, and everyone loves a comeback. Sign here to be the champion again, Mr. Blackburn."

He didn't think. He just acted.

We're here at the final stage of the Manzanita System division championship with Scott Blackburn. He's been called the last man standing, the final human contender in a sport now dominated by robots and post-humans. How're you doing today, Scott?

It's been a hell of a match, Wendy. The high gravity and fire winds always make shooting Manzanita a real challenge. I'd like to thank my sponsor, Krasnov Multinational, for sending me with quality gear that holds up even in these tough conditions.

Scott, you're currently forty-eighth out of fifty shooters on the board. That's a long way down from your peak showings—

The competition has gotten better.

Yes, exactly. Fans are wondering if this will be the last time you ever compete in Open Class, and if that's the case, could this be the last time that any unaugmented human competes at this level? Is this the end of an era?

Not if I can help it.

When Bryan Thomas Schmidt approached me about a sci-fi sports story for Galactic Games, it was really easy for me to decide I was going to write about competition shooting. I'm not particularly athletic, and that was the only sport I've ever actually been really good at. I did well, especially at three gun competition. That's where you use a rifle, shotgun, and pistol to shoot a wide variety of targets over a timed course at various distances. It takes a lot of time and effort to stay really competitive. For a while I was spending every weekend at the range, and a couple nights a week were spent reloading ammunition, but it was fun and the competitors in that sport are a great bunch of people.

However, once my writing career started taking off I had to choose how I was going to spend my limited free time. It was either shoot at that level, or write more books. Writing won. I was never anywhere as committed as the main character in "Shooter Ready," but I've known guys like Scott. Competition is addictive. They're not living unless they're giving 100%.

THREE SPARKS

This story first appeared in Predator: If it Bleeds, *published in 2017 by Titan Books, edited by Bryan Thomas Schmidt.*

I love the Predator movies. When I was offered a chance to write a 30th anniversary Predator story I jumped at it. Since this anthology was about Predators stalking their prey through the ages, I had a lot of options of where I could set it, but as you've seen from a bunch of my other short stories, I kind of love samurai drama. So samurai versus Predator? Hell yeah. How could I not write that?

THEY FOUND THE FIRST BODIES around noon, suspended from a branch high above them, arms dangling. Samurai? They could not tell. It was hard to know someone's social status after they had been skinned.

From the bloat and the stink, combined with the heat, Hiroto guessed they had been dead for three days. He had skinned a lot of game, so even in their sorry state he could tell that this oni was very skilled at butchery. Hiroto was impressed. There were no signs of rope. It would take an incredible amount of strength and balance to haul corpses all the way up there. He had seen great cats cache their kills in trees, but this felt different, as if staged for their benefit. Was it to send a message? Marking territory? He tried not to let his appreciation show. A regular porter should be frightened, so he tried to act that way.

The others, however, didn't have to act.

"Captain Nasu Hiroto, hero of the battle of Dan-no-ura, hero of the battle of Kurikara, master swordsman, and champion archer of the Minamoto Clan. Some say the finest archer in our history, if not, second only to his father. Yet after the war, there would be no peace for him. No. Hiroto took one of *my* ships, and was carried about wherever the waves would take him, always searching for a new battle, for new beasts to slay. Over the years, I heard he was hunting tigers in the jungles of Tenjiku or great white bears in the desolate lands north of Joseon. It is widely believed Nasu Hiroto is the greatest hunter in the world."

There were some exaggerations there but Hiroto did not correct the Shogun's inaccuracies. When the most powerful man in Nippon wanted to ramble, you let him. So Hiroto simply knelt and waited for Minamoto Yoritomo to pronounce his judgment.

"You were one of my most trusted warriors, Hiroto. Why did you leave? After our victory over the Taira Clan, I would have given you great responsibilities."

"I left because you would have given me great responsibilities."

"Your life was mine to spend, Hiroto."

"Spending it teaching children how to use a bow would have been a waste. I am not trying to be facetious, my Lord, but I would have died of boredom. I am not very good at peace."

"Then you picked a fortuitous time to return."

The castle was stifling. It was a miserable day in what had to be the hottest summer in generations. A servant was fanning the red-faced and sweating Shogun. Nobody was fanning Hiroto. He did not rate a fan.

"I should have you executed for your disobedience, you impudent ronin bastard. Yet curiosity gets the better of me. After all these years you returned to Kamakura. Why?"

"I received word that the Shogunate has need of my services."

Minamoto Yoritomo chuckled. "I should have known that the Oni of Aokigahara would bring you out of hiding. Summer began with it murdering a score of my warriors, picking them off, one by one, and leaving them hanging from trees, skinned. Since then, samurai have been rushing there in order to defeat it and win my favor. All have failed. Witnesses whisper of an invisible demon, stronger than any man, which kills by spear, claw, or even bolts of lightning, before vanishing as quickly as it appeared."

"You can see how such stories would catch my interest, my Lord."

"Sometimes, three glowing embers appear upon its chosen victim," The Shogun held up three fingers, then put them against his forehead, fingertips making the points of a triangle. "Being marked by these fire kami are the only warning before it strikes. So many samurai have perished that they believe the oni cannot be defeated by mortal hand. I seem to recall they said the same thing about the Great Sea Beast, before your father killed it with a single arrow through the eye."

"A truly heroic moment."

"I know. I was there. No man has ever equaled his feat . . . including the man who has hunted every dangerous beast beneath the sun. Hmmm . . . Perhaps if you were to defeat the Oni of Aokigahara, you could finally match his legend?"

It might have been in his blood, but that wasn't why Hiroto followed his path. The Shogun may have been a brilliant general, but he did not understand the compulsion to constantly seek out new dangers. "You are wise, my Lord, but what is one little forest demon when compared to a mighty kaiju?"

"You could never resist a challenge, could you, Hiroto?"

He had never fought a demon before. "No, my Lord. I could not."

It was a few days' ride to Aokigahara, the dense forest to the north of Mount Fuji. Despite the blistering sun, Hiroto enjoyed seeing the land of his birth again. He felt eager and alive. Each morning the mountain was a bit closer and so was his next great challenge.

Unfortunately, he was not making the journey alone. The Shogunate had sent a representative, a young warrior born of high status, named Ashikaga Motokane, and his retinue of five bodyguards. Though Hiroto had helped their Lord rise to power, that had been a long time ago. Now, the Shogun's samurai looked upon him as a dishonorable outcast, a wild man, an anomaly in their orderly world.

Worst case scenario, Hiroto would use them as bait.

The map provided by the Shogunate had shown a small village at the edge of the forest, so Hiroto had picked that as their destination. Upon arrival it had proven even more pathetic than expected, simply a collection of rotten huts and stinking pig pens, yet it would provide a final opportunity to restock their provisions. Hiroto also hoped for firsthand information.

The villagers saw the warriors approaching and abandoned their fields to hide in their huts. That was not surprising. Villages like this were often menaced by one conquering army or another, and during times of peace there were always bandits. One farmer remained in the center of the village to greet them. That would be their appointed headman, the presenter of taxes and hospitality.

"The rest of you hang back for a moment. There is no need to spook them further." Of course the Shogun's representative did not listen. When Hiroto dismounted and began walking into the village, Ashikaga Motokane followed, swaggering in the most intimidating way possible.

"I need to ask these farmers some questions."

"Why bother? They'll know nothing."

"You might be surprised."

Motokane looked upon the village with disgust. "They're beneath us. We're authorized to take whatever supplies we require. Let's do it and get on with it." It was no wonder the poor farmers saw little difference between bandits and samurai.

The headman had seen their banner bore the Shogunate's mon, and as they approached, had already launched into a rapid speech telling them how wonderful they were, but that his poor village had paid its taxes, and for them to please have mercy because the terrible heat had caused their crops to wilt and their well to run dry, so on and so forth.

Hiroto didn't have patience for such frivolous things when there were monsters about, so he cut the headman off. "I am Nasu Hiroto. We've come to kill the Oni of Aokigahara."

"You are not the first. The stories are true. Our land is cursed! It is a terrible scourge. We are so thankful more brave samurai came to fight the demon." Only the headman didn't actually sound relieved; if anything he was annoyed. "Many of you have come through here this summer, eating our food, putting our men to work as guides—"

"Yes, I know." The village had probably seen a parade of warriors by this point, but he needed information. "Have you seen it yourself?"

"No, but I have felt it watching. Many have, though. Young Hagi saw it first, perched high in the trees, shaped like a man, but bigger, with a head like an ox. She thought it was an angry ghost and ran away. Old Genzo saw it too. He heard the thunder when it killed the first samurai. It put the three sparks on him too, but Genzo fled before more lightning came! Lucky it didn't chase him because it is swift as a horse!"

Any creature capable of effortlessly slaughtering samurai would have an easy time with a place this defenseless. "How many of your people has the demon killed?"

"Who cares?" Motokane said. "They're just peasants."

The headman looked nervously between the two imposing warriors, unsure whether he was still supposed to speak or not. Hiroto wished that Motokane would keep his idiot mouth shut. These farmers were probably as frightened by hungry soldiers as the demon plaguing their woods.

"I must know, how many of you have died?"

"It is hard to believe, but none, noble samurai. He has only attacked mighty warriors such as you. Our village has not been troubled by Three Sparks."

That name would suffice. "All of those men beheaded or skinned nearby, yet this Three Sparks has not harmed a single person in this humble village . . . Curious."

"Perhaps they're in league with the oni!" Motokane snarled. "Why else would it leave them be?"

The headman immediately threw himself into the dust and began begging for mercy which, with a hothead like Motokane, was certainly the wisest thing possible. "No! Please! We would never! After the killing started some of us left offerings at the shrine to appease it at most!"

"You gave gifts to a demon that was killing my brothers?" Motokane bellowed as he reached for his sword.

Hiroto sighed. Clan officials always made his job more complicated. He wasn't going to get any answers if Motokane started slaughtering villagers. "Please, calm yourself."

"The Shogun will abide no treachery!"

"And I will not abide you interrupting me again." The official may have outranked him, but Hiroto was the one handpicked for this assignment, and his patience was wearing thin. "You said it yourself, peasants are beneath your notice. You and Three Sparks have that in common. Now walk away and let me finish."

Motokane was quarrelsome, but he wasn't stupid. Rank had privileges, but they were a long way from Kamakura. The young man gave the headman one last threatening glare, then let go of his sword and went back to join his troops. *Good.* Hiroto didn't particularly want to murder him, but he would if necessary, and then simply tell the Shogun that the demon had gotten him. "Now where were we?"

"I'm sorry, great and noble—"

"Enough groveling, and stand already. I'm no tax collector." He waited for the farmer to get up. "I'm simply a hunter, and you're going to tell me everything you know about this demon so that I can kill it."

It was hard to tell over the clanking and huffing of Motokane's bodyguards, but beyond them the forest was unnaturally quiet. The wind did not penetrate far into the Sea of Trees. There were no birds singing, no insects buzzing, just the occasional tap of collected humidity falling on leaves.

It was no wonder the place had been considered haunted even before an oni had moved in.

That morning the others had dressed for war. Motokane's retinue were wearing their armor and helmets, with bows strung, spears held high, and their swords at their sides. The Shogun's finest looked like fearsome combatants, a worthy challenge for any demon.

Meanwhile, Hiroto lagged behind them, unarmed and stripped to the waist, with a bamboo pole balanced across his shoulder with a bundle hanging from each end. He had even gone and rolled about in the fields to complete the act. The other samurai thought he'd gone mad when he had left his swords behind, but Hiroto looked and even smelled like a local farmer.

Hiroto tried to appear inconsequential, head down, tired and stumbling from rock to rock beneath his clumsy burden. He would be no threat, especially to a mighty oni. He was simply a porter, conscripted from the village to carry his betters' supplies because the forest was too rugged for their horses. The headman had told him that some of the other would-be demon hunters had done the same, and each time their porter had come running back alone, terrified, sometimes covered in blood, but alive.

In his experience, most beasts targeted the weakest prey. This oni was different. It attacked the strong. He would use that to his advantage.

They walked for hours. It was slow going across such rough terrain. Thick roots waited to trip them. Each warrior was drenched in sweat. The air felt heavy and smelled of moss. The soil was dark and littered with black volcanic rocks. Between the heat and the uneven ground, the samurai were surely regretting wearing their armor, but they were all too proud to show it. Each of them thought that they would be the one to take the trophy back to their Lord, and they passed the time by boasting of what they would do with their reward.

Hiroto just kept his head down, appearing meek and subservient. He reasoned it did not do much good to use his eyes to hunt a creature which was supposedly invisible. Instead, he listened.

In a forest without sound, the faintest things became audible. The oni was quiet, but not as quiet as a tiger. In trees packed too tight for the wind to rustle through, the smallest movement was a clue. Occasionally he'd hear flesh scrape against bark, or the creak of a branch as weight settled on it. There was another sound beneath as well, barely audible, but unnatural, like the chittering of an insect combined with the slithering of a snake across sand. It made the hair on his arms stand up. All of that information would have been lost amongst the noise of a living place, but in the haunted stillness of Aokigahara, it told a story.

They were being followed.

It was somewhere above them and to the right. He tried not to let his excitement show.

"Over here," Kaneto called from the edge of a nearby stream. "There's another."

This body had been there for a few days, and was missing its head, but from his fine clothing and the broken katana lying in the water, he had clearly been a samurai. Motokane knelt next to the corpse and pointed at the emblem embroidered on the sleeve. "I recognize this from court. This is the personal mon of Hojo Murashige!"

Hiroto had no idea who that was, but the Hojo were a family of some importance. The corpse's identity seemed to shake the others.

"He was a fearsome swordsman," Zensuke whispered. "The best of us."

"It didn't just take his head. It ripped out his *spine*." Motokane stood up and glanced around nervously. A full day of nerves and stress had worn him thin. He suddenly raised his voice and bellowed. "Show yourself, demon! Show yourself so I can kill you like the wretched cowardly dog you are!"

Hiroto took a few steps away from the angry samurai. The peasants had spoken of it throwing lightning bolts, and he didn't think it wise to stand so close to the most tempting target. He listened, but if the demon was still watching, it was being especially quiet, or at least quiet enough he couldn't hear it over the shouting. So while Motokane continued to rant and threaten the trees, Hiroto looked for tracks. Sign always told a story.

The black ground was too hard to leave good prints, but the moss, once smashed, grew differently than what was around it. There were the marks of normal sandals, and then much larger footfalls, heavy enough to crush the moss flat. The two had fought back and forth for quite some time, covering a lot of distance. He examined a cut on a tree. From the height and angle, it had come from someone extremely tall. Deep cuts. *Incredible strength.* Twin blades . . . *An odd weapon.* There were other cuts in the barks. The oni fought with a wild and ferocious style. Then he found the dried blood where the oni had finally struck true. He followed the trail. These rocks had been stained green. *Paint?* He touched it. No . . . It had the consistency of dried sap . . . *So oni bleed green. Curious.* The smell was completely alien. He spied something else lying on the rocks, something out of place. He picked it up.

And then Kaneto's chest exploded.

There was a *whoosh-crack* and a flash of light. Motokane's shouting was suddenly interrupted as the bodyguard's blood sprayed him in the face. Bits of meat and armor rained out of the sky, making ripples across the stream. Kaneto dropped to his knees, lifeless, and then flopped forward with a splash.

The wound on his chest must have been incredibly hot because it boiled the stream around it. Steam rose through the giant hole in Kaneto's back.

The samurai's reaction was near instant. Spears were lifted, arrows were nocked, only they had no target for their wrath.

"Where'd that come from?" Motokane shouted.

Hiroto had dropped his bundles, crouched behind a tangle of roots, and was listening carefully. The lightning strike had made his ears ring, but besides the warrior's heavy breathing, he caught a rapid series of *thumps* as the oni danced from tree to tree. It was pulling back to watch from a position of safety . . . toying with them.

That meant they had some time before the killing would resume. The odd item he had found was still clenched in his fist, so Hiroto opened his hand to study it. The thing was too big, it ended in an obsidian claw, and the exposed meat was bright green instead of decaying red, but from the joints and knuckles, it was clearly a finger.

So Hojo Murashige must have challenged the oni to a duel, it had accepted, and lost a finger in the process . . . No wonder it preferred to attack from ambush.

"Why won't this damned thing come out and fight us like a proper warrior?" Motokane grumbled as they trudged through the forest.

"Because it isn't stupid," Hiroto muttered from the back of the line.

"What was that?" he demanded.

They were going back along the same trail they had come in on. Ostensibly to *find better ground to fight on*—or so the official declared. Hiroto assumed it was because Motokane had realized he was in over his head, but he didn't want to lose face by outright calling it a retreat.

Hiroto kept his voice down. It wasn't a low-born porter's place to offer tactical advice to samurai, but he did not feel that the demon was near enough to eavesdrop. "A clever hunter pits his strengths against his prey's weakness. He does not pit his weakness against his prey's strengths."

"Nonsense," Motokane spat. "He's just dishonest like you! Now shut up and keep moving!"

They continued walking, but a few moments later the nearest samurai whispered to Hiroto, "What did you mean by that, hunter?"

"It knows we are strong in close combat. The Hojo was a good swordsman. The demon fought him, katana against some odd manner of dual blade. It won, but left behind a finger. A costly mistake. It will not be so foolish to face one of us head on again."

"Ah . . . I see . . ." The samurai was carrying a tetsubo, a heavy war club, a fearsome weapon which wouldn't do him much good when the invisible oni returned and blasted them with lightning bolts from the treetops. "Unfortunate."

Since Hiroto had assumed most of them would die poorly, he had not bothered to learn all their names, but this one did not seem as dense as the others. "What do they call you again?"

"Nobuo."

His attention had been elsewhere during the attack. "Did you see the fire kami mark your companion? The three sparks?"

"Yes, but I did not react in time. I saw light flickering on his breastplate, but the heat made me slow. At first I thought it was a trick of the eyes. Then it was too late. Kaneto's death is my fault."

He was still not sure what purpose the sparks served. "How long did they linger before the lightning struck?"

"They were already there when I looked over, for how long before that I don't know. Then only the space of a few heartbeats before I was nearly blinded by the flash."

"Hmmm . . ." At first he'd suspected the sparks held some spiritual significance, but now . . . Nipponese archers trained to see their target, then draw and release in one smooth movement, but the archers of the Song Dynasty he had trained with always drew, then paused to sight down the shaft before release. "It sounds as if the demon uses the fire kami to *aim*. This knowledge may prove useful."

They continued on for a time in silence. Hiroto could not currently hear the demon stalking them. He assumed that was because it had waited for them to leave the stream, and now it was skinning and hanging Kaneto from a tree. He had been tempted to stay and wait in ambush, but Motokane had ordered his men to move out. Faced with the choice, Hiroto had decided that live bait was more valuable than dead.

"Hunter, another question."

"Please do not call me that. The oni might be listening."

"Apologies."

Hiroto sighed, because samurai apologized to low-born laborers *so very often.* "What is it, Nobuo?"

"We have seen this hunter's strengths. What are yours?"

"I am a fast learner."

The next attack came at sundown.

Hiroto saw a single leaf fall from a tree fifty paces to their side, then a few moments later a branch vibrated high in a tree thirty paces ahead. The blessing of Hachiman—god of warriors—was upon him, because if they were anywhere other than the unnatural stillness of Aokigahara, he would not have sensed it.

"The oni is here," he whispered.

Nobuo quietly repeated that to the next samurai in line, who repeated it to Motokane, who immediately ruined any chance of an effective response by shouting, "Halt!"

Spears and arrows were readied. The warriors watched the thick undergrowth, wary. Hiroto acted the frightened porter and ducked behind a tree. Several tense seconds passed.

Three flickering sparks appeared on Zensuke's helmet.

"Look out!" Nobuo shouted as he hurled himself against his companion. As they collided there was another whip crack of sound and a brilliant flash. The two samurai fell in a shower of sparks.

Hiroto had seen exactly where that bolt had come from. He quickly dumped the satchels from the bamboo shaft he'd been carrying. His real cargo had been hidden inside all along.

One of the samurai—he had not bothered to remember this one's name—launched an arrow into the branches. To his credit, he was close, yet not close enough. The oni must have felt rushed, because the three sparks did not linger this time, and the bolt struck the warrior low. The resulting blast still sent him flipping through the air. One of his legs flew in the opposite direction.

Careful not to cut himself on one of the specially prepared

arrowheads, Hiroto retrieved his bow. He had it strung and had taken up one of his poisoned arrows before the crippled samurai landed.

The oni was hurling lightning down upon the samurai like he was Raijin the thunder god. Another warrior drew his katana and screamed a challenge, but the oni had learned the hard way what happened when you duel a samurai, so it blew his arm off instead. As Motokane ran away, a tree exploded next to him, and the official was lost from view in a cloud of splinters.

Hiroto had guessed right. The oni concentrated on the warriors and ignored the supposed peasant. Like him, it only enjoyed hunting dangerous game.

That had been a terrible mistake.

Focusing on the source of the lightning, Hiroto raised his bow and brought it down as he drew. The instant his thumb touched his jaw he let fly. The oni was still invisible, but its angry roar told him that he had struck true.

Yet Hiroto did not let up. He had once pierced a great northern bear six times and it had still retained the strength to charge him. Surely a demon would be tougher. In the blink of an eye he launched another arrow, and then another. This time when the oni moved, he saw it. Light seemed to twist and reflect, like staring into a diamond, and for the first time, he saw it was truly shaped as a man.

Another arrow went into its chest. The oni dropped from the tree. Hiroto could not see if it landed on its feet or its back. He would hope for the best and expect the worst.

Zensuke was screaming in pain. Because of Nobuo's quick reactions his sode had been hit instead of his helmet, but there was a glowing molten hole through the iron shoulder plate and the lacquer had caught on fire. Nobuo had taken out his tanto and was slicing through the cords before his friend cooked to death in his own armor.

He could only hide so many of his own arrows inside the bamboo pole, so he picked up Zensuke's quiver as he ran past them. "It is wounded. Follow when you can."

Hiroto leapt through the bushes, arrow nocked, ready to draw the instant he saw light bend. There were insects and lizards which could become the same color as the ground around them; apparently this oni's magic worked far better, but in a similar manner. Cautiously, he approached the spot where the oni had fallen.

There was more of the green blood splattered across the rocks. It turned out that when it was fresh, the oni's blood glowed like a smashed firefly. There was a lot of blood, but considering he thought he had struck it with four arrows, not enough. The light was fading quickly, which would make the glowing blood trail easier to follow.

The other samurai caught up a moment later. Nobuo had gotten Zensuke's burning armor removed in time, but the other samurai's shoulder was a bloody, charred mess. His right arm hung useless. He had to be in terrible pain, but he hid it behind a mask of grim determination, and carried his katana in his left hand.

"That's its blood?" Nobuo gestured with his war club. "Then we can track it!"

"Wait," Hiroto said as he knelt and picked up a broken arrow shaft. It was slick with the green slime. "I coated these arrowheads in a concentrated poison made from the venom of a jellyfish some pearl divers introduced me to. Its sting causes weakness, paralysis, and usually death. I do not know what it will do to a demon, but we will give the poison a moment to work."

Samurai considered poison a cowardly and dishonorable way to kill, but Nobuo and Zensuke did not protest. At this point they only wanted to survive. Surprisingly, Motokane found them a minute later. Hiroto wasn't surprised to see he was still alive—officials were more survivable than rats—but rather, that he wasn't in the process of running back to Kamakura.

"Everyone else is dead."

Hiroto had assumed that by the way it had violently blasted their limbs off. He gave a noncommittal grunt in response to the news. It was time. Hiroto began following the spilled blood.

The poison did not kill it, but either it or the arrow wounds were having some effect. Earlier the demon had been effortlessly leaping from treetop to treetop. Now it was sticking to the ground, and from the relative strength of the glow, it felt like they were catching up.

The ghostly forest was eerie in the dark. There was a full moon, which was enough to keep them from breaking their necks, but not

much beyond that. It made the trail extremely easy to follow . . .
Perhaps a little too easy. If he were wounded, and a hunting party
was following his blood trail, he would use that to his advantage to
set an ambush, or lead them straight into some prepared traps.

"Motokane, you should take the lead."

"What? Why?"

"From all this blood, the oni appears to be weakening and dying.
It should be a man of your status who gets the honor of striking the
killing blow on behalf of the Shogun."

Sadly, Motokane wasn't that gullible. "I don't feel like catching
the first lightning bolt, hunter. Nobuo! Follow that trail."

Like a good dutiful samurai, Nobuo did as he was told. That was
a waste. Hiroto thought the lad had potential.

The trail led them steadily downhill. The footing was treacherous.
Nobuo tried to listen for danger over the clumsy crashing and
slipping of the exhausted samurai. The demon staying on solid
ground rather than shifting branches made it harder to hear. He
thought he caught the hissing insect noise a few times, but could not
be sure.

Nobuo signaled for them to stop. "Hunter, come look at this."

He left Zensuke and Motokane and crept forward. Nobuo had
followed the blood to a narrow path with stagnant pond water to
both sides. Trudging through that mud would make for slow going.
It was a splendid place for an ambush. When Hiroto reached him,
Nobuo was pointing at something ahead. There was quite a bit of
glowing firefly splatter on the land bridge, as if the demon had
stopped for a bit. Even as keen as Hiroto's vision was, it took him a
moment to spot the danger. There was a tiny reflection of blood light
against something metallic hidden among the roots.

It had to be some manner of trap. "Good eye."

But then Hiroto noticed something the less experienced warrior
had not. After setting the trap, the blood continued across the land,
and then turned sharply to the side as the demon had doubled back
through the pond, where its dripping blood would be swallowed
from view.

It was circling behind them.

When the trap was sprung—probably a snare or a spring noose—
against the lead man, the sound would draw their attention forward,

and then it would assault the rear. There were only four of them left. It could take half of them in one move. Hiroto grabbed Nobuo by one of the horns on his helmet, dragged him close, and whispered, "Count to thirty. Then set off the trap." He picked up a rock and shoved it toward him. "Throw this at it."

Then he began creeping back toward Zensuke and Motokane. With luck, he would be in position to put an arrow into the demon as soon as it moved. As soon as he could make out the other two in the dark, he hunkered down, wiped the sweat from his eyes, and waited for Nobuo to finish his count.

There was a thunk as the rock was tossed . . . The whole forest erupted with yellow light.

That was most unexpected.

The demon hadn't set a normal trap. He had summoned the fires of Jigoku. Nobuo had been hurled through the air. Sparks were falling from the sky like rain. It was like being beneath an erupting volcano. Rocks big enough to split a skull crashed through the branches. Hiroto covered his head as fiery debris fell all around him.

Rather than fear, he felt a pang of jealousy. *If I had weapons such as this, there is nothing I could not hunt!*

Hiroto could barely see, but the three red dots climbing up his arm were clear as day, but he lost them as they crawled onto his chest. Instinctively, he flung his body to the side.

The tree he'd been leaning against came apart. Splinters pierced his skin.

He was the one who had hurt the oni so now he was its greatest threat. Somehow it had picked him out . . . The oni could see in the dark!

Hiroto rolled to his feet and ran, trying to put more trees between his body and the oni's fury. Lightning struck. Branches came crashing down. Rocks shattered into a million stinging pieces. Bushes burst into flame. Hiroto dove behind a boulder. When the boulder wasn't immediately cleaved in two, Hiroto risked a peek over the top.

The oni's trap had set some of the treetops ablaze. It was still using its magical trickery, somehow forcing the air to obscure its form, but that did not work so well near a flickering fire. It looked like pieces of broken glass, piled in the shape of a tall man, each bit reflecting the fire in slightly the wrong direction.

Zensuke had seen it, too. He lifted his katana in one hand and charged, screaming a battle cry. The light twisted around where the oni's head must be, facing the new threat. A refracting glow that could only be an arm rose, and two gleaming blades leapt from the end of it.

Hiroto rose, drew back the bow string, and let fly.

The arrow sped across the forest and disappeared into the demon's unnatural form. He heard it sink deep into flesh.

Dead center. A man would perish in seconds, but not this damnable oni. The pile of broken glass and flames remained standing. But everything had a weak spot. Like his father had taught him, *the arrow knows the way.* As it prepared to meet Zensuke, Hiroto nocked another arrow. The long bow creaked, power gathering in his hands. *Find the way.* Hiroto set the arrow free.

This time he had been focused on the arm. If it had no heart, then he would cripple its limbs.

The arrow sailed across the forest. It struck in a flash of blue.

Yet the arm still came down, slicing Zensuke in half.

As the samurai went sailing past both sides of the demon, Hiroto truly saw it for the first time. His last arrow had broken the evil spell! Grey beneath the fire and moon, it was truly a giant, easily two feet taller than the biggest samurai, with a too-large head made of shining metal, hair like a Sadhu monk, and a body covered in a fisherman's net.

When it realized Hiroto was staring right at, the oni reached for its wrist, clawed fingers dancing—probably casting a spell—only there was an arrow shaft blocking the way.

"Enough of your tricks, demon!" Hiroto shouted as he sent another arrow across the forest. That one punctured the demon's stomach. The next struck it in the leg.

The boulder in front of him disintegrated and Hiroto found himself hurled through the air. It turned out the demon didn't need to use the three sparks to aim its lightning after all, though it did help the accuracy.

He hit the ground so hard it knocked the wind out of him. Worse, he lost his bow. From the burning bushes he could see that he was near the edge of the pond. Twenty paces away, Nobuo was lying in the mud, breathing, but knocked unconscious, his helmet visibly dented by the demon's incredible trap.

The oni was coming. It had completely given up on stealth, and its heavy footfalls could be heard crashing against the rocks, getting closer and closer. Hiroto had no weapons. Nobuo's swords were too far. His only hope was to hide and perhaps surprise it . . . He was an excellent fighter with just his hands, but his opponents weren't usually as big as a horse.

Gasping for breath, Hiroto crawled into the reeds. As he tried desperately to fill his lungs with air, he found himself wishing he had a hollow reed to breathe through. Now that would have been handy for hiding. As the demon got closer, he held his breath and sunk beneath the muck.

He was trying so very hard not to move to avoid ripples, not even daring to exhale because it would make bubbles. Even with his eyes open he could see nothing through the thick silt, but he felt the water vibrate as the demon stomped right past him. Either it hadn't seen him, or it was going to finish off Nobuo first instead.

Hiroto's hand bumped into something. Wooden, but sanded smooth. His fingers drifted along it until touching the first embedded metal spike . . . Hachiman had smiled upon him once again.

As he slowly, painfully, silently lifted himself from the murk, he saw that the oni was looming over Nobuo. Arrow shafts were embedded across its body, each wound leaking green. The oni may have been an unnatural being, but its emotions were as clear as any performer telling a story with only a dance. The oni was *furious*. Nobuo wasn't the warrior who had filled its body with painful arrows! It lifted its arm blades to kill him anyway.

Hiroto had been trying to rise as quietly as possible, but something gave him away, maybe it was the pond water dripping from the spikes of Nobuo's war club, or the sucking sound of his body leaving the mud, but regardless, the oni heard. It spun about, braids whipping, drawing itself up, so that it towered overhead.

He never understood why it didn't strike him down in that moment, but the oni paused, just for a heartbeat, confused, as if Hiroto was the invisible one.

Hiroto smashed it with the tetsubo.

He'd been aiming for its metal head, but its sudden movement caused him to strike it in the shoulder instead. Glowing blood flew as flesh was pulverized.

The solid blow would have shattered human bones. The oni lurched to the side, but stayed upright. With a roar he hit it with another overhand strike. The pressure caused blood to squirt from the various arrow holes. Then Hiroto swung the heavy weapon in an arc, striking the oni's extended leg. Something snapped deep within and it went to its knees.

Except kneeling, it was still as tall as Hiroto. The twin blades lashed out. He blocked it with the tetsubo but the demon metal cut right through the wood as if it wasn't there, and still retained the power to slice cleanly through his face.

It was the worst pain he had ever experienced, worst he had ever *imagined*. He fell. The blow had rattled his brain. The world was spinning. All Hiroto could do was hold on. But something else was wrong. Desperate, sick, he reached up, felt along the two burning cuts to the empty socket where his left eye had once been, and screamed.

Through his remaining eye, he watched the oni try to stand, but its broken leg buckled. In his life he had seen thousands of things die. Something about the way the oni was moving told him that it was done for. Hiroto would perish, smug in the knowledge that his killer would follow soon after. The oni began crawling toward him. Hiroto tried to stand, but his body would not cooperate, all he could do was scoot backwards.

"Hunter!" Nobuo had woken up. He was too far to get there in time, but he threw something.

It was a good thing Nobuo's sword was still sheathed, because it landed right in Hiroto's lap.

The oni was bearing down on him. It pulled back its fist, blades aimed at his heart. Hiroto drew and slashed in one smooth movement.

The katana went through half the demon's chest. Green blood flew across the forest in a long arc. The two of them remained there a moment, mangled face to metal face. The demon twitched. The twin blades slowly dropped. He twisted the blade free, and Three Sparks, the Oni of Aokigahara, was no more.

Hiroto was in terrible pain, but he laughed anyway. The summer of death was over. It had been a fine hunt.

As they limped out of the forest, they came upon Ashikaga Motokane, hiding inside the trunk of a hollow tree.

"You're still alive! Is it done?" the official asked as he slowly climbed out.

Hiroto's face was being held together with stiches and dried blood, and his newfound lack of depth perception was making him nauseous. He was not in the mood, so continued walking.

"Were you hiding in there all night?" Nobuo asked.

"Yes. And I was all alone! Because some bodyguard you are!"

Hiroto didn't even look back when he heard Nobuo's sword clear its sheath. There was a gurgle, and then the sound of a head bouncing down the rocks. The young samurai rejoined Hiroto a moment later, cleaning his katana on his filthy sleeve. "When we report to the Shogun, it was a shame there were no other survivors."

"Yes, a terrible shame."

Nasu Hiroto knelt before the Shogun. Their report had been delivered. The magnificent trophy he had presented to Minamoto Yoritomo was on the floor between them. Now they were alone. The Shogun had dismissed everyone else from the room so that the two of them could speak privately.

"The eye patch suits you, Hiroto. What do you intend to do now?"

"If you aren't going to execute me for deserting all those years ago, then I'm unsure."

"When we last spoke, I came to understand something about you. Other samurai try their whole lives to make a mask that never shows fear, that declares they live for battle, hiding their true weakness beneath. For you, there is no mask. You only feel alive when you are hunting something capable of taking your life. Nothing else will do."

Hiroto nodded. The Shogun was truly a wise man.

"Your report has inspired me. I think it has given me the answer to a problem which I have struggled with for the last few years." The Shogun leaned forward and picked up the oni's mask. "We could learn much from the Oni of Aokigahara. Invisible. Calculating.

Hiding in plain sight, then attacking with ruthless efficiency, leaving his enemies filled with dread . . . The ultimate assassin."

"To be stalked by such would bring nightmares to even the bravest samurai."

"Indeed. What if I offered you the opportunity to never be bored again? A hunt which never ends?"

"I am intrigued."

"The Shogunate has many enemies, dangerous men. Often politics make it so that I cannot deal with them directly. The oni has shown me the answer. I have need of invisible killers, inspired by this beast, who make its way theirs. Men who will engage in irregular warfare which most samurai would find distasteful." The Shogun stared into the blank eyes of the mask. "In short, I require men who can fight like *demons*."

Hiroto was becoming excited. "Such an endeavor would have to be done with the utmost secrecy."

"They would be the hidden men, *shinobi-no-mono*, emulating the Oni of Aokigahara to bring ruin upon the enemies of Nippon. Would you build this organization for me, Nasu Hiroto?"

"It would be an honor."

The first ninja bowed to the first shogun.

That's right. It was the Predator who inspired the creation of ninjas. That's my theory, but I'm pretty sure it is historically accurate.

One fun note, I managed to put a shout out to my other samurai versus monster story in here. Though it is completely unofficial because these stories were from entirely different publishers and not in the same universe, if you read "Great Sea Beast" in Target Rich Environment Volume 1, *note that both of these main characters have the same last name, and Three Sparks takes place one generation later. That's because Monster Hunting is a family business.*

RECKONING DAY

This flash-fiction sized short originally appeared in the Monster Hunter International Employee Handbook and Role Playing Game from Hero Games in 2013. It was just a brief little look into the daily life of some of the Monster Hunter International series' most popular characters. Shelly the Orc shows up again in Monster Hunter Guardian.

IT WAS GOOD to be chief.

The noble orc, Skull Crushing Battle Hand of Fury, or Skippy as his human friends called him, was pleased, and for the record, he did not mind being called Skippy. The humans' ways were abrupt and strange, but their oddly short names did save time.

The Tribe was at peace. The scars of their last battle against the evil dead of the foolish human necromancer, Hood, had healed. Word of their righteous revenge had spread across the world and orcs from other tribes had journeyed far to join with their number. The Tribe's warriors were volunteering to go forth into the human world in ever increasing numbers to join the war bands of MHI. The Harb Anger was very pleased by the Tribe's warriors and much honor and respect was given, Harb Anger paid them moneys too, though Skippy didn't really know what to use that for, so they mostly kept it in a big pile which his wives then used to occasionally purchase important items, like new heavy metal albums from iTunes or flea shampoo for their mighty Wargs.

However, Skippy was far too busy to concern himself with such things as human moneys or Warg care, for today was a young warrior's Reckoning Day. Because the gods loved the orcs more than they loved all of their other children, each orc was born blessed with a special talent. These talents varied wildly, but all of them were somehow valuable to ensure a great future for the Tribe. Some orc talent's usefulness were obvious to understand, such as his younger brother's supreme skill in bladed combat, or his own mastery of the human flying machines and his unmatched knowledge of the Air Spirits. Other talents' uses were not so easy to discern, such as his cousin *Rufschertzls'* amazing ability to solve any of the humans' "crossword puzzles," but who was Skippy to question the god's choice for Rufus? Perhaps someday Rufus' ability to make letters fit into small squares would bring great honor to the tribe . . . Naw, who was he kidding? Rufus was a moron.

But regardless, today was another orc's Reckoning Day, which meant that the elders and teachers had finally been able to discern the path chosen by their gods. The young orc would be brought before the chieftain, and his talents displayed. The Old Ways required the chieftain to execute the young orc should his talents be insufficient, but Skippy considered himself a very reasonable and *modern* orc, maybe it was because he lived in America and the Hunters' strange sense of mercy had influenced him, so he'd never executed anyone on their Reckoning Day. He'd even spared Rufus, though he'd been *so* very tempted . . . Like most orc holidays, Reckoning Day was mostly a chance to throw an awesome party, and since Gretchen had already baked a cake, Skippy certainly hoped that today wouldn't be his first Reckoning Day summary execution.

Skippy stood in the center of the village, attended by his wives and his advisors, while the young orc was brought forward. It turned out to be a female, recently arrived with her family, refugees from another tribe. She was squat and dumpy, with misshapen tusks, and one crazy eyeball which kept looking in different directions, and despite the ceremonial fur robes, colorful feathers, and small animal bones which they had decorated her with, she certainly would never get a husband on looks alone, so for her sake, Skippy hoped she'd been blessed with a good talent. Somebody who could cook would be nice. The village could use another cook, because no offense to Gretchen, her cake tasted like ashes in his mouth, not that he would ever tell her that, because even the chieftain couldn't talk bad about his first wife's cooking.

The girl was introduced by his brother *Exszrsd*. That was intriguing. Normally Edward, as their strongest combatant, wouldn't involve himself in a Reckoning Day unless the child had displayed a particularly strong warrior's gift . . . or it was a really crappy talent, since he was their default executioner. Either way, this should be interesting.

Edward addressed the gathering, extremely excited crowd. The girl's parents looked very nervous. The girl seemed ambivalent, which was a proper orc war face. "This is *Slschschlee*."

Skippy snorted. Foreign orc tribes had such silly names. "For our human masters, she will be known to them as Shelly." Everybody bowed at his wisdom. Shelly shrugged. "Let the Reckoning begin."

Edward, being an orc of few words even in Orcish, looked at Shelly and grunted. She nodded, her googly eye squinting in determination. "Her talent did not show for a long time. The gods did not speak to her until she watched the Hunters through the Great Chain Link Fence of Separation and witnessed their preparations for glorious war."

Interesting. So that meant it probably wasn't cooking. Disappointing that, but Skippy nodded for them to continue their demonstration.

His brother snapped his fingers and several of the younger orcs ran forward holding empty beer bottles in their hands. There were six of them, with two bottles each. They cocked their arms back as if ready to throw them into the forest. Curious, Skippy wondered why Edward had just stuck his fingers into his ears.

The orcs hurled their bottles into the air, and a split second later, threw their second. Shelly flung open her fur robe, revealing a leather gun belt with a holster on each side. Two big revolvers appeared in her hands as if by magic. Skippy knew enough about guns to know that these were .44 magnum Redhawks. There was a continuous roar as she fired them both from the hip, and every single one of the flying bottles exploded before reaching the trees.

Skippy's mouth fell open. The Tribe began to cheer. "By the violent tusks of *Gnrlwz*! That was so metal!" And Skippy threw the horns.

Shelly had both smoking revolvers reloaded from speed loaders and put back into their holsters before Skippy had finished his pronouncement. She looked right at him with her good eye, then her googly eye, and then she bowed. Skippy returned the bow, extra low.

"The gods must be pleased with this orc. Now it is time for cake!" *Such dry, ashy cake . . .*

And another Reckoning Day was complete.

WEAPONIZED HELL

This story first appeared in the anthology Urban Allies, *edited by Joseph Nassie, published in 2016 by Harper Voyager.*

Urban Allies was a really interesting idea, where twenty urban fantasy authors paired off, each of us taking one of our popular characters and having them team up with another author's existing characters for a story. Like one of those crossover episodes where two TV shows collide.

I'm a fan of Jonathan Maberry's work and really enjoy his Joe Ledger series (in fact, a story that I wrote for him for that universe appears later in this collection). When I saw that he was involved I asked if he'd want to team up. He said he'd write Ledger if I wrote Agent Franks. That sounded badass.

❖ 1 ❖

Captain Joe Ledger
Department of Military Sciences
Iraqi Desert near Mosul

THEY SAY THAT IN TIMES of mortal peril your life flashes through your mind. Ideally, those memories are not accompanied by shrapnel or bullets.

For me it isn't usually my childhood or images of my family or my ex-girlfriends. I don't have flashes of chances taken and chances missed. None of that stuff. When my life is about to fall apart, what flashes through my head are the details of how in the wide blue fuck I got into this mess in the first place.

Case in point . . .

First, you have to know that the ideal combat mission starts with solid and very detailed intel, with time for training your team, for putting boots on the ground with all of the equipment you need, and to have local assets on hand to smooth the way. An ideal mission has close-range and long-range tactical support, and the cavalry is cocked and locked and ready to ride over the hill to save your ass if things go south.

Yeah, that would be nice.

So nice.

Never fucking going to happen, though. At least not for guys like me.

I run the Special Projects Office for the Department of Military Sciences. Sounds like a bunch of nerds sitting around dreaming up cool gizmos. It's not. The name is boring and there's some misdirection built into it. And, sure, we have geeks and nerds working for us, but they're support. The truth is that the DMS is a covert rapid-response group. We run a couple-of-dozen small teams of first-chair shooters. We go after terrorists or criminal groups who are using bleeding-edge bioweapons. We are a zero red-tape outfit. If they've sent us in then the shit has already hit the fan.

The tricky thing is that this means we have to start running the moment we hear the first rumble of that avalanche. Prep time is what you can manage on the fly. Field support is usually a voice in the earbud I wear: real-time intel that the science and tactical teams are scrambling to acquire while we're running headlong into the valley of the shadow.

I'm sure I mixed a couple of metaphors there, but I actually don't give a cold shit.

I was in Iraq, in a twenty-year-old Humvee going bump-thumpity over a road that was pocked with wagon ruts and blast holes from IEDs. My driver, Rizgar, was a friendly, a Kurd with knife scars on his face. Four of his buddies were in the back. My own crew, Echo Team, was in a fast plane somewhere over the ocean. Too far away. Rizgar drove like his lifelong dream was to die in a fiery crash. My balls had climbed up inside my chest cavity and I'd found religion five separate times during near misses with boulders, craters, and the burned-out shell of an old Bradley. Rizgar had to swerve to keep from hitting a goat and—still at high speed—leaned his head all the way out the window and yelled at the animal who was now fading in the dust behind us.

"*Kerim bimzha, heez!*"

I understand enough Sorani to know that it was a vile thing to say, even to a goat.

I was yelling, too, trying to have a conversation with my boss, Mr. Church. He'd snatched me away from the mission he'd sent me over here to handle—taking down a black-marketer named Ohan who was selling recovered Soviet chemical weapons left over from the Afghan war in the eighties. Church said he'd catch up to me in motion. I was, in fact, in motion.

"What's the damn op?" I demanded. "My guy in Baghdad said he could put me in a room with Ohan and—"

"We've been following a false lead," said Mr. Church. "Ohan is not in Baghdad. We have reliable intel that he is in a village outside of Mosul."

"It was reliable intel that said he was in Baghdad."

"Nature of the game, Captain," said Church. "We have very high confidence in this sighting."

"What's the source of that intel? Our friends in the Agency? Another of those hotshot Delta gunslingers? Everybody's seeing Ohan lately."

"The identity of our source is classified."

Even though Rizgar could hear my end of the conversation, the feed into my earbud was filtered through a 128-bit cyclical encryption system that God couldn't hack.

"Declassify it," I growled.

Church—being Church—ignored that request. He said, "Operatives on the ground have confirmed the presence of Ohan heading into the village. We believe he is going to meet an ISIL team to hand off a bio agent recovered from an excavated burial site."

"Whoa, wait . . . repeat that? Someone's using a burial site as a lab—?"

"No," said Church. "Sketchy reports indicate that a biological weapon has been harvested from the burial site."

"What kind of bioweapon? Are we talking mycotoxins or bacteria?"

Graves and tombs were famous for all kinds of dangerous spores, molds, fungi and similar microscopic monsters. The whole Curse of King Tut's Tomb was a prime example. Lord Carnovan, the Englishman who backed Howard Carter's expedition to find Tutankhamen, died of a mysterious illness after entering the tomb and being exposed to a fungus that had been dormant in the tomb for thousands of years and reactivated by fresh air. Other recently opened tombs in different parts of the world revealed pathogenic bacteria of the Staphylococcus and Pseudomonas genera, and the molds Aspergillus niger and Aspergillus flavus. Very nasty stuff. Obtaining and weaponizing diseases so old that modern humans have no acquired immunity for them is a popular hobby for the world's mad-fucking-scientists. Of which there are way too many.

"The nature of the threat is unknown at this time," said Church. "I need you to make an assessment and to keep it out of the hands of the ISIL team operating in that area."

I was still dressed for plainclothes infiltration of the Baghdad hotel where I was supposed to intercept Ohan. My cover was that of a South African mercenary acting as a go-between for a party wanting to buy some of Ohan's nasty toys. I had my Sig Sauer and a Wilson rapid-release folding knife, but I was not in full combat rig. I was dressed in khaki trousers and one of those canvas shirt-jackets with lots of pockets. No helmet, no long-gun, no grenades. None of my favorite toys. And not nearly enough body armor. And, more to the point, no hazmat suit or even a Saratoga Hammer suit. Nothing to protect me if this was an active biological agent, particularly an airborne one.

"Sure," I said, "I'm on it."

I hate my job.

Rizgar pointed to a small cluster of buildings visible through the heat shimmer a couple of miles up the road. Even from that distance we could see that things had already gone to shit. A fireball suddenly leapt up from amid a group of parked vehicles, lifting them, tossing them away with fists made of superheated gasses. Over the roar of the Humvee's engine we could hear the rattle of gunfire.

❖ 2 ❖

Special Agent Franks
United States Monster Control Bureau
Iraqi Desert near Mosul

SPECIAL AGENT FRANKS of the United States Monster Control Bureau was not known for his patience—especially when he had a mission to complete—but having random terrorist assholes flip his armored vehicle with an IED really put him in an even fouler mood than usual. His driver and interpreter, assigned to him from the Iraqi Army, had been killed on impact. From the noise of gunfire and bullets striking metal, the rest of the convoy was taking fire. Annoyed, Franks had crawled out of the upside-down flaming MRAP in order to vent his frustrations on whoever had been stupid enough to ambush him.

Quickly assessing the situation, Franks realized it had been a really big bomb. It took quite a few buried artillery shells to toss an 18-ton vehicle on its roof. The explosion had flattened several of the houses at the front of the village. There was a blackened crater where the road had been. The enemy appeared to be a bunch of goons wearing ridiculous black pajamas, armed with AKs and looted M-4s. It was an L-shaped ambush. They were firing from prepared positions in the village and from a ravine that ran parallel to the road. Their Iraqi drivers, rather than push through the ambush zone, had hit the brakes. Now they were taking heavy fire. It was another example of why Franks preferred never to work with locals, but he'd been overruled. His superiors didn't like his idea of diplomacy.

Four hostiles, one armed with an RPG, had moved up on Franks' vehicle to get a better angle on the rest of the stopped convoy. The hostiles hadn't been expecting survivors, let alone a giant killing machine who was completely unfazed by the blast. Franks killed the first hostile before they'd even realized he was there, another two before they could react, and the last one as he was trying to run away.

And Franks hadn't used a weapon yet.

The rest of his convoy was made up of MCB personnel and their Iraqi Army escorts. It appeared that most of their vehicles were hit, though none as badly as his had been. Intel had said this area was under ISIS control, but they'd not been expecting resistance away from the dig site. As usual, their intel was wrong. He had to act fast or his strike team would be rendered combat ineffective, and they still had a mission to complete. His men would clear the ravine. His rifle had been crushed in the wreck, so Franks took the rocket-propelled grenade launcher and an AK-47 from the men he'd beaten to death and went into the village.

They'd set up a PK machinegun on the second floor of a mosque and were raking it over the convoy. There had been something in the briefing over the rules of engagement about not damaging religious buildings and blah, blah, blah, but Franks never bothered to read those things. So he blew it up with the RPG. Then he went house to house, shooting every hostile he saw. Since Franks had reaction times that made most normal humans look like sloths, clearing out their firing positions was a piece of cake. He only had to gun down a dozen of them or so before the ambush broke and the remaining scumbags were running for their lives.

His radio had been broken in the crash, but from the noise, it sounded like his men had the road and ravine under control. Franks had seen a lot of casual barbarity in his life, but he knew ISIS were overachievers. Chasing them down was not his mission, but Franks really didn't like them. Sure. He liked hardly anyone, but these assholes were special. So he picked up another weapon and went looking for trouble.

He found it.

The ISIS fighters regrouped in a small market. Their leader was rallying the troops, shouting in Arabic—one of the many Earthly languages Franks had never bothered to learn—so the motivational speech wouldn't have been noteworthy except this human had the stink of demons all over him.

So their intel had gotten one thing right. The insurgents had made a pact with demons. *Now this is more like it,* Franks thought as he flipped the Kalashnikov's selector to full auto and hosed down the market.

❖ 3 ❖

Captain Joe Ledger

I MADE A PUSHING MOTION with my hand. Rizgar grinned and obliged by pushing the pedal all the way down to the floor. He steered with one hand and beat on the roof of the car with the other—the signal for his team to get ready.

We were driving straight into the heart of a full-blown battle, and it was going south on the good guys really damn fast. I could see a knot of men in American BDUs hunkered down behind a shattered convoy of bullet-pocked vehicles. They were taking heavy fire, but they were still in the game. Bloody bodies littered the ground around the vehicles, most with weapons still clutched in dead hands.

All around the convoy, crouched down behind cars, using broken stone walls for cover, stretched out on rooftops, and even kneeling in the street were fighters in the distinctive black of the Islamic State of Iraq and the Levant. ISIS, ISIL, call them what you want. Sons of bitches who seemed to come out of nowhere and were cutting a bloody swath across the Middle East. Well armed, well provisioned, and dishearteningly well trained. Maybe thirty of them alive and twice that number dead or wounded. This battle had been clearly raging for a while. The contractors in the convoy had fought like heroes, but there simply weren't enough of them left to win this.

Rizgar, his four shooters, and Mama Ledger's firstborn didn't seem like a big enough crowd to make a difference. But let me tell you, shock and awe comes in all shapes and sizes.

Rizgar had picked the right angle for our approach. The contractors could see us but we wouldn't be in their direct line of fire. The ISIL fighters had to turn to fight us on their quarter, which decreased the suppressing fire on the convoy. Distract and weaken. Rizgar slewed around to allow the maximum number of our guns to fire at once and we hit them real damn hard. Two of Rizgar's men came out of the Humvee with RPGs on their shoulders. One targeted a building on the corner of the square, a spot where half a dozen of the black-clothed figures were grouped. They saw the grenade coming at them, they tried to move, but feet don't move fast enough to dodge rocket-propelled explosives fired from fifty yards. The explosion killed four of them, tearing them to rags; and it turned the building into deadly debris. Every man inside the blast radius went down. Some dead, some dazed.

The second RPG struck an old Ford Falcon behind which three shooters knelt. The blast lifted the car and dropped it on them. And that left a clear line of approach for me. I ran up the middle like an offensive fullback, my Sig Sauer held in a two-handed grip. I am a very good shot because SpecOps soldiers who are bad shots get killed. I hit everything I aimed at. Might not have been the highest scores on a gun range, but men went down.

Rizgar and the others fanned out, firing automatic weapons at the ISIL team. As soon as the contractors saw what was happening they shifted their focus from defensive fire to a fresh assault. Clearing the way for us. One of them came out of an open door firing a Kalashnikov. He was a brute, a bull. Six-eight if he was an inch, and he looked like Frankenstein. But the son of a bitch could shoot. ISIL fighters spun away, blood exploding from faces and throats and chests.

They say war is hell. Sure. It absolutely is. Even if you like combat. Even when the sound of gunfire is your lullaby—which, for the record, it isn't to me. But there is a part of me—my shrink and I call him the Killer—who shares my head and my soul with my other aspects, the Modern Man and the Cop. And the Killer loves it. In times like this he is fully alive. And maybe so am I.

I hate that it's true, but it is true.

When I burned through all three of the magazines I had for the Sig, I drew my rapid-release knife and took the fight to close quarters. Using the men I killed as shields while I cut them apart, shoving them into their comrades, taking the long reach to do short, ugly cuts, going for effect rather than finesse. Slashing and slicing because stabbing will get your knife stuck and get you killed. There is a balletic quality to knife fighting when you do it right. You cruise on that edge between total awareness and a kind of Zen zero mind.

The ISIL team fell apart. Rizgar's men were brilliant, savage, and merciless. The Kurds have old scores to settle with the kind of men who join ISIL. And the contractors, buoyed by our arrival, took the fight to the bad guys in terrible ways.

We won the fight.

Until . . .

Until the whole day changed.

I cut the throat of one of the last ISIL fighters and saw that there was a teenage girl crouched down between two of their vehicles. Not armed, not dangerous-looking. I moved in close, hoping to grab her and pull her to safety. She cringed back from me, arms wrapped around her head, and at first I thought she was a captive, maybe someone from the village being used as a hostage, or one of the unfortunate ones who would be dragged off and used savagely until her mind or body snapped.

Then I saw her eyes.

They were dark and filled with madness. Total, absolute madness.

And then they weren't.

The brown irises changed as I watched. The brown swirled like paint being stirred. Dark brown, then a medium brown flecked with gold, then sparks of red, and then they turned completely yellow. Cat yellow. Fire yellow. Her face, which had been contorted in terror at the madness and destruction around her, twisted, reshaped, became something else. Not another expression . . . it became another face.

Another *kind* of face.

Still a woman's face . . . but not a human woman's face.

It's impossible to describe, even now, even thinking back on it. There are things the human mind cannot process. Or refuses to accept.

The girl rose to her feet and in doing so stopped being a girl at all. Her spine curved into a monstrous hump, almost like a camel's hump; her leg bones broke with gunshot sounds and then re-formed, taking on the knobbed angles of a goat's legs. And her arms grew long, the fingers splaying and stretching, the nails extending as they tore through the nail beds in splashes of bright blood, then thickened into black talons.

But her face.

Good god, her face . . .

The nostrils flattened and flared, her eyes sunk into shadowy pits so that the hellish light burned like real fire. Her cheekbones cracked and shifted, forming sharp ledges, and her jaw stretched as she smiled at me. Smiled. So incorrect and stupid a word for what was happening. The mouth grinned wide as row upon row of new teeth ripped their way from her gums until she had the dripping maw of a shark.

All of this in a few seconds.

All of this as the last pocks of gunfire tore the air.

I stumbled backward from her—from it.

One of the ISIL fighters lay dead at her feet, his throat sliced open by the knife held limply in my hand. The woman seized his wrist and with a jerk like someone cracking a whip, snapped the arm loose and then tore it from its socket. Blood and bits of tendon splashed on me, and in a moment of truly bottomless horror I watched the woman raise the severed arm to her mouth and bite. Bones crushed between those rows of teeth. Meat burst and blood ran down her chin.

"Jesus Christ," I breathed, and for a moment I was frozen in absolute horror.

◈ 4 ◈

Special Agent Franks

Franks didn't know who the new arrivals were, but one particular man could certainly fight. He'd been doing pretty good slicing up black pajama-clad assholes until he ran into a possessed woman. When she shed her face, he froze. It wasn't a surprise. Most humans choked when they saw real demonic possession for the first time. Franks would have stepped in to save the man, but he had to duck to avoid getting shot in the head by a terrorist. A 7.62x39 rifle bullet at close range had a decent chance of penetrating his armored skull and might have rendered him temporarily combat ineffective, and thus unable to complete his mission. In other words, getting his brains blown out would have been inconvenient.

Drawing his Glock 20, Franks put a controlled pair into the shooter's chest, then turned back to face his demonic target. Franks figured the newcomer would have been torn limb from limb already, but surprisingly, the man had snapped out of it and gotten right back in the fight. He was staying ahead of the claws, and even managed to counterattack and slash the creature.

Not bad, Franks thought as he went over, grabbed the demon by her hair, swung her around in a blur, and hurled her through a mud brick wall. Bones splintered and the wall collapsed in a spreading cloud of stinking dust.

"What the fuck was that?" the man shouted.

"Demon."

From the accent, he was an American. From his skillset, he might be useful. He looked up, and up, at Franks. "Who the fuck are you?"

"Special Agent Franks. MCB."

The man scowled like he'd never heard of the MCB before, but they were both Americans getting shot at in northern Iraq, so it was obvious they were on the same team. "Captain Joe Ledger. DMS."

Department of Military Sciences personnel were probably cleared high enough to get read in on this one. He'd do.

"That's nice," Franks stated as he walked toward the pile of rubble. The bricks were shifting as the demon struggled free. This were a tougher strain than expected—

THWACK!

The rifle bullet smacked into Franks' leg. It punched a neat 30 caliber entrance hole, deformed as it struck his hardened femur, and burst back out the side. Blood sprayed everywhere. Franks immediately picked out the shooter who had appeared on a nearby rooftop, aimed, and shot him before he could get off another round.

"You're hit. Get to cover!"

But Franks just looked down at the fist-sized exit wound in his thigh and frowned. That was what he deserved for stopping to have such a lengthy conversation with Ledger. He lifted the dangling flap of skin and meat and shoved it back into the hole. "Just a scratch."

Ledger seemed a little put off by that.

That wound was going to drastically slow him down, and he'd probably need a replacement leg when he got home, but worst of all, getting shot had cost him several precious seconds he could have used killing things. The demon shook itself free from the rubble. It took one look at Franks and Ledger standing there, realized it was outmatched, and fled.

Without any hesitation and armed only with a knife, Ledger went after the monster.

This one has style, Franks thought as he limped after them.

❖ 5 ❖

Captain Joe Ledger

SO, OKAY, this is me running through the Iraqi desert with a guy I am pretty goddamn sure isn't human, chasing something I'm absolutely positive is a demon. Yeah. Actual demon. Psychologically speaking, I am seriously fucked. I mean . . . demons!

Shit.

The thing fled from us, running like the wind out of the village and onto the sands. Franks ran well for a guy built like a bridge support. Well, but not fast. I ran faster, outpacing him. I'm over six feet and I go about two-twenty, but I'm built like a ball-player. If I had even a smidge of talent I could have played third base. I can run my ass off, and I pulled ahead.

Here's the thing. Running faster meant that I was going to reach the apparently unkillable desert demon sooner than the definitely unkillable guy who actually stood a chance against this thing. As plans go, that sucks ass. But the Killer was in gear and he didn't give much of a fuck what the odds were. He'd tasted blood and he wanted more.

So I ran.

The woman—thing, whatever—cut right behind a ruined wall and fled into the open desert, heading for a clump of palms clustered around a goat pen. The goats screamed and panicked, crashing into the rickety slats of the corral, leaping over the bars as they fell, jumping on each other to escape what was coming. The demon leapt the fence with ease and crashed among them, slashing right and left to clear her path. I saw heads and legs and red chunks fly into the air. It was as if the goats had run into a threshing machine. Their screams sounded like the terrified shrieks of children.

I was five paces behind her. Even though she tore through the goats it still slowed her. When she raced to leap over the rear wall of the corral, I was there. My Wilson has a 3.75-inch blade, which is great for fighting people—the weapon was so lightweight that it allowed my hand to move at full speed. But when cutting at a fleeing target it was inadequate. The tip of the blade drew a seven-inch line across her upper back, but the cut didn't go deep enough to destroy the muscles. Droplets of red-black blood spattered me and all my cut accomplished was to make her stumble. Her left foot caught the upper fence rail and the demon fell face forward into the dust on the other side.

Fell . . . and rebounded, rising into a crouch, spinning around to hiss at me, eyes bright with madness and bloodlust, claws slashing the air. I launched myself into the air for a diving, slashing tackle.

And then something hit me like a thunderbolt, slamming into my side, driving me at a right angle to the demon. I fell hard and badly, smashing into the fence post, spinning amid a cloud of splinters, feeling fire explode on my side as something tore at me. Then I was down, rolling over and over with a second woman.

A second demon.

❖ 6 ❖

Special Agent Franks

ANOTHER POSSESSED WOMAN was on top of Ledger, trying to gouge his eyes out. The two of them were rolling through the mud and shit, trying to kill each other. As entertaining as that was, Franks wasn't in the mood to dick around, so he aimed carefully and shot the creature square between the shoulder blades. The silver 10mm blew a hole through her heart, but rather than die, she screeched and reared back. Ledger reached up with his blade and slashed her throat wide open, half a second before Franks shot her through the side of the head. The demon rolled off of Ledger, thrashing and spraying.

Well, these things were proving to be obnoxiously tough. Franks grabbed one of the kicking legs and dragged the monster away from Ledger while the first demon circled back through the pile of dead goats. Ledger would just have to deal with that one while Franks figured out just how much of a hellacious beating he had to administer to finish an Alghul for good.

❖ **7** ❖

Captain Joe Ledger

I FOUGHT THE DEMON the way I'd fight a wild animal. I've had some experience there. Wild animals and genetically-modified animals. Years ago I faced down mastiffs that had been transgenically altered to give them scorpion tails. I've faced genetically-engineered vampire assassins and some other rude and nasty shit. This was my first encounter with something supernatural, but if it existed and if it could bleed, then some of the laws of nature had to apply. That was useful, that gave me a firm piece of ground in this shit storm where I could stand. And Franks had bought me a moment. So I used it.

The demon tried to end it fast by rushing at me with those claws.

Fool me once, motherfucker . . .

As she darted in I twisted and marked her from wrist to shoulder with picks—short, hard taps with the wicked point of my knife that opened bleeders and ripped apart nerves—and with quick, circular slashes to the muscles for reaching and grabbing. The demon howled in pain and darted back. Tried again, got cut again, and darted back once more. Blood the color of red bricks flowed from a dozen cuts.

If this was a person, I might have used the effect of a pick or slash to close to killing distance, but the wounds were hurting it—just not enough. Those arms still reached, still moved with obvious speed and power.

"Stop fucking around," growled Franks.

"I'm. Not. Fucking. Around," I snapped as I dodged a series of vicious slashes.

"Don't you have a big boy knife?"

"Fuck you."

He laughed a cold, heartless, mocking laugh and tossed something to me. A knife. A Ka-Bar USMC Mark 2 combat knife whose blade flashed in the sunlight. I faked left and lunged for the blade, snatched the handle, dove into a roll to give myself time to grip it properly, rose and spun. I did a fast swap so the Wilson was in my left and the much bigger Ka-Bar was in my right.

"Silver," barked Franks, then he had to concentrate on his own battle.

Silver. Did that work on demons? I had no fucking idea. What do I know about any of this shit?

The demon, though, she stared at the blade and hissed.

She knew.

Yeah. She absolutely knew.

I felt myself smile.

The Ka-Bar was bigger and heavier, but I've fought with them many times. You lose a fraction of your speed, but when you reach out and touch someone they get the message. I switched my grips on both knives so that I held them with the blades spiked down from my fists like the claws of a praying mantis.

"Come on, beautiful," I said to the demon. "Let's dance."

Okay, it was corny but I was having a moment.

So was she.

With a banshee howl the demon flung herself at me.

❖ 8 ❖

Special Agent Franks

HE HATED WHEN DEMONS were strong enough to warp the flesh of the possessed. They always seemed to sprout claws and fangs, just to be pricks about it. This one had scratched him and tried to bite a hole through his armor before he'd slugged her in the head enough times to crack her skull and turn her brains to mush. Franks hoisted the dazed demon high overhead, and with a roar, flung her down, through the fence, and against the packed earth so hard that the snapping bones could probably be heard back at the convoy.

The Alghul lay there twitching, beaten, glaring at him with eyes filled with hatred. She opened her mouth and hissed at him in the Old Tongue. "*Traitor.*"

"Yeah, whatever," Franks said as he reached down, got a handful of blood-soaked hair, and cranked the demon's head brutally to the side. He'd been planning on twisting her head clean off to shut her up, but simply snapping the neck seemed to do the trick, and he felt the ancient malignant spirit driven from the possessed flesh.

❖ **9** ❖

Captain Joe Ledger

THE DEMON tried to end it by driving all ten claws into me like a storm of daggers. I pivoted and parried, using the little Wilson to push the outside of her left arm to one side while also hooking and trapping her wrist. I used the Ka-Bar in a hard, sweeping overhand slash that sliced through scalp, ear, left eye, cheek and mouth. I put muscle into it, using my inverse grip so that it hit like a heavy punch as well as a slash.

It drove her to the ground. Hard. Dark blood exploded upward, and everywhere a drop struck my exposed skin, I could feel it burn.

Even hurt she tried to turn, but I stepped on her elbow, pinning it and her to the ground to spoil the turn. I stabbed down into the base of her skull to sever the spinal cord. The silver-coated knife bit deep and hard.

The demon screamed so loud that it knocked me back. She screamed so hard that blood burst from my nose as I lay there, hands clamped to my ears. The scream made the palm trees shiver and tore fronds off of them. Debris rained down on me as the scream rose and rose and . . .

The silence was immediate and intense.

For a terrified moment I wondered if my eardrums had simply burst.

But, no.

No.

I got shakily to my knees and immediately vomited into the dust. Then I sagged back onto my heels, pawing blood from my lips and chin, blinking past pain-tears in my eyes.

Franks stood there, wide-legged, chest heaving only slightly, sweat glistening on his skin, eyes dark and intense and amused.

"What," I said, "the fuck was that?"

His expression was ugly and unfriendly. "I told you, Ledger. Demons."

"First—and don't take this the wrong way—but fuck you and your demons."

He shrugged.

"Second—since when are demons an actual thing?"

"I thought DMS knew all this stuff."

"No, we goddamn well don't."

There was a twinkle in Franks' eyes. "Your boss does. What's he call himself now? Mr. Church? You should ask him."

I tried to get to my feet, failed, and he caught me under the arm and jerked me upright. I slapped his hand away and stepped back.

"Who are you? How do you know about Church? How do you know about demons, for Christ's sake? And, just in general, what the fuck?"

"The fuck," said Franks, "is that ISIS has gone old school."

"Meaning what?"

He pointed into the desert. "The answers are out there. If you want in, you need to come with me now."

"No, first I get answers." I stepped away from him and tapped my earbud to get the channel for the tactical operations center. "Cowboy to Deacon."

"Go for Deacon," said Church.

"Two words," I said. "Franks and demons."

He said, "Ah."

He gave it to me in bullet points, but they hit like real bullets. Agent Franks. Monster Control Bureau. A group that responded to supernatural threats in the same way that the Department of Military Sciences responds to terrorists with high-tech science weapons.

Real.

All real.

If there was a note of apology in Church's voice for not having read me in on this earlier, I sure couldn't hear it. As I listened, Franks stood apart, checking his weapons and trying to look as casual as a towering freak of a monster killer could look.

"Franks is in the family," said Church. "You can trust him. He's one of us."

"One of us? Is he even human?"

Church paused. "At this point, Captain, would that even matter?"

❖ 10 ❖

Special Agent Franks

"HOW DO YOU KNOW Mr. Church?" asked Ledger.

"We've met," Franks said. "He offered me a cookie."

"Yeah. He does love his vanilla wafers. We have a pool going that there's some kind of code in that whole cookie thing. What he eats, how he eats them, what he offers to other people."

"You're overthinking it."

"Pretty good chance," said Ledger. "Equal chance we're not. He's a spooky bastard."

They walked. The sun was an open furnace.

"Most soldiers, even SpecOps, would have died," Franks told him.

Ledger cut him a look, but only shook his head.

"You fight okay." By Franks' standards, that was a huge compliment.

"I intend to go home and cry into my pillow," said Ledger. "Maybe wear sweats and eat a whole thing of Ben and Jerry's. Or get drunk. Drunk is a real contender for how I intend to process this shit."

❖ 11 ❖

Captain Joe Ledger

I'M A BIG, tough, manly man, but there are times I just want to go and hide. Like when I'm in the middle of the Iraqi desert, having just waded through a brutal fire fight and some Frankenstein-looking cocksucker tells me that demons are real and we have to go chase one of them.

It doesn't help one little bit for me to remind myself that no one drafted me. I signed on for this stuff. Well . . . maybe not *this* stuff, but a good soldier doesn't get to choose his wars.

But, really, man . . . demons?

There is not enough bourbon in all of Kentucky to make that fit into my head.

Franks asked, "Have you heard of Alghul?"

"Sure," I said. "It's a monster from Arabian folklore."

"They're more than that."

I glanced over my shoulder in the direction we'd come. "Oh," I said. "Shit."

"*One Thousand and One Nights* has some truths. Alghul exist. They're mostly female demons who haunt graveyards, digging up fresh corpses to feed on. They lure men to remote spots and attack them. Like mermaids." He cut me a look. "Yes. Mermaids are real. They love human flesh."

"Jesus. Disney got that wrong."

"Alghul are ferocious, but rare. Most were imprisoned. Until now."

"So . . . ISIL is doing what? Recruiting desert demons?"

"Of course." He said it so matter-of-factly that it jolted me. I studied his brutish face, looking for some trace of humor or even irony. Nothing. He was as frank as his name.

"Okay, okay, so they *are* recruiting desert demons. How, though? If these Alghul are so vicious that they were imprisoned, why don't they chomp on the ISIL dickheads? I'm sure they're every bit as tasty."

"I don't do cultural evaluations," he stated. "Dark magic probably."

"And they can shape-shift? When I saw the first one she was an ordinary girl. Sixteen, seventeen, maybe. Then suddenly she wasn't a girl."

He nodded. "They prefer to use virgins as hosts. Demons enjoy corrupting the pure."

There had been a lot in the papers about ISIS fighters kidnapping women, forcing them into marriages with their people, or consigning them to rape camps. As insane as it was, I could see the ugly shape of it. ISIS was fierce but it wasn't massive. It did not really have a home country. It couldn't put a million-man army in the field to oppose the growing coalition of international forces. Even though many of ISIL's leaders were former Saddam officers and the equipment they used was stolen advanced tech, they were still comparatively small. They could fight a guerilla war but there was no way they could achieve a decisive win or hope to hold their territories for very long. They needed a wild card. I was dealing with some of this stateside with ISIL teams stealing technologies like portable EMPs and drone tech. This was new, and if it was something they could repeat over and over again, then this was a game changer.

❖ 12 ❖

Special Agent Franks

THE SUN BEAT DOWN on their heads, and then the rocks beneath them radiated the heat back upwards. They were travelling cross-country to avoid being spotted. It was a brutally hot day and he was sweating profusely beneath his armor. Franks didn't mind. Discomfort was one of those mortal concepts he had never really grasped. Compared to the endless void of Hell, a little mortal suffering was a small price to pay to have a body.

Captain Ledger was human and must have been dying in the agonizing heat, but he didn't seem like a complainer. They'd set a tough pace across rugged terrain, as fast as Franks was willing to risk without further aggravating the bullet hole in his leg, but Ledger had kept up. In fact, he seemed to enjoy the challenge.

So Ledger could fight extremely well, hadn't been scared of an Alghul, and was tough. It was too bad he was with a different agency, because Franks found himself thinking that he could use a man like this . . . But unfortunately, it turned out Ledger was also a smartass.

"So, Franks," said Ledger, "my people tell me you saved the world once."

"I heard the same thing about you."

Ledger shrugged. "Hasn't everybody?"

"No," Franks stated flatly.

But Ledger was undeterred. "That sea monster off the California coast with the nuclear sub. That was one of yours, wasn't it?"

"Classified." Franks had been working with tough guy secret agents of the US government since Benjamin Franklin had performed his first exorcism, so Franks was used to the inevitable dick measuring to see if an agent's rep was legit. "How'd you like the Red Order?"

"No comment."

"Thought so."

They made it less than half a kilometer before Ledger tried to make conversation again. What was it with mortals and their need to break perfectly good silences?

He was a little out of breath from the climb, but he kept pace. Ledger tapped his earbud. "I'm getting a lot of nice backstory on you, Franks. Here's a fun fact. My intel guy says that people who work with you have a tendency to die horribly."

Franks snorted. If Ledger wanted to talk, they might as well talk about the mission. They would be there by sundown. "We're only a few clicks from the target. The ancient Assyrian city of Nimrud."

"I heard ISIL bulldozed it. I guess that's the sort of thing psychopaths do." Ledger snorted, seemingly disgusted by the thought. "They're destroying priceless historical relics because they think it's an insult to their skewed view of their religion. The word 'fucktard' comes to mind." He paused. "Though, I suppose something out there raised a flag, otherwise my boss wouldn't have sent me here."

Franks thought that Ledger was probably talking about intel pinged by the DMS' fancy secret super computer, MindReader. The DMS used it to predict problems by looking for patterns in the massive information streams gathered by the various covert intelligence networks. Franks wasn't sure how well that actually worked for them, but it had brought Ledger here, so maybe there was something to it.

"MCB got a tip. Terrorists found the lost Prison of Shalmaneser. It was built in 1240 A.D. to house the king's enemies." Franks snorted. The mortal ones had turned to dust a long time ago. It was the immortal ones he was worried about.

"Which is why you're here, I suppose. Church tells me he intercepted communications from an ISIL tactician who'd cut a deal with someone at Nimrud for a new super weapon. You know, man, we gunslingers in the post 9-11 federal agencies are supposed to share information about stuff like this."

Franks just grunted. He'd never been good at sharing.

"Let me guess," Ledger persisted, "this lost prison holds more of those Alghul. How many are we talking about?"

Fourteen thousand corpses of the desolate plains, an unholy army that was legend among all the jealous Fallen, until King Shalmaneser had found a way to cast them from their physical bodies and entomb them in the Earth, but Franks couldn't tell Ledger that or how he knew about it, because there was classified, and then there was *classified.*

"A lot," said Franks.

"So much fun hanging out with Chatty Cathy." Ledger sighed.

❖ 13 ❖

Captain Joe Ledger

WE REACHED THE ANCIENT PRISON of Shalmaneser just as the sun began sliding toward the western horizon. Long fingers of darkness seemed to reach out toward us from the shattered rock walls, broken trees and parked vehicles. Our approach was cautious and circumspect. I reached Bug at the TOC and asked for whatever an eye-in-the-sky could tell us.

"Read forty heat signatures, Cowboy," he said, using my combat callsign. "Thirty-four are steady, six are variable. One minute they're normal, then they shift from low-temp to really hot. Not sure how to read that. Maybe they're underground and thermals can't get a solid lock."

I told Franks and he shook his head. "As the Alghul takes over, they burn hotter. The variations in thermal signature mean that the demons haven't fully taken hold. Human spirits are hard to destroy. Even assholes like these."

I had the impression that an explanation that long caused him actual physical pain. Getting trapped in an elevator for six hours with this guy would be a hoot.

We made maximum use of ground cover and came in on a line the satellites said was as close to a dead zone as we'd get. Franks never seemed to tire as we crawled over rocks and through dry washes and up sandy slopes. I felt like I was melting.

There was a small camp built inside the remnants of a medieval building that had collapsed centuries ago. The ISIL vehicles were hidden under desert camo tarps, but we saw a half-dozen empty slots where the vehicles from the fight in town had been parked. We hunkered down to study the layout while Bug fed me what intel he could grab from the satellite.

"How many sites are there like this?" I asked, nodding to the Assyrian ruins.

"Too many," Franks grimaced, or maybe it was a smile. Really hard to tell with a face like his. "Most stay lost."

"So why haven't we heard about the Alghul until now?"

"We have. MCB find stray Alghul, we put them down. They're here. Somebody hears a woman calling at night. Goes to look . . . The bodies are torn apart. Blame it on war. Nobody looks at a corpse over here and thinks 'demon.'"

"Um," I said, but I had nowhere to go with that.

"A few days ago a girl taken captive by ISIS returned to her village as a monster and slaughtered everyone. MCB found out. Intel says this is the source."

"We shut this place down, and we shut down the threat?"

Franks shrugged.

"And here we are," I said. The shadows were lengthening and the heat of the day was already beginning to shift. Once the sun was down it would get very cold very fast. "So, what's the plan? Soft infil? Gather some data and call in an airstrike?"

"No. Explosives only kill the body. We need to kill the demons."

"Shit. Let me guess, only silver does the trick."

"It varies, demon to demon," he said. "With the Alghul, it is silver or the hands of a true warrior."

"Isn't that just peachy. What if there are a lot of them?"

Franks shrugged again.

"Okay," I said, "there are forty hostiles in there and my team is hours out. We're two guys. So again I say, what's the plan?"

Frank handed me a Glock and two spare magazines. I still had the silver-coated Ka-Bar. Franks had taken enough firepower from his convoy to launch a frontal assault on the gates of Hell. He pointed to a pair of guards walking sentry outside of the opening to the ruins.

"Kill everything. How much more plan do you need?"

⸎ 14 ⸎

Special Agent Franks

Franks gave Ledger a few minutes to get into position before he started walking right up to the front of the dig site. The site was a haphazard maze of crumbling ancient buildings, twisted rock, modern prefabs, and heavy equipment. It was crawling with insurgents and absolutely reeked of demon stink. He didn't know how many humans had already been possessed by Alghul, but it looked like they'd practically formed a line to wait their turn to go down into the prison. The tactician was smart, only letting one volunteer descend into the depths at a time, because possession wasn't pretty, and it might make the others lose their nerve.

Idiots.

Construction spotlights kept most of the area well lit, but there were plenty of shadows for Ledger to work in. Franks had thought about taking out the generator first, since he could see in the dark, but so could the Alghul.

There was a Toyota pickup truck with a machinegun mounted in back blocking the road. The man on the gun saw the darkened shape of Franks approaching, pointed, and began shouting something. Franks shouldered the SCAR, put the ACOG scope's glowing green triangle on the man's chest, and launched a .308 round through his heart. The guard spun around and toppled from the bed of the truck. Franks kept walking.

The sudden noise had gotten everyone's attention. Another man had been sleeping in the cab of the truck, and he bolted upright, glancing around, confused, until Franks' second bullet went through the driver's window and blew his brains all over the passenger's side. A man in black pajamas and white sneakers ran around the truck. He had just enough time to fire a wild burst from his AK before Franks shot him once in the chest. He tumbled forward, skidding to a stop on his face.

There was movement all over the front of the camp now. *Excellent.* If they were all paying attention to him, then Ledger could get a shot at the ISIS tactician before he could create any more

Alghul. Just in case Ledger needed more time, Franks slung his rifle, hopped into the back of the pickup, worked the charging handle on the big 12.7mm DShK machinegun, and turned it on the camp. Franks was really good at being distracting.

❖ 15 ❖

Captain Joe Ledger

THERE ARE TIMES you have to nut up and say "fuck it."
So I nutted up and said fuck it.

❖ 16 ❖

Special Agent Franks

THUMP THUMP THUMP THUMP THUMP
The massive bullets tore right through the sheet metal of the prefab buildings. Lights shattered. Men died. Orange muzzle flashes rippled across the camp as they returned fire. Franks methodically swiveled the heavy machinegun toward each one and mashed the trigger, ripping apart bodies and cover. An insurgent ran from the ruins with an RPG over one shoulder and took a knee. Franks tore him in half and the rocket streaked off into the darkness.

As the last of the belt of heavy rounds cycled through the gun, Franks heard a new sound over the pounding. The screams were unnatural, like a sandstorm processed through tearing human vocal cords. *Alghuls incoming*, Franks thought as he saw the twisted figures loping across the camp on all fours toward him. *About damned time.*

❖ 17 ❖

Captain Joe Ledger

I MOVED IN, low and fast, running with small, quick steps to keep my aim level, firing the borrowed Glock in a two-handed grip. The ISIL tactician ducked backward, grabbed the shoulder of one of his guards and hurled him at me. Part shield, part weapon.

I put two center mass and dodged around him to get to the tactician, but there were more of the fighters. So many more.

They screamed at me in half a dozen dialects and began firing their AK-47s, filling the tomb with thunder. But they were panicking, too. In surprise attacks panic is the sword and shield of the attacker and it bares the breast and throat of the attacked. The swarm of bullets burned the air around me. I did not panic. I closed on them and fired, taking them in turn, shifting to interpose one in front of the other, making them pay for their fear that made them miss when I did not.

I could hear carnage and destruction behind me. Franks was a goddamn tank. I think he scared me more than what we were fighting. If he was an example of the MCB operators, then what the fuck *else* could they put in the field? I mean, I'm top of my game for what I am— a black ops gunslinger—but I'm flesh and blood. I couldn't shake off the kinds of damage he was wading through. Even so, I heard him grunt, saw out of the corner of my eye as some of the enemy fire hit him hard enough to tear chunks away, to slow his advance. Could he die?

Probably.

I damn well could.

And so could the fighters in this tomb.

Franks and I had proved that.

Then in one of those moments of combat improbability that offers proof that the gods of war are perverse sons of bitches, a heavy caliber round hit the side of my gun. The force tore the gun from my hand and nearly took my trigger finger with it.

The tactician had two burly guards with him and they were all eight feet from me. Their guns were swinging toward me.

I had no time at all, and I gave them none. Eight feet is a long step and a jump. I leapt into the hair, slapping the barrel of the closest AK aside a microsecond before he fired, and at the same time I hooked the shooter around the back of the neck, shoving him sideways. He crashed into the second shooter and I landed on the balls of my feet, pivoted, snapped out a low flat-footed kick to the second man's knee. The joint splintered audibly and it tore a shriek from him. I gave him a double-tap with my elbow, one very fast and very light hit to the eye socket to knock his head backward and a second much harder shot to the Adam's apple. He fell gagging and trying to drag air in through a throatful of junk.

The first shooter tried to slam me across the face with his rifle, but he wasn't set for it. I slapped the swing high and ducked low, chop-punching him in the groin, then rising fast and hitting him in the throat, too, this time with the stiffened Y formed by index finger and thumb.

That left the tactician facing me.

He did something cute. He pulled a knife.

So, what the hell, I pulled mine.

He was pretty good. Fast, strong, knew some moves.

Pretty good is great if you're fighting in a back alley or in the dojo using rubber knives. Not when you're fighting for your life.

He tried to drive the point of his knife into my chest, maybe hoping to end it right there. I clubbed the knife down and away with a fist and used the Ka-Bar to draw a bright red line beneath his chin. I whirled away to avoid the spray of blood.

❖ 18 ❖

Special Agent Franks

FRANKS CRASHED THROUGH THE CAMP, keeping up a steady stream of fire on the charging Alghuls. The contorted bodies were nearly as fast as he was, and it was taking several solid hits to put them down.

Beneath their tearing uniforms, their skin quickly dried and cracked apart, and unholy yellow light poured through the gaps. Bones twisted into points and ripped through their fingertips. As the possessed around them shed their humanity, the mortal ISIS fighters lost their nerve and fled into the desert. Not all of them made it as, overcome with bloodlust, the Alghul fell on them, tearing them limb from limb, and painting the stone walls with blood. Franks would have shot the survivors in the back as they ran away, but he couldn't spare the ammunition.

There was a ripping noise as an Alghul tore through a canvas tent to get at him. When it appeared, the yellow glow leaking through its tearing visage reminded him of a candle inside a jack-o'-lantern. But when he knocked it down and then stomped its chest flat with one big combat boot, what came squirting out wasn't much very pumpkinlike at all.

"Franks! Over here!" He turned to see Ledger standing in a doorway to an ancient stone building. He no longer had Franks' Glock and instead held a Russian Stechkin automatic pistol he'd picked up from one of the dead ISIS fighters. Behind him, stairs led down into the darkness. Ledger glanced up as a shadow crossed him. An Alghul was spider-climbing up the rock above him. Ledger calmly raised his Stechkin and fired several rounds through its face. "I found the prison," he said as the Alghul landed next to him with a sick thud.

And the rest of the Alghul must have realized it too, because they'd quit tearing the terrorists' guts out and shoving them into their mouths long enough to all focus on the American intruders. There were at least a dozen of them left, and they all ran shrieking toward the doorway.

"Whatever you're going to do, do it fast." Ledger grimaced as an Alghul swiped at his eyes with its claws. He shot the creature repeatedly as it stumbled away. Then Ledger darted forward and punctuated the attack with a deep slash from the silver Ka-Bar. The demon shrieked and crumpled to the stone floor.

Franks shoulder-checked another Alghul into the ground and then dumped the rest of his rifle's magazine into its body, sending up gouts of blood and sand. "Don't let anything past this point," he told Ledger as he shoved by him.

"I sure hope Church was wrong about your allies tending to die horribly," Ledger muttered as he got ready to hold off a horde of demons on his own.

"Not really," Franks said as he went down the stairs.

"That's not helping," Ledger shouted as he kept shooting.

❖ 19 ❖

Captain Joe Ledger

I SWAPPED OUT a spent magazine for a fresh one just as a wave of Alghuls rushed at me.

The Modern Man inside my head more or less screamed and passed out. The Cop backpedaled because this wasn't his kind of fight.

But the Killer . . . ?

Well, hell, I think he was waiting for the right moment to take the wheel and drive us all to crazy town.

And I liked it. They rushed at me. And I . . . fuck it. I rushed at them.

I let the gun barrel lead the way but I chased the bullets into the crowd. The heavy rounds punched holes in foreheads and burst eyeballs and painted the walls with dark gore. If we'd been in a wider space they could have circled me and cut me apart. This was a narrow stairwell and it worked for the kind of close-range fighting I do best. When the slide locked back, I simply rammed the barrel into the screaming mouth of one of the Alghuls and then slashed her across the throat. As she twisted down to the ground I reached past and quick-stabbed the next one in the right eye and then the left. One-two shallow thrusts with the sharpened clip of the Ka-Bar. The demon staggered back, clawing at its face with black talons, and I knee-kicked it into the others, jamming and crowding them even more. I grabbed a fistful of hair and drove the knife into the socket of a throat, gave the blade a quarter turn and ripped it free.

The dead and dying monsters toppled against the others, pressing them backward, transforming their savage attack into a clumsy rout. I jumped onto them, riding the falling, tumbling, bone-snapping avalanche down the stairs. Claws tore at me, the stone walls and the stone steps pummeled me, teeth snapped at me, but I rode a magic carpet of destruction down to the bottom. This was my moment and although they were demons from some twisted corner of hell, I was the red king and the knife was my scepter.

Then something massive crashed past me, striking the last of the demons like a runaway truck.

Franks.

He was splashed with blood and there was a wild light in his eyes that was no more human than the monsters we fought. He smashed them with fists the size of gallon pails; he stomped on them. I saw him tear an arm from its socket in exactly the same way the first Alghul had done back at the village.

It was all red madness.

I was the only one down there who was human.

If you could call the Killer human. He was like a demon howling inside my head, and through my mouth and with my voice.

But I was wrong.

I wasn't the only human down there.

I saw a man standing at the rear of the chamber.

He was dressed in strange clothes, all of gold and jewels and leather, like someone who had stepped from a history book. In a flash of insight I realized that he was probably dressed as a shaman or sorcerer from the courts of King Shalmaneser, emulating everything down to his garb so that there was no chance of getting his horrible ritual wrong.

He was the one responsible for all this death. He was the one who had taken all of these innocent girls and turned them into monsters. He had participated in a kind of spiritual rape by opening them to the demons who destroyed their souls while stealing their flesh. The depth of this crime—this *sin*—was bottomless. If he lived, if he escaped, then all of this destruction, all of this pain, was for nothing. He would start it up again somewhere else. He would ruin more lives, and by doing it, hand ISIL a weapon more dangerous than any nuke.

Behind the sorcerer was a doorway in the living rock of the cavern. It was open and beyond it I could see flames. Maybe there was a bonfire in there, but I don't think so.

I think I was looking straight into the mouth of Hell itself.

One after another of the Alghul came running from the flames to join the fight.

"*Franks!*" I screamed, pointing.

The brute had three Alghuls tearing at him and he bled from at least fifty deep cuts, but he turned, saw me, saw where I was pointing. Saw the sorcerer.

I saw him stiffen. I saw the moment when he understood what we were seeing.

Franks reached up and ripped one of the Alghul from him and used her body as a club to beat the other two into shattered ruin. Then he lowered his head, balled his fists, and charged toward the sorcerer.

Leaving the other ten Alghuls to swarm at me.

But I kicked myself backward and stepped on something that turned under my foot. It was one of Franks' guns. A mate to the Glock he'd given me. I snatched it up, vaulted the rail and dropped fifteen feet to the floor. My knees buckled under the impact, but I tucked and rolled as best I could. The Alghul shrieked like crows and swarmed down the steps toward me. The sorcerer pointed at me with a ceremonial dagger and at Franks with a scepter.

"*Kill them!*"

The demons closed around me like a fist.

I raised the pistol and took the shot.

One bullet.

There was only one round left and the slide locked back.

The sorcerer stared at me. All the Alghul froze. The world and the moment froze.

The sorcerer had three eyes. Two brown ones and a new black one between them. Two of the Alghul stood behind him, their faces splashed with blood that was redder than theirs.

We all lived inside that frozen moment for what seemed like an hour. Or a century.

And then the sorcerer fell.

❖ 20 ❖

Special Agent Franks

IT REALLY PISSED HIM OFF when stupid mortals fucked around with things beyond their comprehension. This idiot had probably pieced the spell together out of some forbidden tome. He'd gotten the costume right but the actual magic words written in blood on the walls were the equivalent quality of Crayon scribbles. The workmanship was so shoddy they were lucky he hadn't sucked northern Iraq into another dimension with this half-assed summoning spell.

Ledger drilling a hole through the summoner's brain had stopped the ritual. No more would cross over. However, they were still up to their eyeballs in Alghul, but since the path was still open, Franks had a solution to that little problem.

This next part wasn't in any of the MCB's manuals.

Franks walked to the shimmering portal, and placed his hands against the edges. His gloves immediately burst into flames. Even though they were all around them, the humans couldn't sense the disembodied, but Franks could. He saw that the Alghul's spirits were still tethered to this prison. In this place of power he could apply the might of his will against theirs.

"*Your invitation has been revoked.*" Franks declared in the Old Tongue. A hot desert wind ripped through the ruins, sand blasting the bloody marks from the ancient walls. The demons shrieked as the void ripped them from their newfound flesh and sent them hurtling back into the darkness.

And then he shut the door.

The flaming portal disappeared in a flash. Every possessed body instantly collapsed into a limp, wet heap.

Well, that worked better than he'd expected.

Ledger was panting, covered in blood, and surrounded by corpses. He looked to Franks, incredulous. "What the fuck just happened, Franks?"

"Mission accomplished."

❖ 21 ❖

Captain Joe Ledger

I WANT TO SAY that it was an easy wrap. I want to say that Franks did his magic mumbo jumbo and the world became all shiny and new and cartoon animals frolicked around us.

I'd love to say that. Just once.

The truth was that there were still some possessed ISIL foot soldiers out there.

Franks and I are alive right now because we earned it.

I'm telling you this now as I sit on an equipment box in Camp Baharia in Fallujah. There are a lot of U.S. military around me. Echo Team finally arrived, so I have my own people there. In that place, with that much muscle around me I should feel secure, should be able to take a deep breath.

But I think it's finally hit me.

There are demons. Real demons.

There are monsters. Real monsters.

We stopped a threat unlike anything I'd ever imagined could be real in this world. The gateway to Hell, or to wherever those demons came from, is closed thanks to a monster that stands alongside ordinary humans like me.

That doorway is sealed, but when I asked Franks if that meant that demons could no longer come into our world, he did something that I didn't think he could do.

He laughed.

And, brother, it was not the kind of laugh you ever want to hear.

No, it was not.

So I sat here, waiting for my ride out of this place, for my ride home. The night is heavy and vast. I used to think the shadows were nothing more than lightless air, that nothing lived in them, that nothing could.

Now I know different.

Holy God, now I know different.

"Weaponized Hell" is one of the two collaborations in this collection, and because writers are a weird bunch, every collaboration works out differently. But to give you an illustration of what a consummate professional Jonathan Maberry is, that entire story you just read was written over just a few days. We had agreed to do this story and then had done a bit of brainstorming together, but we are both really busy with lots of active projects so the deadline for this one kind of snuck up on both of us.

When the editor reached out to see how it was going, it was like, uh oh. Crunch time! Of the two of us, Jonathan had the more pressing schedule that week, so I hurried and wrote a rough of each of Franks' scenes, leaving gaps where I thought Ledger bits would make sense. That night Jonathan took it, wrote his scenes, inserted a few new cool bits I hadn't thought of, and kicked it back to me. Then we spent the last day sending it back and forth, polishing and tweaking each of our characters' dialog and actions when they appeared in the other writer's scenes.

I think it came out really good.

Agent Franks is one of my most popular characters, and Jonathan gets him. In fact a year after this story came out, I got Jonathan to write an Agent Franks point of view story for the Monster Hunter Files anthology, and he gave me a World War Two Agent Franks vs. Nazis story that was great.

SON OF FIRE, SON OF THUNDER

The other collaboration in this collection is "Son of Fire, Son of Thunder," written by me and Steve Diamond, for the Crimson Pact *anthology in 2011, which was edited by Paul Genesse, and published by Alliteration Ink.*

This is one of my very first short stories, and only the second piece of fiction Steve ever wrote. I did the scenes from Diego Santos, Freelance Exorcist. Steve wrote Lazarus Tombs, FBI.

Staff Sergeant Diego Santos
Behavioral Health Department, Main Clinic,
Marine Corps Base Quantico

IN TWO YEARS, fifty-six days, fourteen hours, and ten minutes I will be brutally killed by a demon.

I've watched my own death in my dreams nearly every night since I was eight. I'm used to waking up because of teeth breaking my skin.

You might think that sounds like a tough break, but don't shed any tears on my behalf. The rest of you poor saps have to live with doubt and worry and fear. You have to think about finding a career, marrying the right woman, raising kids, working hard, planning your retirement, getting cancer, and shit like that. Me? I know the exact minute when I'll be ripped to bits.

Just lucky, I guess.

There's only one downside to knowing the exact moment when your life will end horribly.

I hate when people waste my fucking time.

The psychologist had been asking me questions for fifty-two precious minutes. I'd finished telling him about kicking doors and fighting house to house in Fallujah, and one particular story where I'd shot a guy in the neck right when he was about to light me up with an AK, when the doctor asked, "And so how did that make you feel?"

How was it supposed to feel? How should a normal person answer? I did my job. How's it supposed to feel when you do a good job? I am a United States Marine and I have been trained to close with, engage, and utterly destroy the enemy, and I am *extremely* good at my job. I've deployed to Iraq three times, Afghanistan twice. As soon as I get home I volunteer for the next open billet. Better me than anyone else, I've got nothing better to do to prepare myself until the appointed time, and mostly because I can't die until I've fulfilled the holy mission assigned to me by Almighty God.

But that wasn't the answer this man was looking for. He wasn't worthy enough to understand the truth. I needed him to think that I *wasn't* crazy. I had to keep the demons secret. It wasn't time for the apocalypse yet.

"It was very frightening, sir."

I watched the doctor's face as he glanced down to scribble a note on his legal pad. *Just write that I'm normal and quit screwing around.* I'd always assumed that a psychologist's office would have a couch for the patient to lay down on, but I just had a stuffed chair and he sat behind a desk. He looked up at me and it was obvious he knew I was full of it. I've always hated lying. It's easier to just not say anything at all than to make shit up. "I've read your file."

They say that if a shrink declared a Marine sane, he'd be unfit for duty, but I had a reputation for crazy even by our standards. My last CO had decided that I must have a death wish, and that was how I'd ended up here, off to see the wizard. Mandatory Evaluation Time. "I would expect so, sir."

"An impressive list of commendations and fitness reports, but these After Action Reports . . . a complete disregard for personal safety, placing yourself in harm's way, not just volunteering for every dangerous assignment possible but making up new ones. There are serious worries about your stability. Did I even read that last one right? Attempting to draw sniper fire?"

"It makes them easier to spot and neutralize, sir."

"And the most recent incident?"

I scowled. It would have been certain death for anyone else . . . I couldn't tell him that one of the Afghans had been possessed. "An opportunity presented itself. I acted."

"You acted alone against an entrenched, numerically superior foe, after your rifle platoon had been ordered to wait for reinforcements." He looked me right in the eyes. "Are you trying to get yourself killed, Staff Sergeant?"

"No, sir." My answer was completely truthful this time. I'd accepted the hour of my death. It would be blasphemous, not to mention impossible, to thwart His will.

The doctor's Blackberry buzzed. He picked it up and read the display. Our time was up. "That's it for today, but I want to schedule another session for tomorrow. Same time. We'll pick up where we left off."

More wasted time. But I was stuck here, spinning my wheels until it was decided that I wasn't a danger to myself or the Corps. "Of course, sir."

I didn't wake up screaming. Oh no. I knew how to keep the screams inside. The trapped screams turn into heat, and I simply lay there uncomfortable and twitchy. I'd learned how to do that a long time ago. You didn't want to get the reputation as the guy that woke up screaming from nightmares every single night. You might get sent in for a Mandatory Evaluation or something.

Her apartment was close to the freeway so a lot of ugly light snuck around the edges of the curtains. Flat on my back, sweating, breathing hard, I stared at the ceiling for a while, remembering the feeling of razor teeth in my neck, of claws digging through my guts, the crack of my breaking bones still vibrating in my ears. It was always the same. Sometimes there were new bits, unusual clues that I'd never noticed before, small things, but there was nothing new tonight. Just me dying while a few familiar faces watched helplessly at the ragged edge of the apocalypse. I didn't know those witnesses' names, and I'd never met any of them in real life yet, but I knew them so well that they were truthfully my oldest friends.

The girl stirred next to me, lifted one hand and sleepily stroked my chest. She bumped my crucifix, my dog tags, and ended up touching the Eagle, Globe, & Anchor tattoo over my heart.

The reason I'd enlisted was because I'd seen that tattoo in my Vision. Apparently God wanted me to be a Marine, and since I had a destiny to fulfill, I'd gotten inked the day after I'd gotten out of boot camp.

"You're hot," she mumbled. Her hand went flat and her palm was cold on my fevered chest as she drifted back to sleep. I couldn't for the life of me remember her name, though she'd said she was a dental hygienist. We'd met in a bar a few hours ago, she was lonely and alive, so I'd followed her back to her apartment. It didn't matter that I couldn't remember her name. When you've got so little time, there's no point.

Man's got to pass the time somehow.

Special Agent Jarvis "Lazarus" Tombs
FBI National Academy, Quantico

THE CHILDREN.

I still see them every night in my nightmares. Truthfully, I'm lucky if I have a nightmare where all I see are monsters and demons running around killing everyone. I would rather see that type of death and destruction than the eyes of those children again, haunting me.

Tonight was the fifteenth night in a row that I got to relive a grotesque dream version of the day six months ago when I found the house of the thing—the demon—that had abducted my son. It takes no effort to recall the feeling of walking into that house and seeing the walls covered from floor to ceiling in portraits and photographs of children. There were thousands of them. The children, still alive, trapped within their own personal "still life."

My son was included among them.

But my nightmare doesn't follow the reality of the memory.

I stand in the entryway, feeling the heat of the fire as it consumes the house. Flames spring up where the walls meet the floors. This time, the photos on the walls are utterly alive. The captured children pound on the photos from the inside, screaming silently to be let out. In the dream tears stream down my cheeks because I know I can do nothing to save them. Those tears will be on my face when I wake up. It's the same every time.

In my hands I hold the picture of my son on a backyard swing set. His picture too is animated, and he swings back and forth, laughing. As chilling as the screaming faces in the other pictures in the home are—in my nightmare I can somehow see every single one throughout the house—they are nothing compared to the laughter of my son. It is mocking and demonic, like the thing that trapped him in the picture.

The flames get hotter. They now cover the walls, burning and melting the pictures of thousands of children. Impossibly, I see each child catch on fire within their pictures, dying in agony. I can hear them all saying over and over, "Lazarus Tombs has made his choice!"

And over it all I hear my son laughing harder and harder.

I look back down at the picture in my hands. My hands catch fire, and I know the rest of me is burning too. The picture of my son is unyielding. Nothing can free him from the photo except me.

But I won't free him.

Tonight my nightmare ends the same way it always does. All the children are dead, the ashes of their pictures heaped around me in piles. Before my own body crumbles to ash, my son stops laughing and speaks to me from the photo.

"Dad, will you set me free so I can kill everything?"

Special Agent Lazarus Tombs
Personal Dormitory, FBI National Academy, Quantico

I WOKE UP gasping for breath.

The horrifying feeling from that nightmare never dulls, no matter how many times I experience it. Wiping the tears from my cheeks, I swung my legs off the side of my bed. On the nightstand, I keep that picture of my son. I looked so hard and long for him after he was abducted, but never thought that finding him would leave me feeling like a failure. He was right there in the photo, held there by the power of an incredibly powerful demon.

I had two choices. I could say a specific phrase given to me by the demon and set my son free. But if I did, all the power that demon held would take over my son. He would lose his identity and become that demon reincarnated. And then I would have to hunt him down and kill him.

Or, I could leave him in the picture until I came upon a solution that would allow me to free him without consequences. The reality is that I constantly question whether or not the demon was telling me the whole truth. Why should it? What if its threat was nothing more than a bluff? A way to torture me with doubt and temptation?

And tempted I am. Every minute of every day.

The hope of a solution was what brought me to one of the dorms of the FBI National Academy in Quantico, Virginia. Usually I taught classes here every other year, but this time I was here as a counselor for the classes of cops and deputies that were invited to the National Academy. As a counselor I ate with the attendees, went to classes with them, shot with them, and watched for the ones that had potential. Every cop sees weird and scary stuff out there in the world, but these days the weird and scary were getting worse and worse. My division at the FBI, the Paranormal Sciences Division—or PSD— kept track of all paranormal activity, which was on the rise. Significantly. We needed recruits who could deal with the paranormal, and at the very least we needed eyes and ears out in the world that could keep us updated. The FBI National Academy was a perfect cover. We invited those that had some promise or who had actual paranormal experiences.

I reached over and picked up my son's photo. Six months and no real leads. I'd hoped that some of the attendees this year might have something, but I knew I was grasping at straws. A deputy from Sacramento had called me with a rumor about phoenix ashes. But how do you find a phoenix, if one even exists?

It would take a miracle to save my son from his current fate, but believing in miracles isn't out of the ordinary for a guy like me. How can I not believe in them considering I've died and come back from the dead twice already?

My thoughts cut out as the photo warmed unnaturally in my hand. This happened every now and again. What did it mean? Was I running out of time?

I put the picture back down, more than a bit unnerved. I needed a distraction. My clock read 8:00 A.M. As my father always said, it was never too early to get some shooting in. It would get my mind off the nightmare, and it would be a good time to get some time in with some of the cops and deputies. One had hesitantly mentioned encountering a sandman before. Another potential recruit who was here at the Academy, a girlie cop from Chicago, killed a demon in a meth house. Her hair and nails threw me at first, but Detective Cynthia Weber was one of my top prospects of the year.

I was out the door before my clock read 8:05 A.M.

Staff Sergeant Diego Santos
Rifle Range, Marine Corps Base Quantico

"GOOD MORNING, Staff Sergeant Santos."

"And a good morning to you, Gunnery Sergeant Moss."

Moss was a solid, tough, bald, mean bastard with a lazy eye. I was rather fond of him. Fleet Assistance Program had put me working for him while I was under Mandatory Evaluation. We got along because Moss liked anybody that had a reputation for being good at shooting people, and I helped him keep the range squared away. Moss was a no BS, get-the-job-done sort of Marine. I wished I could tell him what was out there, waiting, but God hadn't picked me to be a prophet. He wanted me to be a warrior.

"You look shittier than usual, Santos. Late night?"

"Of course, Gunny."

"Was she pretty?"

I shrugged. "Enough."

"Are you *trying* to be a stereotype? You know it isn't mandatory for you young guys to have every bad habit. With the diseases that's out there, that sort of behavior will kill you one of these days." Moss was happily married with half a dozen kids. I just enjoyed the crappy range coffee and finished off my morning cigar. "If smoking don't get you first."

PT studs like Moss always frowned on the smokers, which was understandable, but it wasn't like I cared about my long term health. "What's today?"

"Training wheels, baby steps, hurt feelings. The short bus should arrive soon." That meant we would be working with the newly minted officers. To be fair, by the point the butter bars got to Moss' range, they were usually disciplined enough not to do anything stupid. There were bound to be some prior service Marines in the mix to make my job easier. Range work was nothing like combat. We both knew that, but you had to start somewhere. "Watch the city boys. They're usually the worst. Don't know shit about shooting."

"I grew up in a city."

"Yeah, but you're from East LA. I bet you got lots of fam fire hanging out the window of a lowrider spraying down the hood with an Uzi." Moss grinned. He loved jerking my chain.

"I was an altar boy." That much was true. I'd hoped that maybe I could've learned something useful about how demons worked from the priests, but they'd been blind as everyone else. It had always been frustrating keeping my knowledge secret. I'd mostly wanted somebody to talk to that *got* it.

"Uh huh . . . Sure you were, Santos." He looked around to make sure we were alone. "They should just let me write up your psych eval and save everyone some time. I recognize your condition. You suffer from an acute case of *does not give a shit*. You were born to fight. Combat is where you belong. Some officers just can't wrap their little minds around the fact that men like you exist."

That was a hell of a compliment.

"Doesn't help that you're a scary little motherfucker. You always got this disturbing look on your face, all shifty, like you're deciding if somebody is worth stabbing. You should try to smile once in a while."

I tried.

"Jesus . . . Okay, don't do that every again."

"Ooh-rah, Gunnery Sergeant."

"Let's get the lockers open. Gonna be a busy day."

It might seem odd that they'd FAP somebody they were worried about being suicidal to work on a range with live ammunition, but this was the military. I knew of a guy in the Army that was being counseled for clinical depression and they'd assigned him to be a parachute rigger.

Demons have a smell. It is hard to describe, and it's been different each time I've found one. Sometimes like burning plastic, or dried blood, or the sickness in an old folks home . . . I think they had different species and each one had their own nasty fragrance, but there was always something underneath that just cried demon.

This time it was like old road kill.

It took me a moment to pick it up. Firing ranges have a strong smell to them anyway. Sweat, oil, dust, and the overpowering carbon stink from thousands of rounds of 5.56. Even on an outdoor range, if there wasn't a breeze, it would collect and hang around you like a cloud. But even then, I could smell the demon stink.

I'd been coaching a trainee when I took a step off the line. It was close. And then there was another, slightly different scent, and then a third, and then more. "It can't be . . ." I'd never encountered more than a single demon at once.

"Staff Sergeant?" the recruit asked.

We still had two years and fifty-five days until the battle for the end of the world kicked off. This couldn't be right. "Cease fire! Cease fire!" I shouted.

Immediately the command was relayed and repeated down the line. Moss shouted it into his bullhorn. One last round went off a split second after the command went out, and in any normal circumstances that Marine would've been chewed a new asshole.

I took my headphones off and ran down the concrete slab. The smell . . . Where was it coming from? It was so close I could taste the rot in my mouth. It was coming from the FBI side of the range.

Moss appeared at my side. "What is it?"

I couldn't just say that the forces of hell were loose in Quantico, but I had to do something. "Listen . . . You hear that?"

"What?"

There wasn't any yet, but I knew there would be soon enough. "Screaming."

Special Agent Lazarus Tombs
Indoor Shooting Range, FBI National Academy, Quantico

I STOOD IN ONE OF THE ACADEMY'S indoor ranges, arms folded, watching members of my class put round after round into paper targets at twenty-five feet. Ten of my class of twenty-seven were here, each of them having been personally targeted and recruited to attend this session. There should have been eleven with me, but Deputy Helen Collins from El Paso had just discovered she was expecting. My boss, Frank Shields, had passed down the mandate that starting today Collins wouldn't be visiting a shooting range until after she was a new mother.

Regardless, I was pleased. The world was taking the straight road to ruin, and no one seemed to really care or even notice. The Bureau needed help. Hell, the whole world needed help. Most of the Academy sessions only would net one or two cops and deputies who could take the stress of dealing with the supernatural.

I had ten in the room with me. *Ten.* That meant that potentially ten more cities and towns would have a slight extra bit of help when real-life monsters began running around in their neighborhood.

It was also potentially ten more people that could keep an eye out for ways to fix my son's . . . situation.

On the far left Sergeant Tim Danielson—Reno PD—was burning through magazines at twice the speed of everyone else. He'd just been promoted for "exceptional bravery in the line of duty." His superiors didn't know the half of it. Danielson had responded to a domestic dispute that had turned into stopping a possessed couple on a killing spree. I was going to try to properly recruit him to work with me. Next to him was Cynthia Weber. She was trying out a smaller caliber Glock 17 and seemed to be subconsciously competing with Danielson. It was close. I wanted her for the PSD, but had a feeling she had too much love for Chicago. But that didn't mean I couldn't try.

The rest were probably going to be sent back home after receiving some specialized training from myself and a few other experts at the PSD. They'd each have my direct line with instructions to call with any questions or concerns.

I felt The Itch.

Stiffening, I felt the hairs on the back of my neck stand on end. I only felt The Itch around supernatural creatures or paranormal hot spots, and it usually meant things were going to get bad.

The muffled popping of ten sidearms was suddenly accompanied by a dull thudding behind us.

At the door.

The others began hearing it too, and soon they had all stopped firing and were watching the door with me.

I took one step towards the door then froze as a portion of it bulged inward. I pulled my Glock from my holster and took aim. Something was coming through, and The Itch in my head was maddeningly intense. There was no way this was going to end well.

The door flew inward, and a demon followed.

Demons come in all shapes and sizes. Some were intelligent and some were dumb as bricks, but they were all killing machines. This one had a long snout like a mutated dog with red-stained teeth bristling from its maw, with skin that was red like it had just crawled out of Hell the way they describe it in church. It was also the biggest demon I'd ever seen. At least three times my own mass, and seven or eight feet tall.

The demon smiled, then charged us.

A continuous roar of gunfire greeted the demon's sudden movement. The rounds—a mixture of .40 and .45—pounded into the creature, slowing its momentum, but it wasn't enough. Bullets thudded into the demon's black hide but didn't cause any visible harm. The demon shielded its face, keeping me from hitting it in any of its vulnerable areas, and leapt into the line of police officers to my left.

A cute, petite blonde—Lieutenant Alice Thompson from the NYPD—was the first to go down, ripped open groin to neck. Blood sprayed into the air and splashed onto the two deputies next to her. One froze in shock at the blood—Captain Carson from Minnesota— and had his head taken off by a casual swipe of the demon's clawed hand. The other deputy—Blinds, from Miami—stepped forward and emptied a full magazine into the creature's chest from three feet away. As he thumbed the magazine release, the demon grabbed him by the neck and flung him against the far wall of the indoor range. He was dead when he hit the steel trap. The demon slashed at another of the cops in the room, and the officer went down, clutching his belly to keep his insides from spilling out.

One officer—by the name of Jorge Castilla—ran for the door. Weber screamed after him, calling him a coward as she reloaded, but I could hardly blame Castilla. Some people just couldn't handle the up-close violence these kind of creatures could dish out.

The demon was slowing down. Inky, black blood was dribbling out mostly from the rounds Blinds had shot at close range. If this went on for much longer we'd all be dead. I shoved another magazine into my Glock as the demon leapt onto a cop from New Jersey, tearing out his throat with its powerful jaws. The demon jerked its head to the side and snapped the man's neck for good measure.

It turned its head and made a deep, guttural sound.

Laughter.

I extended my gun and put two shots through its left eye.

It collapsed like a puppet that had its strings cut.

Danielson and the other living rushed to the side of the cop holding his internal organs and tried keeping him alive. I reached up and pulled off my ear protection. Sounds of screaming through the open door to the range assaulted my ears. The scent of blood, gunpowder and sulfur were making me lightheaded and nauseous. I ran to my duffle bag and pulled out three loaded magazines—the rounds were all hollow-points and would have difficulty penetrating the hide of any demon that was more than a few yards away.

I left the officers behind and walked out into the bright late-morning light. To my left two more demons were playing tug-of-war with Jorge Castilla. A small mercy was that he was already dead from a dozen slashes and bites. I leveled my gun and fired in one motion. The rounds thudded into the left demon's torso, and I was rewarded with a shriek of pain. The two monsters dropped Castilla's corpse and started in my direction, smiling.

"Tombs! Tombs! Tombs!" the one on the right rasped. It sounded . . . *delighted.*

They *knew* me.

Staff Sergeant Diego Santos
Rifle Range, Marine Corps Base Quantico

I'M A STAFF SERGEANT. It isn't like I can order around very many Marines in the grand scheme of thing, but luckily for me, the chaotic noise of battle coming from the FBI side of the range was unmistakable. I reacted first, but the others caught on pretty quick.

Moss got back on his bullhorn. NCOs dragged their men off the line, and one sharp lieutenant decided that somebody needed to go investigate.

Since I'd already taken a vest in my size off the range display, thrown it on, and was shoving loaded magazines into the pouches, I must have looked like the logical choice. Once again, just lucky I guess, because I was going anyway. Moss, God bless his ready-for-violence soul, had done the same thing, though surely he was thinking it was a terrorist attack or something. Two other vets were just as on the ball and the four of us were ready to go within a minute of the first inhuman bellow drifting across the fence from the FBI side.

Armed with range loaner M-16A4s and M-4 carbines, we took off. Even the PT stud had a hard time keeping up with me. I always seem to move faster when demons are around. Just motivated, I suppose.

We were scouts, but I already knew what we would find.

This was the only part of the base where the Marines bumped up against the FBI Academy grounds. It made sense to share a backstop. The smell was stronger here. Men and women were shouting and there were random bursts of gunfire. We crouched behind a concrete bulwark at the boundary.

Moss about had a heart attack when he saw his first hell spawn. This one was seven feet tall, red, with muscles that seemed to be constructed out of living strands of barbed wire. It was too busy yanking some poor dude's entrails out to notice the four men in MARPAT watching it. Moss ducked back down. He actually turned grey for a second and I thought the hardened Marine was going to puke. No matter how tough you are, demons always had that effect on people their first time. "Easy, Gunny. They feed on fear. Makes them stronger."

"What the fucking fuck—What is that?"

"Demon."

"Demon?"

I risked a quick peek. I'd seen one like that back in LA on leave last winter. God had shown me where it slept so I'd beaten that one to death with a pipe wrench. "Shoot for their eyes, mouths, soft bits. Try to engage from a distance. They're super fast and their claws are nasty."

Moss was shaking his head, but not in disbelief. There was no way he could delude himself about what he'd seen. There's something about the sight of a demon that slugs you deep in your primal instincts. There was no denying the sheer, unearthly wrongness of them.

"Take it out," Moss ordered.

We rose and opened fire. I'd zeroed the Trijicon on the loaner M-16A4 myself. The chevron landed on the red beast's head and I stroked the trigger. The scope bobbled a bit, then settled back down, and I popped another 5.56 into its face. It took a several more hits before black sludge erupted from between the strands of fleshy wire. The demon took two awkward steps on its goat legs, and fell over. One of the lance corporals put a few extra into it to be safe before we ducked down.

"They're not so tough!" the lance corporal shouted.

I changed mags and stowed the partially spent one. "That was the weakest kind I know of. They're quick, but not durable. The others will be worse. Especially if they've got any of the ones that can look like people . . . You know, these feel like they just got here. They're disoriented. If we can pop the son of a bitch that brought them in, we can stop this fast."

"How can you tell who that is?" Moss hissed.

God will show me. "I just will. He'll be close."

"Damn it, Santos . . ." Moss looked at the two hyperventilating lance corporals. I had to hand it to them, they were doing okay. I'd peed my pants the first time I'd seen a demon, but then again, there's a lot of difference between a scrawny eight-year-old and a Devil Dog. "Kerchek, Whitney, haul ass back. Tell the LT everything Santos said . . ." and when he realized how strange the report would sound, he added, "*Convince* him." He looked at me next. "Your crazy ass is with me."

The other two got up and ran.

Moss' hands were shaking, but he was a Marine, which meant that no matter how awful or terrifying it was about to get, he was programmed to kick serious ass. "How do you know—"

"Altar boy. Remember?"

"Now you smile? Stop. You're freaking me out."

We moved out, crouched but quick, weapons shouldered. Combat waddle they call it, but it's normal for your body to crouch when it thinks it is about to get hit by something. One of the mottled green bastards with a head like a triceratops came out from behind a cinderblock wall. I swiveled at the hips, the Trijicon moved over and I blasted the fucker. *POP. POP. POP.* Moss moved up beside me. *POP. POP.* Sludge splattered all over the wall and the dinosaur-headed thing went down hard.

I could feel the source up ahead. I knew from His holy wisdom that these were just slaves. Their master was here, whipping them on. I'd run into assholes like this before. How any human being could heed the call of the darkness, I would never know. "This way, Guns." He looked up from blasting one of the red ones long enough to grunt an affirmative.

Terrified men and women ran past us, wearing the khaki pants and blue polos of the FBI Academy trainees. Some were fighting, and most of those were being torn apart. Arms, legs, heads, organs . . . body parts were everywhere. There was so much blood that my Danners were leaving tracks in it. It was a slaughterhouse. "That way. Go that way!" Moss waved the survivors toward the Marine line.

We kept on dropping monsters. The movements were practiced and mechanical, moving and shooting, dropping mags and reloading while the other Marine provided cover. Heat waves shimmered over the barrel of my rifle, but they just kept on coming. We'd picked up a few armed FBI on the way, and the knot of us made our way forward.

Twenty yards away, two of the big, gangly dog-faced demons had just got done pulling some poor bastard in half, and now they were loping toward another Fed. He was shooting a pistol at them, but they were shrugging it off. I'd never heard one of the inhuman looking ones speak before, but one of these was repeating the word "*Tombs*" over and over again.

The Fed looked familiar . . . "*Dios mio!*" He was in my Vision! He was one of the witnesses to my death. I recognized him easily. I'd known that face for twenty years. The demon was almost on him. There was no time. "Guide my hand," I whispered as I fired, and He did. The demon tilted its hideous dog face just in time to catch a 5.56 up one nostril. The bullet must have fragmented perfectly because half its skull disintegrated into a cloud of rapidly expanding fragments.

The second one looked right at me, dodged to the side as I fired again, then turned tail and ran. Surely going to its master, probably to warn it that a Vengeful Sword of the Lord had arrived to send them all back to the festering pit. The Fed went after the demon. Of course he did. He was like me. He couldn't fall until his appointed hour.

Moss on the other hand, far as I knew, was imminently mortal . . .

"Gunny!"

"Yeah?"

"Could you stay here and wait for the others?" He outranked me and you do not tell a Gunnery Sergeant what to do. "Please?"

Moss growled at me. "You seem to know what the fuck's going on here, Staff Sergeant."

"I do."

"Go and fix it then!"

I went after the Fed. He disappeared around a concrete wall and I followed. I was more excited than I had been in years. I'd found one of the witnesses! I was making progress. This was proof that I was following the Lord's path.

Special Agent Lazarus Tombs
FBI National Academy, Quantico

THE DEMON on the left cocked his head as if hearing something. Then its head exploded.

I don't think I'd even seen a demon with a look of shock on its face before, but I guess there was a first time for everything. The demon wiped away its companion's brain matter that had splattered everywhere then looked toward the origin of the shot. I followed its gaze to the far left where a Marine was sighting down a rifle. The demon threw itself to the side as the rifle boomed, then turned and sprinted in the opposite direction.

I threw a quick wave of thanks to the Marine and sprinted after the fleeing demon.

The demon loped away from me heading south. It was an odd feeling chasing it, since usually the demons were the ones doing the chasing. I had thirty rounds left for my Glock spread between two full mags in my pocket—not the ideal place to be carrying them—and the half-full mag in the gun. Hopefully I wouldn't need any more than that for one demon.

I sprinted through the campus noticing sickening patches of red decorating the sidewalks and walls of the buildings I was passing. A mangled leg stuck out from some bushes to my right. In the distance I could hear screams of terror and pain from people around the campus, and growls and howls from more demons.

Where had they all come from? One person couldn't have summoned this many, which told me this was a coordinated effort.

I caught a flash of another demon ahead. Behind me I heard the sounds of running, so I shot a quick glance over my shoulder. It was the Marine.

At least I had some sort of backup. There were at least two demons ahead of me now. Maybe more.

What were they after?

The so-called experts in the field said that demons were mindless predators that lived to hunt and kill. I knew demons could have far more intelligence. All demons were dangerous, but it was the intelligent ones that were scary.

And these knew my name.

I couldn't have been running for more than a few minutes when I came around a bend and saw one of the FBI's research buildings. Most people knew that we conducted all sorts of tests on materials, biological agents, and weaponry here. There was also an area at the back where we held most of our information on the supernatural.

Fifty yards from the building, I slowed to a stop. There were no screams around this part of the campus, and the silence was just as eerie. The main research building ahead was two floors above ground, but I knew there was subterranean storage and laboratories as well. On a typical day there could be upwards of a hundred people inside.

One hundred people that had likely never actually seen a demon. All their work was controlled. *Theoretical. Safe.*

The double doors at the entrance were a pile of shattered glass, on top of which was the unmoving body of an agent in standard HRT gear. *Geez.* Even those guys hadn't been ready for this. I ejected the half-full magazine and replaced it with a full one.

The sound of footsteps came to halt beside me. The Marine. "I'll take left," he said. He actually sounded eager. *Psycho.* But he was a well-armed psycho, and I found myself wishing for a rifle like his—

an M16 from the brief glance of it I got before he began moving quickly to the left side of the wrecked door.

My Glock 23 felt a bit underpowered at the moment, but what could I do? I moved to the position on the right.

As I got to the door I shifted to a left-handed grip on my gun and peered around the corner. There wasn't just one guy from HRT dead in the doorway.

There were eight.

They were cast about like broken dolls, necks and limbs bent at impossible angles. I've seen my share of bloody scenes, and this wasn't even the worst, but somehow being on the FBI Academy's campus made it far worse psychologically. The walls of the entryway were painted in blood. The frightening thing was the lack of damage from gunfire . . . and the quiet.

Practically at my feet was the trailing HRT member's discarded weapon, an M4. It was a little shorter than the Marine's own rifle, which I hoped would give me a slight bit more maneuverability if it got to close-quarters fighting.

Of course if it came to that I might already be dead.

Again.

I checked the magazine. Completely full. I motioned for the Marine to cover me so I could pull the extra magazines from the corpse. I'd worry about feeling like a grave robber later. For now I needed more ammunition.

We entered the building, leapfrogging one another for covering positions. Glass crunching under our feet was the only sound. The entire area looked as though explosives had been set off. Cubical walls were shredded, and sparks still flew from the exposed wires of shattered computers and other electronics. Bloody bodies and bloodier body parts littered the wreckage.

The lack of natural sound was unnerving, but it didn't seem to have any effect on the Marine. His eyes were constantly scanning. There was something about him that was different. It was like The Itch in my head wanted to have a reaction to him, but couldn't because of all the supernatural interference in the room.

I guided us toward the back of the building where the secure access to the Supernatural Development Studies rooms—always abbreviated SDS in the acronym-friendly FBI.

The entry to the SDS was a gaping hole. Inside, the place was a total loss. Any information not backed up to hard drives was gone. All physical material was destroyed. Was this the reason for the attack?

Then we heard the demons' howls.

And they were close.

Staff Sergeant Diego Santos
SDS Research Building, FBI National Academy, Quantico

IT WAS AN AMBUSH.

And there was only one thing to do in an ambush.

Fight your way through it.

The demons spilled out of every doorway. They came out from behind desks and filing cabinets. They pushed over cubicle walls and charged. It was an unstoppable force of demonic fury. A normal response would have been to give in to despair, curl up, and die. However, I was not normal. I was on a mission from God and had been trained by the United States Marines Corps. Fuck these stupid demons. They didn't have a chance.

I had been born for this.

Special Agent Lazarus Tombs
SDS Research Building, FBI National Academy, Quantico

THERE WERE DEMONS EVERYWHERE. Dozens of them. They'd lured us into a kill box, but we were holding our own. The Marine seemed to know the demons' weak spots and was exploiting them with deadly accuracy. He was obviously the superior shot, so I took neck and body shots to slow them down, then he would finish them. Heads erupted in geysers of gore. The stench of sulfur and blood was enough to make me gag. I focused on breathing through my mouth, and pulling the trigger in three-shot bursts.

Then they started coming through the ceiling.

I swung my rifle and caught a demon through the armpit as it dropped three feet behind the Marine. It crumpled to the floor whimpering. Two more dropped down in front of the Marine, one of which he smashed in the face with the stock of his rifle, and the other he shot through the eye from six inches away. I used the final burst from my own rifle to put down the creature the Marine had stunned.

Pushing my last magazine into the rifle, I opened up on the remaining demons.

They were getting closer and closer. I shot one through the mouth as it launched itself at me. Its black blood sprayed onto my face and into my eyes. I screamed as it burned my eyelids. I squinted through the liquid and continued firing at the now hazy shapes of demons. They were fewer now. Much fewer.

We were actually winning.

I pulled the trigger and nothing happened. Empty.

The rifle dropped from my hands and I drew the Glock in time to shoot one of the last demons five times in the face.

And then there was pain.

I looked down at my chest and saw a clawed hand stuck into it. *Huh. Those are huge claws.*

My gun slid uselessly from my grip. My vision seemed to get even weirder. Couldn't focus. The Marine was shooting everything that still moved.

And now there was a guy walking toward us. My boss, Frank Shields. Finally we had a little backup. I was on the ground, on my side. Numbness was spreading through my chest. What was Shields doing? Even at the point of blacking out, The Itch grabbed my attention and made me focus on my boss. Shields raised his gun, and I saw the muzzle flash over and over as he shot the Marine.

I couldn't see the result. My vision tunneled until all I saw was a hazy blackness. I knew this feeling.

I was dying.

Again.

Third time's the charm.

I took one last breath, then nothing.

Staff Sergeant Diego Santos
SDS Research Building, FBI National Academy, Quantico

EVEN IF TOMBS had been wearing a soft vest, those needle-tip claws would still have slid right through. The demon's hand came out, red and dripping. The Fed took a couple of faltering steps, looked back at me seemingly surprised, mouth hanging open, eyes wide. The demon chuckled then shoved the Fed down.

He couldn't die. It wasn't his time. I had faith. I lifted the M16A4 as the demon charged and took it apart, walking 5.56 rounds through it until it spilled over and slid to a wet stop at my feet. My rifle was empty and I reached for another magazine as I hit the release button.

Somebody shot me.

The bullet hit me in the MTV and the vest stopped it. Then a second bullet struck my rifle and knocked it from my hands. Several more bullets whipped past as I fell on my ass.

I looked up to see another blue and khaki Fed at the end of the room, and the stink on him told me that this was the asshole that had summoned these demons. He had a Glock in his hands and was walking toward me, covering me like he was going to arrest me or something. Old habits were hard to break.

The man from my dream was down. His eyes were open, flat and empty. Those were dead eyes. I'd seen it hundreds of times. He was gone.

It couldn't be.

I struggled to my feet as the summoner closed on me. He seemed surprised that we'd torn apart his monsters. The room was littered with bullet-riddled, discolored demon bodies. He flicked a cold glance at the body of the Fed. "Tombs is dead? Will wonders never cease? The mistress will be displeased. We needed him still."

"Your mistress can go fuck herself. He's not dead."

The pistol moved back to me. The summoner was old, a senior agent, probably just another dumb shit cultist seduced by lies and pride. Probably a plant by the other side, trying to sneak one of their own into a position of authority. Up close I could see the name "Shields" embroidered on his polo. "They talked about your kind!" he said when he finally got a better look at me. The cockiness was replaced with nervousness. They always reacted like that when they realized what I was.

"He's not dead," I repeated. "This is a test of faith." I took a step forward. "This is a test of my dedication."

The asshole shot me again. The bullet slammed into the Kevlar weave covering my shoulder. I grunted, swayed back, then righted myself and took another angry step forward. The gun was shaking. I was unnerving him.

"*B'nai regesh!*" Shields snarled in what I recognized as Hebrew.

"I've been called that before." I took one more step. "Among other things. The last asshole I met like you called me *Boanerges*." Ten feet away, the Glock went off. He missed. The bullet tore up carpet between my boots. His rapidly blinking eyes betrayed his terror. His grip and stance were sloppy. "It means 'son of thunder.'" One of the triceratops-looking demons was dead nearby. I put my boot on its bony neck shield, grabbed one of its horns, and wrenched hard on it until it cracked and broke free. I stepped off the demon's corpse and held the wicked horn low at my side. It was dense and cold. "I am a faithful servant. I am your earthly judge."

He took a clumsy step back. "Your god is young and weak!"

"Keep telling yourself that." Another step closer. "You think you idiots are the first to try to move in on His turf?"

"I'm going to kill you!"

"I've seen the thing that kills me, and you ain't shit compared to it."

He jerked the trigger. The bullet grazed my left forearm, just above my watch. I looked down at the nasty crease as blood ran down my hand. It hurt like a son of a bitch, but then I realized where I'd been struck. I started to laugh. "Fuckin' A!" It was a sign.

"What!" The summoner cringed. "What?"

"I've seen that scar in my Vision for years! I've been wondering when I was going to get it. About damn time." I nodded respectfully. "Thank you."

Now terrified, Shields tried to keep the gun up as he kept walking backwards. I followed. His back hit the far wall. "Stop! We've already got what we came for." We were so close now that there was no way he could miss. The end of the .40 was a gaping hole aimed right between my eyes. "The vessel has been prepared. The end is near. Your god can't protect you."

"Let's find out."

CLICK.

The demon summoner actually squealed like a little girl, but his training took over and he executed a malfunction clearance drill. He thumped the base of the magazine, grabbed the slide and racked it back to clear the dud round, but it was already too late. I knocked the muzzle aside and slammed the demon horn through his neck. I twisted the horn back and forth, widening the wound. Hot blood struck me in the face. Shields' Glock hit the carpet as he sagged against the wall.

I held him there and peered into his eyes, trying to understand what would cause a mortal man to believe the lies of the Rusted Vale. Those eyes were filled with terror and doubt, emotions I could no longer comprehend. "Told you so." He tried to respond, but his mouth was too full of blood and it just spilled past his teeth and down his chin. "When you get to Hell, let your masters know they can't win here. He won't let them."

Shields slid down the wall, still staring at me with a fanatic's fervor. I waited for him to die, just to make sure there were no other tricks.

I could hear sirens outside, but no more gunfire. Gunnery Sergeant Moss had come up behind me while I'd been distracted. He joined me, standing over the corpse, but didn't say anything.

"So, how much of that did you catch, Guns?"

"Enough to know that I don't want to know." He bent over and picked up the .40 cartridge that had been ejected from the Glock. He looked at it and then handed it over. The primer had been solidly dented by the firing pin. "About that psych evaluation . . ."

It wasn't anything to worry about anymore. "My enlistment is up soon. I've got a feeling I'm supposed to go do something else for a while." I looked back at Tombs, who was still obviously dead. This was turning out to be more complicated than expected, but I had faith that everything would work out in the end.

Special Agent Lazarus Tombs
Personal Dormitory, FBI National Academy, Quantico

I OPENED MY EYES to a view of a ceiling, and my brain reminded me that I should be dead. I instantly panicked and tried to sit up. This situation wasn't anything new to me, but just because I've been dead before doesn't mean I enjoy revisiting. The last time I'd died I had woken up on a surgical table with half my chest sliced open.

Three months of therapy followed.

My body screamed in protest, and if felt like a cleansing fire was coursing through my veins. The fire was familiar, the same as it had been the last two times I'd woken up from the dead. It hurt more than anything, but at the same time felt absolutely wonderful. I knew where the wound was that the demon has inflicted on me, but I was more than a little afraid to look down. I didn't really know if my mind could cope with seeing massive surgical cuts or another huge Y-incision. There was no putting it off. I looked down at my chest.

A clean white bandage was wrapped around my middle. No blood was soaked through. Confused, I looked around and realized I was in my room.

I also noticed the Marine I'd seen earlier lounging in one of my chairs. He had a cigar in one hand and a glass of amber liquid sitting on the table by him.

"You do this?" I asked pointing at the bandage.

"Yep."

"Thanks."

"No worries," he said taking a puff on the cigar. "I figured saving you the bullshit of waking up all cut on would save you some sanity. And a trip to a shrink. What a waste of time that is."

I nodded in agreement. "While I do appreciate it, how'd you know I wasn't totally dead?"

He cocked an eyebrow at me. "You *were* totally dead. I just knew it wouldn't take."

"Oh?"

"Dreamed it." As if that were the only answer possible.

I looked at him a little closer and felt just the faintest hint of The Itch. He was touched by the supernatural. Barely, but touched even still. Who—or *what*—was he?

"I also saved this for you," he said. He reached forward and pulled an ID wallet off the table and tossed it to me. It was mine. "Came out of your pocket when you got killed. Says your name is Jarvis Tombs. I'm Diego Santos. Nice you meet you."

"Call me Lazarus. Or just Tombs. No one calls me Jarvis. And thanks again."

"Lazarus?" he asked with a smirk. "This 'death' thing happen before?"

"Twice." That wiped the smirk off his face. "Really, though, how'd you know I'd come back?"

"Told you. I dreamed it. Don't like repeating myself."

"Then clarify it for me," I said laying back down.

"Look, I know when I'm gonna die. To the minute. I've seen it coming in my dreams—a Vision—for years. And you're in my dream. You're there when I die. Good enough?"

He wasn't big on explanations, and I could think of one hundred follow-up questions. I didn't bother even trying to ask them. I sighed and rubbed my face. I should just be happy that Santos had spared me the therapy.

"I gotta say though," he continued, "that's pretty crazy you not being able to stay dead. You're not a zombie, are you? That'd be some messed-up shit, and I'd probably have to shoot you in the head or something."

"Not a zombie," I said chuckling. It hurt, but in a good way that reminded me I was alive. I turned my head left to look at my son's picture.

The frame was there, but the picture was gone.

I jolted back up, hissing in pain, and grabbed the frame. I blinked a few times just to make sure I wasn't hallucinating. There were two black marks on the front of the frame, one on each side. Fingerprints burned into the frame. I flipped the frame over and saw corresponding marks for the rest of a person's hands. I lifted it closer to my face and sniffed the prints.

Sulfur.

Demon. Or someone that had summoned the demons.

"What's going on?" Santos asked.

"Someone—a demon or something—stole the picture of my son," I said. This was unbelievable. What if he was accidentally freed?

What if that was the reason why the picture had been stolen in the first place? To free my son. How powerful would he be?

"There was a girl who came out of your room when I was bringing you here," Santos said. "She had a picture in her hand. Thought she was your girl or something." He described her to me.

Helen Collins. She must have been one of the summoners. The pregnancy had just been a cover. When I investigated some more—and I'd go room by room if needed—I was sure I'd find one or two more of the bastards. I had a sudden vision of Frank Shields lifting a gun and shooting Santos. He must have been a summoner too.

"That was Helen Collins," I said, shaking my head. "She was one of the summoners along with the agent who shot at you. What did you do to him?"

Santos smiled. It was almost as frightening as the demons we'd killed. "Oh, you mean Shields? Didn't have my rifle. Had to improvise with a demon horn. Too bad you missed it."

"Yeah," I said. "Too bad." *Psycho.*

"I need to make a few calls," I said trying to stand. "My bosses need to know what went down here, and that they've been infiltrated. Who knows what else has been compromised?" I rubbed my eyes, exhausted. "And then I *need* to get that picture back." I was fuming inside. My son had been taken again. I'd *failed* him again.

The people that took my son were going to die for this.

All of them.

"I'd like to know what went down here too. Those were the same kind of demons from my Vision. In fact, they kill me in" —he looked at his watch—"two years, fifty-five days, twelve hours, and forty-two minutes. Give me the detailed version."

"It will take a while, and we'll have to talk on the move."

He smiled. "Tombs, for you, I have time."

I wanted to include this story because it was written really early in my career. Despite us both being total newbies, I think it came out pretty good. Steve and I ended up writing several Tombs and Santos stories over the next couple of years.

Earlier I talked about collaborations and how each one is different. Steve is super easy to work with. I originally met him when all I had published was my first novel, Monster Hunter International, *and he interviewed me for his site* Elitist Book Reviews. *Back when I still had a day job, we ended up working together as accountants at the same defense contactor. Since then Steve has written several more shorts and the YA horror novel,* Residue.

Currently, the two of us are collaborating on a new novel for Baen Books. Think WWI Eastern Front, in a world with dark fairy tale magic, so it's sort of a Trench Warfare Fantasy, where we are telling the story of a crew who goes into battle in a suit of magical power armor made out of dead golems.

EPISODE 22

This story originally appeared in Aliens: Bug Hunt, *edited by Jonathan Maberry, published by Titan Books, in 2017.*

This is set in the Aliens universe—which I've been a fan of since I was a little kid—and is about the adventures of the Colonial Marines. So in this collection I've already got an official story that I wrote for Predator, and now Aliens. If I ever write something for the Terminator franchise then I'll hit the ultimate 1980s trifecta. Since becoming a writer I've gotten to mess around with everything I thought was awesome from my childhood.

Considering there's actually a GI Joe character based on me—Spreadsheet, GI Joe's accountant—that's probably accurate!

I was the oddball writer in this particular anthology. Everybody else wanted to write about the Colonial Marines kicking ass and taking names, but as a gun nut I wanted to write about the real hero of the movie Aliens, *every gun guy's favorite sci-fi movie prop, the M41 Pulse Rifle. Having been a guest on a couple seasons of* Joe Mantegna's Gun Stories *on the Outdoor Channel, I had the perfect idea for how to tell that story too.*

Saga of the Weapon, Season 1, Episode 22
The M41A Pulse Rifle

The M41A is one of the most successful combat rifles in history, and has become a potent symbol of American military might, not just on Earth, but into the furthest reaches of space. It has seen battle on every continent and dozens of worlds. It is beloved by those who use it, and feared by their enemies.

However the adoption of the Pulse Rifle was controversial, and the story of its evolution is filled with tragic errors that cost many Colonial Marines their lives.

Join us now as we discuss the history of the legendary M41A Pulse Rifle, on *Saga of the Weapon.*

There's nothing like the sound of a Pulse Rifle. It's like a maniac is running a jackhammer on a steel drum. That's the sound of freedom.
—Lance Corporal Chris Johnson, USCM

Today's Colonial Marine takes having a reliable and potent rifle for granted, but it wasn't always so. When the USCM was formed in 2101, their standard issue infantry weapon was the Harrington Automatic Rifle, with one Weyland Storm issued per squad.

Marines now don't realize how good they have it. Back in my day, you had basically two choices. Have a handy little rifle that ran slicker than snot—the HAR—but bounced its feeble little bullets off your enemies' body armor, or have a rifle that would put them down no matter what, but only when that complex hunk of junk wasn't broken down or hopelessly jammed because a speck of dirt got into the action. You ever pull the side plate off a Storm? It looks like an old-fashioned clock in there. When Marines talked about something working like clockwork, we sure as hell didn't mean the Storm.
—Staff Sergeant Mike Willis, USCM

Personally, back in the '60s I carried a HAR, because I'd rather know it would go bang every time I pulled the trigger, than have this super advanced killing machine that could track enemies across the battlefield from a satellite feed, but was so fickle that if you looked at it funny it would crash. Nothing sucks more than waiting for your rifle's operating system to reboot while a thousand Swedish insurgents are shooting at you.
—Corporal Cheryl Clark, USCM

After the battle of Kochan and the long campaign on Miehm, there was a clear need for a next-generation infantry weapon to arm the United States Colonial Marines. It needed to be rugged enough to survive the rigors of combat in a wide variety of planetary ecosystems, and fire a potent enough round that it could defeat newer forms of advanced body armor. The 6.8mm armor piercing round of the beloved HAR was simply too anemic, and the Storm was just too fragile. After many campaigns with inadequate equipment, the USCM put their foot down. Enough was enough.

I was there when General Phillips threw a fit in front of Space Command. He said that if his men were going to fight against the insurgents, what did he expect us to do? Tickle them to death? Watching a bunch of four stars yell at each other was way over my pay grade, but it was a hell of a show.

—*Captain Trent Miller, USASF*

The Marine 70 Program shook up everything, and small arms procurement was no exception. The commission that was created to study the need for new replacement weapon systems immediately met fierce resistance. The Weyland-Yutani Corporation filed a lawsuit, alleging that the Colonial Marines were simply misusing their Storm rifles, and it was their lack of following the proper maintenance guidelines that was causing the reliability issues.

Yeah . . . Those pogues actually blamed us. Can you believe that? Abuse and neglect, they said. Guess what, you corpo-monkeys, this isn't a clean room at your factory. Proper maintenance kind of goes out the window when you've flown halfway across the galaxy, to be neck deep in blood and mud and guts for weeks, and have to beat a man to death with the butt of your rifle—seriously, who puts circuitry in a stock?—and the unit armorer is a little indisposed because he stepped on a land mine that morning. Well excuse me that I didn't have the proper factory-approved widget to fix it! At that point if a Marine can't fix it with a hammer and duct tape, it ain't going to get fixed.

—*Sergeant Mario Cordova, USCM*

Ultimately, amid allegations of bribery, corruption, and blackmail, Weyland-Yutani dropped the lawsuit, and the new small arms appropriation committee got to work.

You know what they say about things designed by committees, right? Well, that's where we were heading. You should have seen the original list of requirements. It was ridiculous. The specs weren't written by combatants. They were mostly wish lists from staff officers who'd never seen the inside of a drop ship unless it was parked at an air show, and specs inserted by lobbyists requiring gizmos that only their company happened to make. There were so many suggested bells and whistles screwed on that you'd need a wheelbarrow to carry the rifle.

—Construction Mechanic 1st Class Mike Raulston, USASF

It was a time for bold concepts. Many of the more advanced technological aspects proposed by the committee would later be incorporated into other weapon systems, such as the stabilization mechanism of the M56 Smart Gun, but it threatened to bog down the current rifle project in red tape.

However, there was a ray of hope. While various mega corporations were preparing their new weapon systems for trials, a retired Colonial Marine, Jonathan LaForce, was working on the prototype of the rifle that would become the legendary M41. By day he made ends meet running a food truck, but his nights were spent in his humble workshop. A distant cousin of legendary gun designer John Moses Browning (see *Saga of the Weapon, episodes one, four, fifteen, and twenty*) Corporal LaForce had served with distinction at Miehm, and knew firsthand the needs of the modern warfighter.

If you're a Marine, when you're saying your prayers, you better tell whoever it is you're talking to that you're thankful for LaForce. That man was a mechanical genius. We're lucky he was a gun nut, and not into space ships or something. Sure . . . We'd have some awesome space ships, but my Pulse Rifle has saved my life more times than I can count. Thank Odin for Corporal LaForce.

—Gunnery Sergeant Aimee Morgan, USCM

LaForce started with the familiar layout of the HAR, utilizing an integrated pump-action grenade launcher, but the similarities end there. The sonic "shaker" burst weapons used by the rebels on Miehm to disable the Marines' HARs had shown the need for a firing mechanism that couldn't be disrupted by outside sources. So his new design started with a unique electronic pulse ignition.

This feature would go on to cause the M41As infamous nickname.

Pulse rifle isn't in the official designation, we all know that, but since it was a pulse that ignited the primer, the name just kind of stuck. Marines do that kind of thing. My great-great-whatever grandfather carried a Pig and his dad carried a Tommy Gun. It sounds cool, it works, it sticks. The problem with calling the M41 that name though is always some dumb boot hears we get issued pulse rifles and gets all excited thinking it's going to be shooting laser beams or something. What do they think this is? Sci-fi?

—Lance Corporal Tripp Dorsett, USCM

The specifications required the new weapon to use caseless ammunition, but this presented several challenges. LaForce believed that standard ammunition was a better choice, because sustained fire of caseless ammunition causes a rapid buildup of heat, which could cause stoppages or even premature parts breakage. In a rifle using standard brass-cased ammunition, the ejecting cartridge case serves as a heat sink, and some heat escapes through the ejection port. However, the committee specified all submissions had to be totally sealed from the elements. LaForce's solution to the overheating problem was using advanced materials for the internal mechanism, and ultramodern, cooler burning propellants for the ammunition.

LaForce was issued several new patents. Among them was the visionary rotating breach design, which not only cut felt recoil in half, but allowed the use of his new U Bend Conveyor magazines. This brilliant system made his weapon far more controllable than competing designs, even while using more powerful ammunition.

We had the best engineers in the business all competing to come up with a new gun, and some retired Marine, who doesn't even have an engineering degree, shows up to the trials with this cobbled-together piece of junk that looked like it got built in his garage. I found out later it literally was built in his garage. Here we were, the sharpest designers in the military industrial complex, all representing corporations with millions budgeted for R&D and marketing, and he walks up to the line like he belongs there, and pulls this ugly thing out of a case, and goes to town.

Phase one was just a demo shoot for some of the officers. No big deal. Until LaForce opens up with that beast. Everybody knows what a pulse rifle sounds like now, but this was new back then and we'd never heard anything like it before. Nothing gets your attention like the noise a pulse rifle makes. Every head on the range swiveled in that direction.

He'd chambered it in 12mm Darnall, a monster of an old caseless hunting round that can shoot through a genetically modified rhino, just to prove that he could. Show-off. This thing was shooting bigger bullets and more of them, with less recoil and still shooting better groups than every million dollar prototype on the line . . . It blew our socks off.

The competitors found out later that LaForce hadn't been invited by the committee at all, but had snuck into the initial test firing. He'd saved the life of one of the Marine testers during the battle of Kochan and had called in a favor to get onto the range as an "observer." I had gone to MIT and spent thirty years designing firearms on the most advanced CAD programs in the Solar System, and there were twenty others like me there, but we all got our butts kicked by a hobbyist whose day job was selling barbeque.

—Michael Ankenbrandt, Daihotai Engineering

LaForce had the clearly superior design, but no ability to manufacture it. After a demonstration where the prototype was frozen in mud, and then fired six thousand rounds without a single malfunction, LaForce received an official invitation to the competition. He was also approached by several of the competing arms manufacturers and offered huge sums of money for his patents. Surprisingly, he refused them all, declaring at the time that he was in it to help his brother Marines, not to get rich. At the time there were even rumors of an attempted break-in at LaForce's workshop to steal the prototype, followed by an attempt at deliberate sabotage, all of which was blamed on—and vehemently denied by—Weyland-Yutani.

With a working prototype in hand, and USCM interest in his design, LaForce approached Armat. The once-respected company had fallen on hard financial times, yet retained a reputation for never skimping on quality, and always doing its best to support the soldiers it supplied. Luckily for LaForce, Armat, and America, this would prove to be a match made in heaven.

If you look at the history of small arms development, what came first, cartridge or rifle, is usually a chicken or the egg kind of proposal. Sometimes you design a platform to fire an existing cartridge to spec, other times you have the weapon system and you shoehorn in the best round you can fit. This time we got lucky. As LaForce was designing his Pulse Rifle, Armat had been making some real breakthroughs in chemical engineering and projectile materials. This allowed us to really push the boundaries of terminal ballistics.

Our new experimental 10mm x 24 caseless approximated the ballistics of the old .300 Winchester Magnum sniper round in a far shorter and lighter package, with a bullet that could penetrate most modern body armor, and an explosive payload inside that would absolutely wreck whatever was hit. The issue was that it produced too much recoil energy to control on full auto in an assault weapon-sized package, so we were primarily marketing it for crew-served weaponry. When LaForce came to us with a light rifle platform that could easily handle the recoil of our new experimental 10mm round, our executives bet the future of the company on manufacturing the Pulse Rifle. The rest is history.

—*Mordechai Yitzhak, Armat Technician*

Armat was able to utilize more advanced materials for the next prototypes, which drastically lowered the weight, while also increasing the already impressive durability. Their new propellant compounds were able to decisively solve the LaForce prototype's greatest weakness—heat dissipation. The Armat rifle easily won the rest of the competition, passing all tests with flying colors. The newly designated M41 was put into production, and entered service with the Colonial Marines in 2171.

However, all was not well. Some of the early batches of 10mm ammunition were subcontracted out to other manufacturers. It is unknown who changed the propellant design, and later congressional inquiries never discovered the culprit, but regardless of who was at fault, this mistake cost Colonial Marines their lives, and gave the early production M41s a bad reputation.

(Warning, the following footage from LV-832 is intended for mature audiences only. Viewer discretion is advised.)

It was a nightmare. All of the wild life on LV-832 is gross, mean, and cranky, but the colonists there were hard as nails. You had to be to survive that shit hole. There is only one thing they ever needed to call in Marine support to deal with, and that was a swarm. There's this one species, imagine a carnivorous moose-sized critter with tentacles instead of antlers. Individually, not so dangerous. Only it turns out that every seven years they have a population explosion, swarm, and eat everything like locusts.

My platoon was supposed to protect this one settlement on LV-832 during the swarm. No problem. We're in a fortified position. We've got these fancy new Pulse Rifles. Just stupid alien animals. Nothing we can't handle. Right?

Then we heard the thunder. It was like ten million hooves on the rock, and this . . . wave. That's the only word. Just a wave of angry green flesh comes rolling down the mountain at us. It was far worse than the projections. Corporal Richards was our forward observer. He died horribly, trampled into bloody chunks in seconds.

We opened up with everything. Our only hope was to carve a hole in that wave of meat, to pile up enough dead to make a wall.

But then our Pulse Rifles started to choke. Only the swarm kept coming.

—1st Lieutenant Hank Reynolds, USCM

The horrific incident on LV-832 was not isolated. Wherever the improperly formulated ammunition was shipped, problems occurred. As the weapons would begin to heat up, the propellant would expand and stick, causing malfunctions. Or worse, cook off prematurely and detonate inside the conveyor magazines, often with catastrophic results.

You ever see what a 10mm explosive round does to a man? It penetrates a bit then explodes. The secondary wound channels are nasty. You can stick a softball into the hole. Yeah . . . Real nasty. Oh, we love them now. But back in '71, imagine having that same explosive round cook off inside your rifle, right next to your face. Or worse, I heard about one dude where his Pulse Rifle cooked off, and it caused a sympathetic detonation with his grenade launcher. Marines were scared of their own rifles. Some of the guys took to carrying short-barreled shotguns on them for when things got close.

—Lance Corporal Daniel Walker, USCM

Rumors began to swirl of Colonial Marines found dead on the battlefield, with their Pulse Rifles disassembled, killed while desperately trying to clear a stoppage.

To their credit, Armat did not try to pass the buck. Instead, they sprang into action, discovered the cause, alerted Space Command, and tried to track down the bad lots of ammunition. By the time the hearings began, the M41 was working as intended. However, the bad reputation lingered in line units for quite some time, and the topic is still hotly debated among gun enthusiasts today.

Design changes were immediately instituted to make the M41

less ammunition-sensitive and more cooling vents were added to the shell. The integrated digital ammo counter was given a dimmer switch, because Marines had taken to covering the early versions with masking tape to avoid giving away their position during low light maneuvers. This variant was designated the M41A, which remains the standard issue rifle of the US Army and Colonial Marines to this day.

With the bugs worked out, the M41A began to earn a different kind of reputation.

Our Cheyenne hit the hot LZ like a meteor. There were so many missiles and so much flak that the night sky was lit up like the Fourth of July. Before the skids had touched ground we already had tracers coming in from three directions. We lost two men before we could even unass the transport. Our APC ate a rocket and we lost our lieutenant. The DeLorme rebels were ready for us, dug in, and itching for a fight.

My platoon's orders were to take and hold the main plaza on the coastal platform. We encountered fierce resistance every step of the way. They were well funded. Most of the rebels were wearing top of the line carbon-weave armor, but our Pulse Rifles punched them anyway. Then the DeLorme Corporate Security Teams were wearing these heavy, servo assisted, armor suits. Tank boys we called them. Right hard bastards, every one of them. Except, even when our 10mm bullets failed to penetrate the plates, the impact and micro-explosions were enough to throw them off long enough for my Marines to close and finish them off through the rubberized gaps at their joints. The muzzle doesn't climb much, and the M41 is so acute, we'd just hammer the tank boys until we pierced something vulnerable and they dropped.

It was street to street, house to house. We'd catch sniper fire from a window, launch a grenade through it, and keep moving. We reached the plaza, and found out that we were it. Nobody else had made it through the drop. We had to hold that position or the whole mission would fold.

The battle went on all night, and the rebels kept throwing everything they had at us. We shot our Pulse Rifles until the muzzles were glowing orange, and they never stopped, never jammed, not so much as a hiccup. Cheyennes were doing high-speed flybys and dropping crates of U Mags and grenades on us so we could stay in the fight.

That was the first time I used an M41A. It didn't let me down then, and it has never let me down since. After DeLorme, I've taken a Pulse Rifle to every godforsaken planetoid, orbital, moon, backwater colony, and bug hunt you can think of. I've used it in zero G. I've used it underwater. Polar wastes to burning sands, abuse it, drop it, burn it, and the M41A won't ever quit on you.

The Pulse Rifle is the only rifle tough enough for a Colonial Marine.

—*Staff Sergeant Michael Newman, USCM*

The M41A has gone on to earn the respect of every warrior who has used it . . . or faced it. This mechanical marvel has taken its place in history as one of the finest combat rifles ever fielded. The Pulse Rifle is known for going anywhere, doing anything, and accomplishing the impossible. Seldom has a weapon so encapsulated the bold, unstoppable nature of the men it is issued to, as the M41A Pulse Rifle.

This has been *Saga of the Weapon.*

V-WARS: ABSENCE OF LIGHT

This story first appeared in the anthology V-Wars: Night Terrors, *edited by Jonathan Maberry, published by IDW Publishing in 2016.*

The V-Wars series is about a virus which reappears and spreads across the world, reawakening latent DNA and turning people into vampires, and the resulting war between mankind and the vampires. It is currently being filmed for a show on Netflix. This is the second story that I wrote in that series. The first appears in Target Rich Environment Volume 1.

THE MOB PUSHED AND SCREAMED and chanted their slogans, stinking of sweat, adrenaline, and excitement. The air was moist from recent rain evaporating off of sweatshirts and hoodies, and hot from hundreds of packed-in bodies. Marko and his vampires passed between the protestors, and the hardest thing in the world was not killing them all.

These humans are nominally on our side. These are the useful idiots. Killing them—now—would be a waste of resources. Marko had ordered his men to hurt as few of the protestors during the op as possible. He'd had to beat that lesson into his soldiers. Some of his men were more feral than others, so in a few cases, the beating had been literal. Some of his recruits struggled with the concept of discipline.

The street was absolutely full of bodies. Most of them were young, impressionable and passionate. The ones who were showing their faces thought they could make a difference, naively believing

157

their slogans, hash tags, and painted cardboard signs were going to change the world. The protestors hiding their identities were just eager to break shit. From the smell he could tell that some of their backpacks contained all the fixings to make Molotov cocktails. So far the masked hooligans were behaving themselves. The broken glass and burning cars would come later. The day belonged to the activists. The looters believed the night belonged to them . . . In reality it belonged to the vampires, and as tempting as it was to show these idiots who was really in charge, a riot made one hell of a good distraction.

The other side of the street was a sea of flashing red and blue lights. Seattle PD had learned their lesson about protests a few times over the last decade, and that was before I1V1 kicked societal order in the balls. The cops were ready behind batons and shields, tear gas launcher and pepper balls. If it weren't for all of the news crews recording the *peaceful protest* the street would already be filled with gas. The cops and the looters both knew what was coming next, but there were *rules* to the fall of an empire. If the forces of law and order jumped the gun, morons would rant on Twitter, politicians would feign outrage, and a bureaucrat somewhere might be inconvenienced. Pretenses had to be kept up. So the street-level decision makers would be forced to coddle the mob until the situation spiraled out of control, turned into a complete cluster fuck, and then overreact to contain it. That was the yin and yang of riot control.

All those years the government had spent training him how to overthrow governments, and Marko had never realized just how entertaining it would be to screw with his own. Before he had turned, Marko had been Army Special Forces. His job had been to train and lead indigenous forces behind enemy lines. *Force multiplication*, they called it. Now he was training vampires. He'd collected these individual predators and molded them into a real unit. Same tactics, new war.

One of his vampires appeared at his side. Even with the bandanna covering his face, he could tell it was Basco just from how smoothly he moved between the humans. Basco had been a tough bastard when he was still human. Making him bloodthirsty and fast as lightning had only made him an even better soldier. "In my country, we'd run a belt-fed across a mob like this. A hundred rounds and problem solved."

"Where's the fun in that?"

His vampires were wired, tense and ready. They were hungry. Not just for blood—he'd kept their feeding to a minimum so as to not tip off the local authorities—but for action. They'd been planning this op for weeks, ever since word of the vaccine experiments had leaked. The news conference this morning had simply bumped up their timeline. The protestors had already been here anyway. His men had already been working the locals and stirring up the radical elements, so it hadn't taken much of a push to get the riot kiddies fired up. His people had been bussing them in all day.

Marko was wearing a black hoodie and a plastic Guy Fawkes mask. The irony of a bunch of lefty atheists using a Catholic fanatic as their symbol caused him no end of amusement, but he was guessing there weren't a lot of War College grads in this bunch. He needed the mask because the NSA was certain to be running facial recognition programs against the footage. As a bonus the hood hid his radio headset. "Target is in sight."

The Iwashiro building didn't look that impressive. It was just another plain old office cube. The real prize was inside. There were a hundred medical research companies looking for the Holy Grail but if the rumors were true, Iwashiro Biomedical had been making real progress on understanding the vampire virus—mostly because they had zero ethics—and according to this morning's press conference, they'd made a real breakthrough.

"*Sniper is in position.*"

"*Breaching team is in position.*"

Every mutation was different. Some of his best soldiers couldn't operate well in the sunlight, so they'd move once the sun was safely behind the buildings to the west. At the same time his kill teams would start taking out vital employees who hadn't come to work today because of the protests. If everything went according to plan, by the end of the night the technology to produce a screener would be in vampire hands, and every human who understood how to make more would be dead. "Assault team, blend in and wait for my signal. We've got sundown in thirty."

The angry mob was here because Iwashiro had been caught doing illegal experiments on vampire *volunteers*. Some girls wearing duct tape over their mouths—symbolic of who knew what—went marching past, waving signs that declared VAMPIRES ARE PEOPLE TOO.

Marko smiled behind his mask. *No . . . We're so much better.*

"Look at all those hippies."

"Just try not to run any of them over, Solo," Matt Kovac told their driver.

"General May hates when I run over civilians. Look at all that flannel. I can't tell if they're homeless or college students." He honked the horn as twenty people jaywalked in front of them. Somebody threw a beer can at their car and it bounced off the hood. "You little son of a bitch!"

"Be cool, man. It's a rental. It's on the company card."

"It's the principle of the thing," Solo muttered as the kids flipped them the bird, but eventually they meandered out of the way so he could keep driving. "Big Dog's team gets to pop tangos while we have to grade rent-a-cops. Fantastic. Hang on, police checkpoint ahead."

Toolbox was in the backseat. He leaned forward to see better. "Cops are diverting traffic like it's a parade or something. Can you believe this nonsense, Show?"

Kovac didn't like his call sign, but Showdown had stuck. Get in one Mexican standoff with a crazy vampire, and pretty soon everybody in V-8 was telling exaggerated stories about it, but as a new team leader, it had helped establish cred with the vets. It usually got shortened to Show for brevity's sake.

V-8 was the military's elite special response unit for vampire problems. Their personnel were some of the finest operators available, recruited from every branch of the service. Kovac had been Army SF himself, following in his deceased father's footprints. It wasn't until after he'd been with V-8 for a while that he'd learned his father wasn't exactly *deceased*.

"Pull over there."

The four of them were out of uniform—rocking the business casual as Solo put it—and driving a Honda. Normally when V-8 rolled up on a site, they were hard to miss—what with the armored vehicles and top-end military gear—but the General had told them to be discreet today. If Kovac had realized that the streets were going to be filled with cops in helmets, face shields, and vests, they'd have brought their fun stuff. It was a sad comment on the state of the world that they wouldn't have stuck out that much.

Kovac rolled his window down and showed his ID to the police officers on the corner. "How's it going, Officer?"

"Mostly vandalism and graffiti so far but they're just getting warmed up," the cop said as he read the card. Behind him, a stoned white guy dressed in tie-dyed clothing and sporting dreadlocks was trying to put a peace sign bumper sticker on the cop car's windshield. "Aw, stop that! You guys go through. My boss said to expect you. Head that way."

The cops moved a wooden barricade and waved them through. Solo drove between a SWAT van and an MRAP, honking so that the riot squad would get out of his way. They got some surly glances from the other side of those Lexan face shields. They could see a lot more of the protestors now, and Kovac was surprised to see how damned many of them there were.

"Glad that's not our problem," Kovac muttered.

People were milling around in groups and the atmosphere was charged. The rumble of crowd noise was overwhelming. Iwashiro Biomedical had been working on a vaccine for I1V1, which just about every sane person would agree was a good thing, but if people could throw a fit about animal testing, they got downright pissed when a company got caught illegally testing drugs on vampires.

"Today's lesson is if you're going to do stupid shit, don't get caught!" Solo exclaimed.

"Like these assholes care about the civil rights of vampires. Okay, maybe the chicks do, but there are two kinds of guys who come to things like this," Toolbox explained. "The ones who are trying to impress the activist girls so they can get laid, and the ones who want to break a window and get a free TV . . . Mute here was an observer in Libya with me. Those protests were sure different than this, huh?"

Mute spoke for the first time since they'd left the airport. "More AK-47s."

"Yeah, and not so many pussies sporting anarchy symbols."

Since it was the focal point of the protestors' outrage, the cops had formed around the front of the Iwashiro building. The police here didn't know who they were, but their car had been let through, so that was good enough to make a hole for them to pass.

"Weak-ass metal fence around the perimeter. Couple of decorative concrete planters would stop a car bomb from getting right under the facing," Solo said as he gave the place the once-over. "Not exactly impressed on first glance. A little bit of creative landscaping would make this place a lot harder to crash . . . and make it look nicer too. My dad's a landscaper. I should give them his card."

Inside the visitor parking lot was a little guard shack manned by rent-a-cops. The glass wasn't even thick enough to be bullet resistant. The guards inside looked nervous and distracted, which was understandable since there were a few thousand people a couple hundred yards away who thought their employer was the capitalist antichrist. "What's your business here?"

He held up his ID. "Captain Matthew Kovac, Vampire Counterinsurgency and Counterterrorism Field Team. You should be expecting us."

"The Army guys?"

"I'm Navy, but I let them hang out with me," Toolbox said quietly enough the guard wouldn't hear.

"That's us."

The guard pushed a button and the flimsy bar lifted. It was the kind of thing kids could push out of the way when they didn't want to pay for parking. Solo drove up to the front of the building and parked. "Can you believe that? A laminated ID card I could make at Kinko's gets us right in without question. The General was smart to send us to review their security, because this place sucks."

"Be diplomatic," Kovac warned as he stepped out of the car. The four of them started toward the entrance. "It's their invention. We just need to make sure they're smart about keeping it safe until it's ready for release. The military isn't officially here. This is a completely civil matter. We're only supposed to assess."

"If they've actually got a working V screener somebody should declare the whole place a national security risk and take it over," Toolbox suggested. "Nobody else has gotten a test to work yet. Can't we just say it's a public health emergency or something?"

"That's over my pay grade. Once the government gets its shit together I'm sure they'll buy the thing, and if not, it'll go to court and the lawyers can fight. General May told me these guys are big donors with lots of Congress friends, so play it cool. He offered to protect it, but the best he could talk them into without a court order was allowing some advisors."

Two men in suits were waiting to greet them at the entrance. Kovac took one last glance back at the protestors. Most of them looked like they were attending a concert, but there were a few knots of them that made his instincts tingle. He'd often felt like that back in Afghanistan, rolling through a village, getting the eyeball from some of the locals that said *you are not wanted here*, and as soon as you were out of the way those were the ones who were planting IEDs. Some of those kids were giving him that exact same vibe now.

Three men in white masks and black hoods were standing toward the front of the mob, arms folded, watching, too still compared to the excitement swirling around them, and Kovac felt the hairs on his arms stand up. A group moved between them, waving red flags, and when they passed, the men in the white masks were gone.

"You can tell that's your son. He looks just like you," Gregor said.

"Yeah, regular chip off the old block." It wasn't a surprise. He'd figured V-8 would get involved, and he'd known Matthew was working in this area. Marko keyed his radio as he moved smoothly through the masses. "We've got pros in the building. At least four. Plainclothes."

May's elite V-8 troops were no joke. They were recruited from the best, and his old friend had done a good job staffing his special unit with the type of get-the-job-done hard asses who wouldn't get unnerved by little things like fighting creatures straight out of nightmares. It hadn't exactly been a shock to find out that his son had gone to work as a vampire killer. He'd always been a pretty straightforward good-versus-evil, protect-the-innocent type idealist, even as a little boy.

Now, somebody with even a scrap of human empathy would have kicked Matthew from his anti-vampire unit once he discovered his father had turned vampire, but General May wasn't the type to let some little thing like personal bonds or family history stand in the way of using the right trigger puller for the job.

"*You want to abort the mission?*"

If they could steal the screener technology it would be a powerful recruiting tool for their new army. He'd heard that the Red Court had already paid to get backdoor access to every DNA database in the world just in case. Far more importantly, the humans couldn't be allowed to have such a weapon. If they could know for certain who among them was destined to become a vampire, there would be no more recruits. The vampires who could still pass as humans would all get caught. They would lose their spies and insiders. Their race would be driven to extinction once again.

"Negative. Stick to the plan." He checked his watch. Sundown was in twenty-five minutes.

Gregor was following him. The big vampire was eyeing some of the pretty girls hungrily. He'd not fed for a while, and his kind had an insatiable appetite. "With May's people here, you think it's a trap?"

"If it is, we'll make them regret it."

"What about your kid?"

That was a good question. Ever since his transformation, when Marko looked for that place where his feelings used to be, there was only a dark empty hole. He had loved his boy. Hell, he'd doted on him. Matthew had emulated his father and tried to follow in his footsteps. Seeing his son wearing the same uniform had been the proudest moment of his life. At the end of his mortal existence when he'd been chained and beaten, and the Syrians had begun to saw off his head, the last thing he'd thought of was his family. Only instead of dying, he'd turned, and never looked back.

When Marko thought of his family now there was *nothing*.

"The mission comes first."

The review wasn't going well.

"You're a security expert? Have you ever fought vampires, Mr. Cook?"

The head of security for Iwashiro Biomedical hadn't been expecting to get grilled this hard this fast, and was stumbling badly. "We had five volunteers here during the early testing phase and I was in charge of managing—"

"Not managed. I'm sure you're a fantastic zookeeper. I said *fought*."

"Well, no. I haven't, though one of our subjects did become unruly as a result of the drugs and caused some trouble, but as you can see outside, we're working in close conjunction with local law enforcement. Between the police presence and our employees, we have a very secure facility."

Kovac had only been talking to this corporate goon for a few minutes and he was already running dangerously low on patience. He could have stormed this facility with a crack team of Girl Scouts. "I don't think you realize that as of this morning's press conference, your company declared it has something that every vampire supremacist in the world wants. You've dealt with volunteers desperate enough for a cure that they'll let you do all sorts of things to them, but trust me, there are plenty of vampires out there who see your research as the effective end of their species, and they'll do whatever it takes to stop it."

"I've been doing this for years and think we're—"

Kovac cut him off. Tagging in Solo was dangerous, because he tended to be colorful in his descriptions, but it needed to be said. "Sergeant Gonzalez, what do you do for a living?"

"I kill motherfucking vampires, sir."

"And what did you do before that?"

"I went to places that supposedly had good security, killed the people there and took their stuff on behalf of the United States Army. I was extremely good at it, sir."

"In your professional opinion, are vampires much like regular security risks?"

"No, sir."

"How would you assess Iwashiro Biomedical's security against a potential organized vampire threat?"

"Woefully fucking inadequate."

"Well, there you go." Kovac leaned back in his chair. "That's pretty close to the assessment I'm going to give to General May, which he'll pass along to the President."

They hadn't even gotten a real tour. They'd been taken right past the entrance to the labs holding the sensitive goodies and upstairs to a conference room where they'd sat down with the CEO and his right-hand man. Cook was obviously proud of his handful of low paid, barely trained, just-over-minimum-wage security guards with their .38 Specials in nylon flap holsters and Fisher-Price My First Walkie Talkie level communication system, but Kovac's standards were a bit higher when it came to protecting one of the most important discoveries in history.

The conference room probably would have had a good view of the street, but they'd pulled the curtains. It was dark out there, light in here, and some chump in the crowd might have been tempted to pop off a few rounds at the enemy. Other than the security guards, the place was nearly deserted. Everyone who could stay home to avoid the protests had done so, except the CEO had proudly told them that the scientists vital to the screener and vaccine projects were still downstairs, bravely working away for the good of mankind, despite the danger outside. That might have sounded great on a press release, but Kovac didn't like having all of their vulnerable eggs in one basket.

Dr. Iwashiro was younger than expected for a CEO, probably only in his mid-thirties. Kovac had watched the morning's press conference on YouTube on the ride over. During that, Iwashiro had mentioned inheriting the company from his father. The CEO had struck him as somebody who was trying to overcompensate to get out of his father's shadow. Being the son of a legend and working in the same field was tough—Kovac got that better than anyone—but that didn't justify taking stupid risks. A few hours ago this man had rocked the world, yet now Iwashiro was listening intently as his security chief was being eviscerated. So far he was playing it close to the vest, and Kovac couldn't tell what he was thinking.

"If you won't accept our protection, at least let us provide a full security workup, Dr. Iwashiro. We understand the potential threats you face. We all come from special operations backgrounds."

"What did you do before becoming vampire experts?"

Vampires were so damned new and odd that he didn't think anyone actually qualified as an *expert*. Luther Swann maybe, as that dude was a walking encyclopedia of vampire trivia, but even then he was wrong half the time. "Gonzalez and I are both Army Special Forces and Morris is a SEAL."

"What's he?" the CEO nodded toward where Mute was sitting. The tall, thin man hadn't bothered to pull up a chair at the conference table, but instead was sitting on a couch by the windows, surfing the internet on a tablet.

"It's so classified you don't even want to know," Kovac said.

"James Bond-level shit," Solo suggested.

"We can also bring in information security experts to prevent outside sabotage." Iwashiro Biomedical had a good IT department. He knew that because General May already had his guys at the NSA working on breaking into their files. But they'd be more interested in stopping corporate espionage. Kovac was worried about the research being destroyed rather than stolen. As a man who'd seen firsthand the horrors of vampirism, he'd love to see the screener technology leaked far and wide. Screw Iwashiro's bottom line, he wanted vampirism eradicated like smallpox.

"I truly appreciate your offer, gentlemen, but this is *my* company. General May was rather demanding on the phone. I believe in cooperation, but you can see why I'd be hesitant to accept your help. Some of my advisors think that V-8 is overstating the danger of some sort of threat in order to gain access to my company's research."

"We've got ninety nine bombings that disagree with your advisors," Toolbox said. "And that's just the stuff you've seen on TV."

"Yes, of course. Coordinated vampire terrorism, and stopping that, justifies *everything*."

Kovac made an honest plea. "I can't share details about national security risks, but there are groups of vampires out there who are far more organized than anyone in the media suspects. Some extremely knowledgeable people have turned." As he said that, Solo and Toolbox gave him a curious look. Everybody on the Field Teams knew about Showdown's dad, but none of them liked to talk about him. "Some of these have been organizing and training cells. Their skillset makes them extremely dangerous."

Iwashiro gave him a patronizing smile. "Oh, I'm sure they are, but since we're on the topic of vampires, there's that old bit of folklore about how they can't come into your home unless invited. Today, we know that's a myth for vampires, but it has been my experience that it is true for the government. This is my house, gentlemen. Not General May's."

The CEO sure was a smug little bastard.

"Look, I'll level with you. I hope you make billions off your screener. I hope you spend the rest of your life sleeping on a giant pile of money in a house made out of gold bars. I just want to make sure the screener is kept safe. I can have the rest of my team here in a few hours and we can get this place locked down."

The head of security came back for more. "We've already got a secure facility. No one is going to try anything when there are hundreds of cops right outside."

"And in a few days when the protestors get bored and go home, the cops will go away, and then a vampire could walk right in here."

"You can't enter without scanning a badge!" Cook was getting upset. It was a good indicator of a man's lack of professionalism when every pointed-out flaw was taken as a personal insult.

"They aren't exactly vault doors!" Solo exclaimed.

Toolbox grinned. "If it was me, I'd just follow an employee up to the door, let them swipe it with their badge, then shoot them."

Solo wasn't about to be outdone. "Or, hell, take out an employee at home and steal their badge!"

"Our employees' personal information is kept private," Cook retorted.

Mute cleared his throat and held up his tablet. It was easy to forget he was even in the room. "Yeah, about that, I just got all of your employees' names and home addresses while we've been sitting here. Your HR director really needs to do something about his wi-fi settings."

"Holy shit, you people suck at this," Solo muttered.

Marko watched the sun disappear. It was remarkable how few vampires were actually light sensitive. *The movies got everything wrong.* "Execute phase one."

Bringing in agitators to rile up crowds and incite riots had been part of asymmetrical warfare since they'd invented the concept. Marko had agents placed throughout the crowd, some vampires, but most were easily duped or paid-off humans. It started simply enough, with windows shattering across several blocks and greedy morons rushing into stores to steal things. The smarter humans in the herd realized that the channel had just been flipped to a different station and tried to get the hell out of the way. The stupid got stuck in the middle, but even the panicked ones were useful meat shields and noisemakers. By the time the rocks and bottles started raining on the cops, the riot had begun in earnest.

Killing the power had been a no-brainer, and any big city grid had its exploitable vulnerabilities. Remote detonation took out a few choice lines and five minutes after the first cop needed stitches from a brick to the face, half the lights in downtown Seattle were out. They could still see though, because by then some cars had been helpfully set on fire, and the flickering orange light and spreading smoke really added to the ambiance.

All around them, angry youths rushed forward, hurling things at the cops. No Molotovs yet though. That was a downer. Marko had paid good money to have Molotovs here. The cops formed up in ranks, shoulder to shoulder, a wall of Kevlar and muscle, and they started forward, like a comparatively gentle, politically-correct Roman legion.

Brave or drugged-up rioters rushed the line, kicking at the shields. Screaming and taunting, dancing around and hurling balloons filled with piss.

And they said vampires were savage . . .

"I love this stuff," Marko told Gregor and Basco. He could tell that both of his lieutenants were feeling the bloodlust too. They wanted to jump in there and start taking heads and drinking from necks like fountains. "Easy, boys. We'll feast tonight."

The cops turtled their way up, shields raised against the falling debris. He could hear the *thunk-thunk* of projectiles bouncing off of plastic. They were wearing their gas masks but they'd not started firing canisters yet. They were probably hoping for a quick clash and break to arrest the troublemakers, and then everybody could go home without any exciting news footage of downtown being gassed.

The main bodies clashed. The Seattle PD must have been drilling a lot, because they kept their formations and did a great job of rotating men in and out as their arms got tired. Groups of cops would part ranks, allowing another squad to rush through, surround some of the really unruly troublemakers, drag them down, cuff them, and drag them out of the fray. They must have had some good leaders in there keeping order. Marko picked out the guy calling the shots and keyed his radio. "These cops are too calm. Sniper team, up the fear. Your target is the tall black guy giving orders at the front of the MRAP. Don't kill him though. I want some screaming."

"*Roger that.*"

Their shooters were hidden in the surrounding buildings, sitting back inside the rooms a bit so they wouldn't be spotted by the police snipers on the opposite rooftops, just like he'd taught them. The suppressed rifle was so quiet that there was no way anyone would hear it over the chaos in the street, but the cop fell over, blood spraying, as the .308 round tore through his knee. Marko had seen plenty of limb hits like that. The bone blew up like a grenade, fragments making all sorts of secondary wound channels. It would probably need to be amputated, but Marko had to hand it to the cop. Other than one quick bellow of shock, he stayed calm, put pressure on it, and began calling for a medic, probably a fellow combat vet. Luckily some of the cops around him weren't as cool, and they started freaking out. By the time they'd dragged the wounded cop behind the armored vehicle, the SWAT cops were looking to blast the shooter, and somebody else had given the order to fire tear gas.

Then flaming bottles of gasoline were tossed toward the line, most shattering in the street, but a couple hit the cops. Those who'd come prepared had melted Styrofoam packing peanuts into the gasoline until it had gained the consistency of jelly. It was poor man's napalm, and that stuff stuck to riot shields and flesh, melting either rather easily.

"About damned time. Breaching team, you have one minute. Move. Assault team, kit up and execute on my signal." Marko and his men unslung their packs, knelt, and began getting their gear ready.

The 37mm tear gas rounds hit the pavement, bouncing, sparking, and spitting. A noxious haze drifted through the street. The stupid humans who hadn't got out of the way in time really began to panic when they suddenly couldn't see or breathe right. A few fools were knocked down and trampled. By the time the gas washed over the hidden vampires, those who were still vulnerable to such things had already pulled on their own gas masks. The rest were taking out firearms, unfolding stocks, and racking charging handles.

Between the flickering fire, the spreading smoke, and the fog of gas, visibility was awful. A constant roar of shouting, screaming, and cursing filled the street. Nobody would see or hear them make their move, and if they did, by the time a response was organized they'd already be gone.

"Breaching team is in the truck."

He knew he couldn't bring up his own vehicle to ram the door with a protest in the way, so he'd had his stealthiest troops sneak into the Iwashiro parking lot last week to check the vehicles that were already there. They'd had plenty of time to make their own keys. The nice thing about being prepared was that even when your timeline got moved up, a professional was ready to handle it.

The cops were pushing forward too fast now. Those that heard one of their own had just taken a bullet had started cracking skulls. The rioters reciprocated and now they had a good old-fashioned slug fest on their hands. The law was pulling away from the target building and leaving gaps in their lines. *Wait for it . . .* Marko watched the whole beautiful thing unfold until all of the angles were right.

"Execute, execute, execute."

Ten vampires set out toward their target and no one even saw them coming.

When the lights had gone out, Mute had pulled back the curtains to take a look outside. His voice was eerily calm as he warned them, "We've got incoming."

There was a crash below them that shook the whole building.

"What was that?" Iwashiro shouted as the four men from V-8 drew their guns. Cook fell out of his chair and hid under the desk. When normal people hear a big bang, their first reaction is surprise, and then puzzlement. In Kovac's line of work it was assess and prepare to return fire.

Mute had his forehead to the glass and was peering down. "They rammed the front door with a truck."

Toolbox looked at Solo, as if embarrassed that he'd not mentioned that method of getting in. "I guess that works too!"

If it had been a car bomb, they'd already be dead. That meant they were about to raid the lab. "Box, call it in, then you and Mute take the north stairs. Me and Solo will take south." They had to counterattack, break the momentum. Time was of the essence. Any delay and the attackers would have to retreat because there were a whole lot of reinforcements nearby. He turned to Iwashiro. "Have your security protect the lab and get the civilians out of here. Let's move."

"Told you so," Solo spat at Iwashiro as they left. The lights came back on within seconds. It made sense that a building that did sensitive medical research had a good backup power generator. They rushed past a handful of confused employees, to the stairs and down, taking whole sets at a time. It was hell on the ankles, but riding an elevator into a potential gunfight was a great way to make yourself the proverbial fish in a barrel. They reached the main floor and headed toward the entrance.

Kovac took cover at a corner and risked a quick peek down the hall. A single headlight was visible through the dust swirling around the broken wall. The guards who'd been posted there had been hit and were lying on the ground, partially crushed by the debris. Solo moved up behind him. "If we're really lucky, that was just a stupid car accident and we'll all laugh at it over beers later." Someone began screaming and it took a moment for Kovac to realize that there was a guard stuck beneath the truck. Solo started to move up, but Kovac signaled for him to hold.

There was a *chuff* of a suppressed gunshot, and the screaming stopped.

"So much for beers," Solo whispered.

There was a lot of movement around the wreck. A man moved in front of the headlight, crouched with a stubby rifle at his shoulder. Before he could ID him as friend or foe, the man put a round into one of the unconscious bodies lying on the floor. *That would be foe.* Kovac leaned out, centered the front sight of the Sig M11 on the man's chest and pulled the trigger. Solo fired a split second later. The man went sideways, hit the wall, but stayed up. He saw them, opened a mouth full of jagged shark teeth and screeched something incomprehensible. They opened up, striking him repeatedly, but he didn't go down.

"Vest!" Kovac warned, but by the time he could sight on his head, Solo had blown the vampire's brains out. That did the trick.

More vampires around the truck began flinging rounds their way. Solo hung his M9 around the corner and cranked off several more shots. The headlight went out. Then Kovac took a turn just as a vampire moved up behind the reception desk. He put a couple 9mm rounds into the wood and was rewarded with a surprised yelp from the other side. That slowed them for a second, but then the vampires came back shooting. Their heavier rounds zipped right through the walls. One of them was on full auto and Kovac had to pull back as several rounds pulverized his corner into dust and splinters.

He heard crashing, fearful cries, and more suppressed shooting. Some attackers must have entered before they'd gotten here. They'd been too slow to establish a bottleneck. There was a flash of movement and Kovac fired at a vampire sprinting across the lobby. That one dove behind cover before he could put a round into him. Some vampires were just too damned fast. They were going to get flanked here. "Fall back."

"Cover me, Show."

He leaned out and started shooting, forcing the vampires to keep their heads down while Solo crossed the hallway. Then he followed. The two of them rushed back into the offices. Employees were running past them, and every bit of movement was making his nerves twitch. "Get out the back! Get out of here!" Kovac held up one hand as they approached a glass partition. He'd seen a dark reflection in it. Someone was moving up the other side, and this one wasn't dressed in a lab coat or a suit. They both took aim and the split second a vampire with a hoodie and a gun came around the side, they lit him up. The glass shattered. One eye socket turned into a gaping red hole and the vampire collapsed in a heap.

The slide was locked back on the Sig. "Reloading." He had two more mags his belt, but they had not come here expecting a firefight. By the time Kovac had shoved a fresh mag into the gun, Solo had moved up on the dead vampire, taken his Tavor rifle, and lifted its bloody clothing to reveal that he was wearing a plate carrier and mag pouches beneath. "Bastards came loaded for a fight."

"Grab it and go. We've got to protect that lab."

There was more unsuppressed gunfire from that direction. Mute and Box had gotten in on the action. They'd dropped two but had no idea how many more there were. From the noise coming through the building, there were several, and from the dead bodies they passed, some of the vampires had gotten ahead of them. Most of the staff had been shot, but a few looked like they'd been ripped apart by wild animals and spread across the cubicles.

The men of V-8 had gotten really good at tuning out that sort of thing while in the zone. You dealt with the images later, once the job was done.

They reached the entrance to the lab just in time to see a grey, twisted, hunched-over *thing* rip a security guard's heart through his ribs. They both shot at it, and Kovac was positive he hit it, but it lurched across the carpet lightning fast and disappeared into the lab. A split second later it came back, cranking off a bunch of rounds on full auto their way. Bullets tore through the desks around them, but Kovac stayed up and shot it in the face that time. There was a splash of blood and teeth, but the thing just shrieked and pulled back, still annoyingly alive.

"I'm hit." Solo said, perfectly calm.

Kovac jerked his head over to see his partner sinking down as his leg slid out from under him. Blood was pumping out of Solo's thigh. "Damn it." He slunk over, trying to stay low behind the desks, until he reached Solo. "How bad?"

"Bad." Solo was pulling his belt off. "Help me tourniquet this before I pass out."

Kovac did. Solo roared in pain when he cinched it up tight. His hands came away slick and red. "Take it easy." He kept risking quick peeks over the desk to make sure the grey vampire wasn't sneaking up while he pulled off his dress shirt to use it as a makeshift bandage. "Keep pressure on that."

"What the hell was that thing?" Solo asked through gritted teeth.

"One of the Indonesian types." He couldn't remember the name but he'd read about one in another team's report. "They're one of the fastest we've seen."

"What do you want to do, Show?"

"Carry you out the back."

"Hell no. That screener can ruin these suckers once and for all." Solo shoved the stolen rifle toward him. "Don't let them take it."

Solo was right. Judging by the continuous gunfire, the rest of his team was occupied at the far end of the building. "Okay. Cover the hall and call Mute and Box. I'll hit the lab."

❖ ❖ ❖

Marko checked his watch. It had been three minutes since they'd rammed the door. They were running out of time. He glanced around the laboratory. He'd memorized the blueprints, but it still felt like he was in the wrong place. It was far plainer than he'd expected. Laboratories were supposed to have all sorts of interesting devices—Tesla coils and bubbling vats, that sort of thing. This was mostly computers and all of the fancy medical equipment looked like white or beige boxes. *Disappointing.*

He'd shot a few of the staff to make the point that he was in control. From the noise coming through the walls, the V-8 soldiers were being a pain in the ass and refusing to die. A couple of his assault team hadn't checked in, which meant they were probably dead. The breachers were holding the front door. Basco was watching one entrance to the lab and Gregor had the other. Meeker was off running an errand, and Doroshanko—who actually understood all this egghead stuff—was screwing around with their computers.

"Sniper team. Status outside?"

"*I don't think the cops have made you yet. The riot is going crazy.*"

That had been money well spent. "Doroshanko, what've you got?"

He'd pulled his gloves off so he could type better. Marko could see the bones of his fingers through his weird, translucent skin. Some mutations were stranger than others. "I've taken most of their research, but there are a few files that have extra password protection."

Marko glanced at the scientists. He'd made them all kneel on the floor in a line. "Which one of you has the password?" They all looked at the floor. "Nobody?" He tore off his mask, went to the nearest idiot in a lab coat and picked her up by the hair. There was a hot pressure in his face as the fangs grew, and then he sank them into her neck. His jaws clamped shut, slicing through the flesh. She kicked and thrashed and screamed as the wonderful blood filled his mouth and painted the walls. He unclenched his jaw, ripped his teeth out, and hurled her across the room. She slammed into a machine hard enough to smash a huge dent in the sheet metal and send sparks flying from it. Droplets of blood sprayed from his mouth as he shouted, "How about now? Anybody got the password now?"

"Market, the number forty-two, underscore, the number twenty, blue!" shouted a young man. "All lowercase!"

"Thank you," Marko said as Doroshanko typed it in. The Moldovan vampire nodded when he was in. "Keep being helpful like that and you might just live through the next few minutes."

Gregor came in, dragging an Asian man by the tie. "Look what Meeker found hiding in a janitor's closet upstairs."

"That boy has a nose like a hound. Ah, Mr. Iwashiro. Just the man I've been looking for. I really enjoyed your press conference."

"Why are you doing this? We're trying to cure you!"

"Cure us?" Marko laughed. "You've got that backwards, Doc. Vampires *are* the cure. I'm preventing genocide here. I'm the good guy."

"Go to hell!"

The CEO had balls, Marko would give him that. He knew he was rather intimidating when he was covered in blood with fangs sticking out and eyeballs filled red, and he'd get the truth out of the doctor eventually, but he didn't have time to screw around. "Gregor, bite off one of his fingers."

"What? No!" Iwashiro cried out as Gregor grabbed his hand. He strained and fought, but Gregor's mutation had turned him into an *asasabonsam,* and that bloodline was ridiculously strong. It was like watching a kid wrestle an adult. Gregor dragged the hand up, pried out a pinky, and smiled, revealing grey, flat teeth. "No! No!" And then Gregor chomped down and bit the finger clean off. Iwashiro screamed.

Gregor spit the severed pinky out. He saw that Marko was scowling at him. "What?"

"I thought you were hungry."

"I don't eat the *bones,* man."

Marko turned back to the weeping CEO. "We've got a problem. You said you had a prototype screener. I can't find it. Your people deny knowing where it is, and I'm pretty sure they're telling the truth." He glanced theatrically at the corpses. "So where is it?"

"I don't have it!"

"Another finger."

Gregor dragged the twitching, bleeding hand back up and shoved the ring finger between his iron teeth. *Chomp.* Iwashiro screamed again.

"Damn. Someone just experienced a drastic reduction in typing speed. Where is it?"

"I'm telling you! There is no screener! It isn't real!"

"Another."

Iwashiro screeched and babbled and fought. *Chomp.*

Gregor spit it at his feet. "I feel like I should be saving these. Make a necklace or something."

"Now you can't flip anyone off. Tell me what I want to know while you can still point."

"There's no screener. I lied! The press conference was a lie! I swear!" Iwashiro was desperate. Gregor clamped the last finger between his teeth, but didn't bite down yet.

"Explain."

"We're stuck, just like all our competitors. We can't get it to work right. We got so much bad publicity from the trials that our stock was in the toilet. I needed to do something or I was going to lose the company. Claiming to have a working screener was just to buy us time."

"You lied to boost your stock prices?" Marko had wasted his time, his resources, and lost some vampires over a PR stunt? He didn't even need to tell Gregor anything that time.

Chomp.

With a stubby bullpup rifle on his shoulder, Kovac swept into the lab.

There wasn't a vampire in sight. Moving quick and crouched, Kovac saw lots of blood, footprints tracking blood, and shell casings, but no vampires. There was a spatter trail from where he'd nailed the Indonesian in the face, and that blood had a purple tint to it, but after a few meters the trail disappeared, and he'd either healed or got the bleeding to stop.

Room after room, nothing. His nerves were spiked. He was ready to react. A fraction of a second after he picked up a target, it would catch a 5.56 round. He'd been fighting vampires for a year, so Kovac knew to keep scanning, not just side to side, but also up and down, because some of these bastards liked to climb walls or stick to ceilings. Some could only be seen in your peripheral vision when they were holding still. Kovac listened, but it would be hard to pick up the stealthiest predator sneaking up on him with all that gunfire-related ringing in his ears. The worst part about operating by yourself was that no matter how good you were, you could only look in one direction at a time.

It had all happened too fast. In minutes the vampires had swept through and killed everyone, and they'd done it with an army of cops outside. It was too brazen, too slick. There was a gnawing feeling in his gut about who was behind this.

Kovac reached a closed door. There was a headless security guard sprawled in front of it. No sign of the head. He kicked the door in.

This room was a mess. It hardly seemed possible but there was even more blood everywhere. There was a pile of dead in white lab coats now dyed red. Judging by the splatter and the waist-high line of bullet holes in the wall, it looked like the scientists had been lined up, put on their knees, and then machinegunned down.

There was so much blood that it was hard not to slip in it. He moved around a table and found Dr. Iwashiro flat on his back, staring at the ceiling, with his chest so torn open that his ribs were visible and his intestines were hanging out. Kovac swore under his breath. The vampires had fled.

Surprisingly, Iwashiro was still alive. On the other side of the red ribs, he could see purple lungs inflate. "I'm sorry."

It was such an odd thing to say when you were laying there disemboweled that Kovac didn't know what to say. He knelt next to the doctor and had to lower his head to hear the whispers.

"This is my fault. I lied. There was never a screener. My . . . fault . . . All a lie." He coughed up blood and went out.

"You son of a bitch." Kovac's phone buzzed. He pulled it out. The screen read *Toolbox*. "Are you guys okay?"

"*Yeah, looks like the vamps are retreating.*"

"Listen. Solo's injured. He's in the hall by—"

"*We're with him now. Where are you?*"

"In the lab." There were footprints through the blood leading away. Three sets of them. "Iwashiro and all the scientists are dead. He just told me there was no screener. I think it was a scam. I've got three vamps on the move. I'm going after them." He stood up and followed the red path down the tile.

"*Wait, Showdown. I'm coming to back you up.*"

"There's no time. They'll get away."

"You just said there was no screener. There's no reason not to wait. You go by yourself you're liable to get killed." They all knew that was true. Only a fool ever went after a vampire by himself, let alone multiple vampires. Solo had gotten his call sign by being stupid enough to do that once. *"Wait just a damned a minute."*

"I can't do that, Box."

"You can't because you think it was your dad that did this. This feels like one of his ops. I know you want to put him down—"

"More than you can ever understand! He's gone evil, Box. I've got to stop him."

"Don't let your anger cloud your judgment, Captain."

"Catch up," Kovac ordered, then ended the call. He needed to concentrate.

They'd only been inside for a few minutes, but the riot had changed dramatically during that time. Maybe they'd been unconsciously spurred on by all the blood-spilling going on right under their noses, but the rioters were really charged up now. Maybe it was all the pent-up aggression and worry since ancient horrors had started rearing their ugly heads again. Maybe the cattle were tired of getting bled and had begun to stampede—Marko didn't know, but shit had gotten real in the street. A bunch of kids had knocked one of the cops out of formation and were beating him like a piñata. A rioter was lying facedown in a gutter, skull cracked open. There were wounded on both sides, and some of the cops looked ready to call it a night and open fire with real guns. It looked more like a battle than a riot and the protestors had transformed into wannabe berserkers.

Into that mess, Marko Kovac melted. He pulled the plastic mask back on, put up the hood, and simply walked away. The rest of his vampires spread out, each of them taking a different route to the rally point and then they'd get out of town. The hungry among them would certainly feed along the way, and they'd earned it. Three of his new recruits hadn't checked in, which meant they were most likely dead or lost. But that's why he'd sent the inexperienced ones to roam the building to cause trouble so his elite could focus on the mission. *What a waste.*

Basco had caught a bullet in the face. It would take weeks for the shattered bones around his mouth to heal, but luckily for him, his kind fed through a spike in their tongue so he wouldn't go hungry. Gregor gave one last nod to his boss, and then his two lieutenants veered off. The last he saw of them was two shadows climbing up the side of a building to take to the rooftops. Gregor had picked up the scent of the college girls he'd fancied earlier and the two of them were going to track those girls down and have a little party. They'd earned it.

As for Marko, he savored the chaos as he strolled through the riot. There was a lot of fear stink over on the cop side. Their carefully drilled formations had fallen apart once they'd got word that one of their own had gotten shot, but there had been no more shots and no sign of the shooter. SWAT cops were spread out behind cover, rifles pointed at the surrounding buildings, scanning for threats. Now that they'd just found out that there'd been a massacre inside the building they were supposed to be protecting, they were really going to freak out.

He didn't know how it worked, but one of the abilities he'd picked up since he'd turned was being able to sense when he was being watched. It was more of an instinct really, a certain knowledge of where humans were looking, and how to avoid being there. In that one instant, he knew there were eyes on him, but this time it was different. Normally he used the instinct to avoid the eyes of his prey, but this wasn't food, this was another predator stalking him. Marko kept his head down and kept walking until the feeling lessened just a bit and the other predator kept scanning.

"*Marko, you've got company,*" his sniper warned. "*One of the V-8 guys is moving your way.*"

He froze in place, surrounded by fools and animals, in a fog of blinding gas and choking smoke, between the burning cars and the angry law, and took stock. The whole city was filled with anger tonight, but it was unfocused, cruel, lashing out stupidly, but piercing through that haze was another feeling, only this anger was the righteous wrath of a warrior, focused like a laser beam, and sharper than any sword.

Marko slowly turned until he saw his son.

Across the mob, Matthew Kovac was searching for him. He was

wearing a bloodstained white T-shirt and had an assault weapon hidden under one arm, concealed in one of the protestor's discarded red flags. The tattered bits were whipping in the hot wind behind him. The image made Marko think of a crusader for some reason. His boy was certainly dedicated enough. Brave too.

"*I've got him in my sights. Want me to take the shot?*"

Matthew hadn't made him yet. He didn't have the senses of a vampire. He was a strong man—a better man that Marko had been when he was still human, for sure—but he was still only a man, so he was out of his league, and he couldn't pick out his target through this chaos, but he sure as hell wasn't going to give up. The boy had never been a quitter.

Marko's instincts had evolved. He'd been blessed to become something more. Vampires had existed before, but they'd failed because they had not had officers like him to lead them. His people, his *true people* needed Marko to survive, to continue training the others, until the day the vampire army was strong enough to rise up and take what was rightfully theirs. Matthew was one of the humans who would end that dream.

"*Marko, I've got the shot. Say the word.*"

Marko knew that if he let Matthew walk away tonight, his son would hunt him for the rest of his life. The smart thing to do was to end this here and now.

Except Marko had found an emotion in that pit he'd thought was empty.

Fatherly pride.

He let Matthew follow him into the darkness. The best would win and the other would die.

"Hold your fire."

Marko Kovac faded back into the night.

PSYCH EVAL

This story first appeared in Joe Ledger: Unstoppable, *published in 2017 by Griffin, and edited by Jonathan Maberry.*

The bestselling Joe Ledger series is a lot of fun, and it is also a lot of books, so when I had a chance to write a story set in that universe I asked Jonathan what were some of the crazy urban fantasy things he'd not touched on much yet. Demons had shown up in "Weaponized Hell," but he'd not really done anything involving them or anything like possession.

Say no more.

And yes, this story was written to a David Bowie soundtrack.

"WHY AM I BEING INTERROGATED?" she snapped as soon as Rudy walked through the door.

"Relax. It's just an interview."

"Then why does the sign say 'Interrogation Room'?"

Rudy pulled out a chair and sat down across the metal table from one of the survivors of Bowie Team. She was obviously suspicious and frightened, but his goal was to help, not make this adversarial. Lieutenant Carver had been through enough already. Rudy's plan was to be his normal, good-humored self, and help this brave soldier through the aftermath of her ordeal.

Unless Mr. Church's suspicion was right, and she was a murderous traitor, because then her fate was out of his hands.

"This room is what the Army had available on short notice. Believe me. I'd much rather be having this conversation in a nice office." As usual, he wanted to make his patient feel safe and comfortable. Only it was summer in Texas, the building's air conditioner was dying, and it was muggy enough in these stuffy windowless rooms that sweat rings were already forming on his shirt. So comfort was out, but Rudy could still try to make her feel safe.

"We've not spoken before, Lieutenant Carver. I'm Dr. Sanchez. You can call me Rudy."

"The Department of Military Sciences' number one shrink. I know who you are, so I know why you're here. But I'm not crazy."

"Nobody said you were."

"I'm not a liar. I know what I saw. I gave my report."

She was clearly agitated. Rudy had read her file on the way over. The DMS mission was so sensitive that every team members' backgrounds had been gone over with a fine-toothed comb. Her record wasn't just clean, it was spotless. Her service record was exemplary. Carver's previous psych evaluation had made her sound as a rock, solid under pressure, but the poor young woman in front of him today had been reduced to an emotional wreck.

He'd watched her through the one-way glass before coming in. She'd spent the whole time staring off into space and occasionally muttering something incomprehensible to herself. Now that there was another person for her to focus on, she was demonstrating bad tremors in her hands. Her eyes kept flicking nervously from side to side. By all accounts Carver had been fine before leaving on this mission, but she'd developed several severe nervous tics in the last forty-eight hours.

"I've read your report, Lieutenant. Do you mind if I call you Olivia?" She didn't respond, so he went with it. "Believe me, Olivia, I'm on your side. After some of the things I've heard from other teams over the years, I never assume anybody in this outfit is lying, regardless of what they say they ran into."

"Do you believe in the devil, Rudy?"

Considering what she'd just been through, with most of her team murdered, and the only other survivors in critical condition, it wasn't such an odd question. "I believe in good and evil. My small part in that struggle is helping good people deal with traumatic events and the horrors they've faced. I'm just here to help you."

Carver stared at him for a long time. It was the first time her tremors had stopped. She responded like she hadn't even heard his words. "I believe in him now."

"You hungry? Want some coffee or something?"

The survivor lifted her arm to show that her wrist was handcuffed to the metal table.

"Yeah, well. Sorry. That's not my call," Rudy explained.

"No. It's his." She looked over at the mirrored wall and raised her voice. "Hello, Mr. Church."

Rudy just shook his head, but he didn't deny who was on the other side of the glass. He'd asked about the necessity of the restraints already—it was hard to make somebody feel safe enough to open up while they were chained like a prisoner—but he had been shot down. Apparently it wasn't clear yet who had done *all* of the killing. Lieutenant Carver could be the survivor of some kind of new chemical hallucinatory attack, or could have been the victim of an unknown terrorist bioweapon, or she could have just had a psychotic break, or even be a traitor who had simply murdered her teammates in cold blood and lied to cover it up. The fact was they didn't even yet know what they didn't know.

Say what you will about working for the DMS, it was never predictable.

"Let's just talk. Tell me about the mission. Tell me about what happened in Mexico."

This part of Sonora looked a lot like Arizona. She was born and raised in Phoenix, so it seemed weird to be rolling hot in an area of operation that looked suspiciously like her hometown. Only back home she hadn't been worried about car bombs or cartel gunfights growing up, common threats the poor folks stuck here had to deal with on a daily basis.

Their convoy moved fast. The black government Suburbans barely slowed as they left the paved road and hit gravel. Carver was at the wheel of the second vehicle in line. The view out the window was creosote bushes and sun-baked rocks as far as the eye could see, just like it had been for the last hour. The only difference was now the ride got bumpier, and she began to taste dust in the air conditioning.

Captain Quinn got on the radio. He said something in Spanish, and the last three vehicles in their convoy broke off. Those were white and green pickups filled with *Federales*. They would be setting up a roadblock to keep anyone from getting in or out of the AO. From here on in, the DMS was on its own. The Mexican government and the US State Department had come to an agreement that all parties were cool with. This was DMS' show. Everybody official was just going to deny that this op ever happened anyway.

Their commanding officer was in the vehicle behind them. Satisfied that they were now speeding toward the target by themselves, the captain switched to the encrypted DMS channels and addressed Bowie Team.

"*We're ten minutes out. You know the drill.*"

There would be silence between their vehicles the rest of the way in. Intercepting even garbled radio transmissions could warn the bad guys something was up. Carver just concentrated on driving. The loose gravel turned to washboard, which threatened to rattle their armored vehicle to death. These pigs didn't have the smoothest ride in the best situations.

Sandbag was riding shotgun. Gator and Corvus were in the back seat. Louie was serving as trunk monkey, ready to pop open the back window and open fire with a SAW.

"You really think there's something to this intel, LT?" Sandbag asked.

"We know Hezbollah has an exchange program going with the cartels for years," she answered. "One side has expertise, the other has more money than it knows what to do with. Smuggling people and weapons across the border is a piece of cake to the cartel, and terrorists get an easy way into the US. It's a match made in heaven."

"Yeah, nothing like sharing your cultural traditions with others, like beheading, or car bombings," Gator interjected.

"Well, now DMS thinks they're sharing something else. Word is a few days ago an unknown weapon was shipped from an undisclosed location in the Middle East to this little town. Once it is ready, they'll send it north. We just don't know what it is yet. Which is why we're going to nab these bastards and find out," Carver stated. She was trying to stay right behind the truck ahead of her without rear-ending it while blinded by its plume of dust. At least the dust was obscuring the view of cactus and endless nothing. "It's one thing to look at this area on the map, another to see it in person. They picked a village so isolated that it's making me worried they're playing with something really nasty."

Her teammates readied their weapons. They were pumped. They'd done this sort of thing many times before, but it was always exhilarating. When they were only a few minutes out, Carver hit play on the sound system. This song was pre-raid tradition for them. Captain Quinn was a proud Texan, so when the DMS had set up a team out of Fort Hood, he had christened it Bowie Team. Of course, his boys had immediately decided that meant David rather than Jim.

"*I'm afraid of Americans*" began playing over the Suburban's speakers.

Carver grinned. *Good.* The terrorist assholes they were hunting should be.

The Suburban ahead of them was slowing down. That didn't make any sense—the village was still a mile away—but she slammed on the brakes fast enough to keep from rear-ending them.

"Get ready." Something was up. It could be an ambush. It could be a barricade. Regardless, speed was their ally. Getting bogged down out here meant the cartel was more likely to see them coming and get ready. "What the hell, Zeke?" she muttered. He was driving the lead vehicle, and wasn't the type to hesitate.

But nothing happened. The point vehicle maintained radio silence, only lollygagging for a few seconds before speeding up again.

"Yo, LT. Check it out." It was Sandbag who first saw what had caused the point vehicle to hesitate. He tapped the bulletproof glass of the passenger side window. "There's a—good lord . . ."

There were telephone lines running alongside the road. The poles were the tallest thing for miles, and so constant flashing by every couple hundred feet that she'd begun to tune them out. Only this one was different. Somebody had been *nailed* to it.

There wasn't much time to assess. Hanging ten feet up . . . adult male, Mexican, mid-thirties, jeans and a flannel shirt, coated in dried blood. Arms extended above his head, dangling with multiple nails—no, spikes—through his hands and wrists.

Then it flashed by. She looked in her mirror, but the body was already obscured by the dust.

Since Louie was in back he'd gotten the best look. "I know the cartel leaves some brutal warnings, but crucifixion? Damn. Fucking barbarians."

Then they passed another pole, and there was another body stuck to it. Female. Twenties. Vultures were perched on the crossbeam above her. There was more swearing and muttering. And then she too was swallowed by the dust.

The next telephone pole had another body hung on it. This one was elderly. Had she been somebody's *abuelita*? And the next. And the next. Every couple hundred feet the spectacle repeated. Men, women, children. The soldiers quit talking. This wasn't a warning. This was a massacre.

Numb, Carver concentrated on the road.

"All the way to the village?" Rudy asked.

"All the way," she confirmed. "Every single pole."

He swallowed hard. "That wasn't in your initial report."

Carver shook her head. "Considering what else we saw, it wasn't that noteworthy."

Bowie Team rolled into the village ready for a fight.

It was dead.

She'd been ready for the sound of gunfire, but there was nothing. There should have at least been a dog barking. There was no movement, no sound other than the wind. There were a few dozen small houses and other assorted buildings, but not so much as a curtain parted for the locals to spy on them. No matter how scared they were, nobody kept their heads down that well.

Ten seconds after dismounting, they stacked up on the little grocery market that their intel had said housed their targets, tossed bangs through the windows, breached the doors, and rushed inside.

"Clear!" Carver shouted after she swept through the back storage room. The smell of death assaulted her nostrils. There were dried blood puddles on the uneven wooden floor, big enough that it looked like they'd butchered a cow in here, but no bodies, and certainly no living terrorists or cartel members.

Somebody had set up a shrine inside the storeroom. She'd seen the painted skull faces in the briefings, *Santa Muerte*, popular with the cartel assassins. Corvus walked over to the shrine and started shoving around the flowers, papers, and dolls with the muzzle of his SCAR, checking if there was anything interesting. All of the crucifixes had been turned upside down. He found a plastic dog bowl. Corvus gagged and backed away from the shrine. There was a pile of glistening, white spheres inside.

"I think those are human eyeballs, LT."

A bunch of little devotional candles were still lit around the shrine. So the occupants couldn't have been gone long.

"They must have bolted," Sandbag said. "Did they see us coming?"

She shook her head. There was only one road out, and nobody had passed them. The terrain was rugged enough that they could have escaped on foot, horseback, or four wheelers, but she wasn't getting that vibe at all. "My gut's telling me nobody got out of this place."

"Yo, LT. I've got something weird here. It looks really old." Gator had picked up an odd-looking silver amulet. He was scowling at it. "Is that Arabic?"

She looked at the antique. It was the head of a goat, with ruby eyes. An unconscious shiver of revulsion went through her and she had no idea why. "Greek maybe? I don't know what language that is."

Gator was holding it in his glove. Suddenly, red droplets of blood appeared on the silver. She looked up to see that it was coming from Gator's nose. He was just staring at it, and didn't seem to notice the rivulet of blood running down his chin. It was like he was in a daze.

"Gator, you're bleeding."

It took him a long second to focus. He slowly looked up from the amulet. "Huh?"

"Did you hit your head or something?"

Gator seemed to snap out of it. He wiped the blood away with a sleeve, and looked at it in surprise. "Naw. Damned dry heat."

Captain Quinn came over the radio. "*Target's in the wind. We're splitting into teams and searching the town. Zeke, take the cantina. Carver, you've got the church.*"

"Roger that. We're on the church." She let go of the transmit button. "Bag that necklace and let's go."

❖ ❖ ❖

"What did you find in the church?" Rudy asked softly.

"He found us." The lieutenant's trembling had gotten worse. He was inclined to give her a sedative, but Mr. Church had been adamant they needed answers now.

"Who is *he*?"

Rudy waited for her to elaborate, but this interview was like pulling teeth. "Tell me about what happened in the church, Olivia."

Abruptly her trembling stopped. The change in manner was so complete, so chilling, that it brought to mind patients he'd worked with suffering from Dissociative Identity Disorder. In the blink of an eye, there was a different person sitting across from him. Only this one was utterly calm.

"Are you okay, Olivia?"

Seemingly curious, Carver tilted her head to the side, a bit too far. "I like eyes. Your eyes are broken, Rudy. I can only see through one of them."

The shift was so sudden, and the question so unexpected, that it put him off his game. "I was injured. I have a glass eye."

Carver nodded slowly. "Your world is flat."

"You mean I have no depth perception. Correct."

She stared at him for a long time. "It makes me sad you're broken."

Despite being summer in Texas, Rudy felt a sudden chill. There was a knock on the other side of the glass. It made him jump.

He tried to hide his relief at having an interruption. "Excuse me a minute." Rudy got up and went to the door. He had to wait for them to unlock it.

There were four MPs waiting in the hall. Mr. Church was by himself in the observation room. He was simply standing there in the dark, watching Lieutenant Carver through the one-way glass, inscrutable as ever.

"What do you think, Doctor?"

"It's too early to tell. She's a severely traumatized young woman who has been through a lot, but beyond that I'm going to need more time to reach her."

"I've received a call from another agency. They are sending a specialist. He'll be here soon."

"What kind of specialist?" Rudy asked suspiciously. "From what agency?"

"The kind you don't ask questions about. His name is Franks. I've worked with him before." Considering how broad and mysterious Church's background was, that was incredibly unhelpful. "Agent Franks is a thoroughly unpleasant individual, but very good at what he does. You'll want to stay out of his way. He's not big on conversation."

"It's unlike you to turn over DMS jurisdiction to someone else. Carver is one of us."

"Is she?"

"What do you mean by that?"

Church glanced at the wall clock. "He should arrive in an hour."

"Then let me keep talking to her until this specialist shows up."

"I wouldn't advise that . . . However, I will admit I'm curious to hear what she has to say. Carry on."

"Okay then," Rudy started walking away.

Church called after him, "By the way, Doctor, we got the preliminary results back on her dead teammates. No toxins, drugs, or biological agents were present in their systems. The causes of death were all straightforward—gunshot wounds, stabbings, strangulation, blunt force trauma, that sort of thing."

"Okay. Anything else?"

"It might be a sticky subject, but I would suggest asking her about the cannibalism."

"*What?*"

"Human tissue was found in some of their stomachs. We have not had the time to get the DNA results yet, but considering some of the bite patterns on the survivors, it probably came from their teammates."

Rudy blanched.

"Do you still want to continue?"

Like he'd told Carver, his small part was helping put the good people back together. Until proven otherwise, he was going to assume good whenever possible. "Yeah, I've got this."

"Very well. Can I help you with anything else, Doctor?"

"Sure, tell the Army to turn down the air conditioner. It's freezing in that little room."

"Really? They were just apologizing to me for the accommodations. According to the thermometer it is over eighty degrees in here."

"Shit." Rudy put his head down, plowed through the hall, past the MPs, and back into the oddest psych eval he'd done in quite some time.

Carver had gone back to shaking and mumbling. It was sad, but that sign of human frailty made him far more comfortable than the creepy mood swing from a few minutes before. Rudy sat back down. She gave him a weak smile.

"Okay, Olivia. Tell me about what happened inside that church."

Corvus kicked the door open and her men swept inside. They had trained so constantly that their movement was like clockwork. Each one covered a sector.

"Clear!"

A minute later the small Catholic church was secured. There was still no sign of the tangos, or any of the locals for that matter. There should have been something.

The church was old, and humble. The wooden walls had been painted white a long time ago, but they were faded and chipped now. Heavily lacquered wooden saints looked down on them. The pews were polished smooth from decades of use.

"Where is everybody?" Louie wondered aloud.

"Nailed to the telephone poles," Sandbag muttered.

"No, this town held more people than that." But that didn't mean she had a clue where they'd gone. Carver had her men take up defensive positions on the doors and got on her radio to contact Captain Quinn. She got nothing but static. *Weird.* "This place is giving me a bad vibe."

Carver turned around and nearly jumped out of her skin when she saw a little Mexican boy sitting on the altar. Sensing her reaction, her men spun around, lifting their weapons.

"Hold on!" she shouted before fingers could reach the triggers. "It's just a kid." He was probably only seven or eight years old, wearing a T-shirt, shorts, and barefoot. "Whose section was that? Damn it, Corvus! Why didn't you clear that?"

"I did, LT. He wasn't there a second ago."

It didn't matter now. They'd found *somebody.* Carver swung her carbine around behind her back and let it dangle by the sling. She lifted both hands to show they were empty. "*Hola.*" She spoke three languages fluently, but Spanish wasn't among them. Sandbag was fluent though. "Tell him we're friends."

Sandbag started talking. He was a big scary dude, but he kept his voice nice and soothing. Only the little boy kept staring at her instead. She found it odd that he was sitting cross-legged on the altar. She wasn't religious, but that seemed really disrespectful. "Ask him what's going on."

Sandbag did. The boy smirked as he answered.

"He says he just got up from a long nap."

"Huh? Where?"

"In the ground, I think. No. A tomb." Sandbag shrugged. "He's not making a lot of sense, LT."

"Ask him where everybody is."

The little boy finally looked at Sandbag and rattled off a dismissive answer. Sandbag seemed really confused by it.

"He says that he forced them to walk across the desert."

"Who did?"

"Him." Sandbag nodded at the kid. "He's talking about himself. He said he did it."

The little boy had an annoyed expression on his face. He said something else, like he was correcting the translator. He spoke for a long time. Sandbag's eyes kept getting wide.

"He says he made them take their shoes off so their feet would bleed on the rocks and thorns, and to not stop until they fell. They're probably dead from thirst by now." Sandbag was distressed. He'd never struck Carver as the religious type, so when he unconsciously crossed himself, it unnerved her. "That was only for the ones who pray. The rest he nailed to the poles."

"Little fucker would need a ladder," Corvus muttered. "He's gone mental."

"He says they brought him here, but they didn't understand what they dug up. He's insulted they thought he was just some mere weapon."

The kid smiled at them.

Then he began weeping blood.

That was when everything went horribly wrong.

❖ ❖ ❖

Rudy realized he was gripping the edge of the table so hard that his knuckles had turned white.

"What's wrong, Rudy?" Lieutenant Carver asked him with unnerving calm. "You seem frightened."

"I'm fine."

"No. You are broken. You are an unworthy vessel."

All the hair on his arms stood up. "You mean my eye?"

"Among other things." She smiled, but it wasn't a real smile. It was more like something was wearing Carver's face as a mask, and pulled the strings to make the face muscles perform the motions it assumed were appropriate. "I've been hidden away so long. The world above has changed. I do not understand it anymore. I was supposed to rest until the final days. Only the Canaanites opened my tomb. By the time I was fully away, they had brought me to the hot lands below."

"Canaanites?"

"I don't care what you name them now. I was weak, without purpose. I have found one again. I will seek out my old enemy, and begin our war anew."

Rudy didn't know where his next question came from. "Why did you come *here*?"

"I heard this one's song. I had to come and see for myself if it was true. Is my enemy here?"

"Who?" It was now so cold his breath came out as steam.

She leaned close and whispered to him.

Rudy bolted upright and headed for the door. He pounded on it. Thankfully the MPs opened it right away. "Keep that locked. Nobody else goes in or out." He didn't have the authority to order them around, but it wasn't a suggestion.

Church was waiting for him in the observation area. "She really seems to be opening up to you, Doctor."

Rudy raised one hand to stop Church. He wasn't in the mood. He was silent for a long time, breathing hard, staring through the glass at the woman on the other side. She'd gone back to trembling, knees nervously bouncing, just a poor, traumatized woman, who had seen her squad turn on each other and rip themselves to pieces.

"Clinically, on the record, I'd say she's severely delusional."

"And off the record?"

"I'm not going back in there without a priest."

Then the lights went out.

"Stay calm." Church's voice was flat.

The logical part of his mind immediately rationalized the power outage. The overworked air conditioner had caused the building to blow a fuse. But the part of him that had just been laid bare and terrified by an alien presence that should not be, knew that wasn't the case.

The lights came back on.

She had left two bloody red handprints on the other side of the glass for them.

"Carver's gone."

The interrogation room was empty. The handcuffs were on the table, still closed, like she just tore her hands right out of them. The door was closed.

Church moved to the hall. The MPs were still there, oblivious but unharmed. He threw open the door, and despite Rudy's admonition to the contrary, they knew not to mess with Mr. Church. He came back out. "Sound the alarm. Find her, but do not engage." The soldiers rushed off. Church returned a moment later, glowering. "She's escaped."

Nothing ever seemed to shake Church, but Rudy was sick to his stomach. "That specialist who's on the way . . . He's an exorcist, isn't he?"

"I don't know if Agent Franks puts that on his business cards, but I suppose that might be among his many qualifications," Church replied. "This is important, Doctor. I couldn't make it out over the speaker, but the last thing she said to you, when you asked her about this old enemy, about why she'd come here, what did she say to you?"

"The song said 'God is an American.'"

MUSINGS OF A HERMIT

This story first appeared in the Forged in Blood *anthology set in Michael Z. Williamson's Freehold universe, edited by Michael Z. Williamson, and published by Baen Books in 2017.*

The idea behind Forged in Blood *is really interesting. Every story features the same sword, as it is handed down to different users, starting in ancient Japan, through WWII, through modern times, into the future and out into space (where it eventually belonged to the main character in the novel* Freehold).

Sometimes the author picks the setting, and other times the author gets picked because he can write a particular setting. In this case I already had a rep for writing samurai drama, and Mike approached me because he needed some stories set in that era.

If you are familiar with this series, it has a very strong theme about freedom and liberty running through it, so I wanted to write about one of the sword's wielders who could never really have those things, yet yearned for them. I wanted to write about a man who had been born in the wrong time.

WHEN YOU HIT A MAN with a sword, it can go clean or ugly. A clean hit and you barely even feel the impact. Oh, your opponent feels it. Trust me. But for the swordsman, your blade travels through skin and muscle as if it is parting water. Arms can come right off. Legs are tougher, but a good strike will cut clear to the bone and leave them crippled. A katana will shear a rib like paper, and their guts will fall out like a butchered pig. Then, with a snap of the wrist, the blade has returned and the swordsman is prepared to strike

again. Simple. Effective. *Clean.* I'll spare you all the flowery talk the
perfumed sensei spout about rhythm and footwork that inevitably
make killing sound like a formal court dance, but when you do
everything just right, I swear to you that I've killed men so smoothly
that their heads have remained sitting upon their necks long enough
to blink twice before falling off.

However, an ugly hit means you pulled it wrong, or he moved
unexpectedly. The littlest things, a slight change in angle, a tiny bit
of hesitation, upon impact you feel that pop in your wrists, and then
your sword is stuck in their bone, they're screaming in your face,
flinging blood everywhere, and you have to practically wrestle your
steel out of them. Whatever bone you struck is a splintered mess.
Usually the meat is dangling off in ghastly strips. Some men will take
that as a sign to lie down and die, but a dedicated samurai will take
that ugly hit and still try to take you with him, just because, in
principle, if a samurai is dying then, damn it, he shouldn't have to do
it alone. It can be a very nasty affair.

The tax collector died very ugly.

I only wanted to be left alone.

Kanemori was sitting by the stove, absorbing the warmth,
debating over whether it was too early in the afternoon to get drunk,
when there was a great commotion in his yard. Someone was calling
his name. It wouldn't be the first time in his long life that someone
with a grudge had turned up looking for him, but this sounded like
a girl. He rose and peeked out one of the gaps in the wall that he'd
been meaning to repair, to see that it was the village headman's
daughter trudging through the snow with determination.

"Go away!" he shouted.

"Kanemori! The village needs your help."

The headman always wanted his help with something, the lazy
bastard. A tree fell on old lady Haru's hut. Or Den's ox is stuck in the
river. Or please save us from these bandits, Kanemori-sama! And
then he'd have to go saw wood, or pull on a stupid ox, or cut down
some pathetic bandit rabble. He knew it was usually just the
headman trying to be social, but it was a waste of his time. He didn't
belong to the village. He'd simply had the misfortune of building his
shack near it.

"What now?" he bellowed through the wall.

"The new Kura-Bugyo is going to execute my father!"

"What did your imbecile father do to make the tax collector angry this time?"

"The last official was honest, but the officials this year are corrupt. They take more than they're supposed to. They take the lord's share, and then they take more to sell for themselves! Father refused to give up the last of our stores. If we do we'll perish during the winter."

Of course the officials were corrupt. That's what officials were for.

The girl was about ten, but already bossy enough to be a magistrate. When she reached the shack, she began pounding on his door. "Let me in, Kanemori!"

"Go away."

"No! I will stay out here and cry until I freeze to death! Your lack of mercy will cause my angry ghost to haunt you forever. And then you will feel very sorry!"

Kanemori sighed. Peasants were stupid and stubborn. He opened the door. "What do you expect me to do about it?"

"You are samurai! Make them stop."

"Oh?" He looked around his humble shack theatrically. "Do I look like Oda Nobunaga to you? I am without clan, status, or even basic dignity. Officials aren't going to listen to me. Do you think I moved to the frozen north because I am so popular?"

"You are the worst samurai ever!"

In defense of the clumsy butchery that passed for a battle against the corrupt tax collector and his men, my soldiering days were over. It had been many seasons since I'd last hit a man with a sword, so I was rusty. When your joints ache every morning, the last thing you want to do is practice your forms, so my daily training consisted of the minimum a retired swordsman must do in order to avoid feeling guilty. Why do more? I had no lord to command me, no general to bark orders at me—the only person who'd done so recently was my second wife, and I'd buried her two winters ago—and if I spent all my energy swinging a sword, who was going to feed all these damnable chickens?

It isn't that peasants can't fight. It is that they're too tired from working all day to learn to fight. A long time ago some clever sort figured that out, traded his hoe for a sword, started bossing around the local farmers, said, you give me food and in exchange I'll protect you from assholes who will kill you, but if you don't, I'll kill you myself, and the samurai class was born. From then on, by accident of one's birth, it determined if you'd be well fed until you got stabbed to death, or hungry and laboring until you starved . . . or got stabbed to death.

Spare me the history lectures. I actually do know where samurai come from. I was born *buke*. I slept through the finest history lessons in Kyoto. You would not know it to look at me now, but I was once a promising young warrior. It was said that handsome Hatsu Kanemori was a scholar, a poet, and the veritable pride of my clan, and high-ranking officials were lining up to offer me marriages to their daughters . . . until one day I finally told my lord I was sick of his shit. Then I promptly ran away before he could decorate his castle wall with my head.

Now, the life of a ronin is a different sort of thing entirely. Samurai live well, but they're expected to die on behalf of their lord. Ronin live slightly better than dogs, and are expected to die on behalf of whichever lord scraped up enough coin to hire us. Being a wave man retains all of the joys of getting stabbed to death, but with the added enticement of being as miserable and hungry as a peasant, up until when you get stabbed to death.

But at least you are your own master.

After he closed his door in her face, the headman's daughter had sat down in the snow, started wailing, and seemed petulantly prepared to freeze to death in his yard in protest. He'd known mighty warriors who had committed seppuku to protest a superior's decision, but this was a new form of protest to Kanemori. He thought about throwing rocks at her until she left, but even a curmudgeon has his limits. So he put a blanket over his head to muffle the noise and took a long nap instead.

When he woke up, the girl was still there. Kanemori was surrounded by stubborn idiots.

"Does your family know you walked all the way here?" he shouted through the hole in the wall.

"No! I snuck out. They will think that I was devoured by wolves. They will perish with sadness! You are so cruel, Kanemori! My ghost will wail like this forever!"

He opened his door. When the orange light of the stove hit the girl, she quit her fake crying.

"You will save our village?" she asked.

"The Kura-Bugyo is an important man. If I report him, it is his word against mine, and I am without status in this district. There isn't much I can do." Before she could start crying again, he hurried to add, "But I suppose I could try."

"Thank you, noble samurai!"

It was a very long walk to the city, and the local governor's representatives would probably just turn him away, but he'd traded with these villagers, at times he'd chosen to help them, and they'd chosen to help him. It was remarkable how well folks got along without being ordered around.

"I will leave in the morning and travel to the city. I can request an audience with the Mokudai about this corrupt tax collector and—"

"There's no time. They're coming for father tomorrow morning. If we walk all night we can get back in time to save him."

Well, that complicated matters. That meant engaging with the tax collector personally, and since Kanemori had no place in this province, the petty official would probably take an interruption as an insult, and the girl's father wouldn't be the only one executed in the morning.

But she had started crying again, and as far as Kanemori could tell, it looked real. Those tears were probably going to freeze her eyelids shut, and then he wouldn't have to just walk all the way down to the village, but carry a blind girl too.

Kanemori sighed. "Stop that awful noise. Fine. I'll try to save your stupid village. Let me get my sword."

I have never been good at taking orders. Petty authority annoys me. I have always had a surly, contrarian disposition. These are not desirable traits in a samurai. A good warrior is supposed to have unquestioning loyalty to his lord, no matter how ridiculous he might be. My problem was that I always questioned everything. When I was a boy, my individualistic attitude helped me collect an inordinate number of beatings. That was good. It made me tough. Because if you are going to make it on your own, wandering a world that is all about surviving as part of a group, you'd better be tough.

Luckily, by the time my family sent me off to training, I'd learned when to keep my mouth shut . . . mostly. I had enough natural talent with a sword that my sensei usually overlooked my flippant attitude. It turns out you can afford to give some inadvertent insults when everyone else is scared to duel you. But that only applies to equals— insult a superior, and you had better have a fast horse nearby.

In this world, every man has his place. You know it, you live it, and you pretend to love it. A good samurai would rather let his superior make a foolish decision unchallenged than bring dishonor to his name. Yes, your leader could be an imbecile giving orders that are sure to lead to ignominious defeat, but you'd better take those orders and die with a smile on your face. That is the way of things. So when you slip up and anger your betters, you need to be very valuable on the battlefield—which I was—for them to overlook it. Sadly, when peace finally came to my home province, my painful honesty outweighed my value with a sword.

Stupid peace.

I remember the day when my father gave me my sword. It had belonged to him, and his father, and his father's father's father, so on and so forth, back to tales of glorious battles long ago, and a family legend of a one-handed matriarch, all accompanied with a proud genealogy that was probably half forgery, and half wishful thinking. But regardless, it was an excellent sword.

I suspect he knew I was unworthy of such a legacy, but every father hopes for the best.

At sunrise the village headman ran down the steps of the storehouse, slipped through the packed snow, scooped up his little girl, and swung her around in his arms before holding her tight. "Iyo! You're alive! We woke up this morning and you were gone. Where have you been? We were so worried about you."

"I went to fetch the samurai so he can save you from the officials," the little girl declared proudly.

"What?"

"Defiant Kanemori! Hero of Sekigahara!"

Kanemori cleared his throat so the headman would notice him. Personally, he hated those titles, but bored peasants like to tell stories. The little girl's head had been filled with nonsense exaggerations about his exploits. During their journey down the mountain, she'd asked him about *all* of them.

Kanemori had walked all night, in the dark, in the miserable cold, lucky he hadn't fallen off a narrow trail to his death, and now he was tired, hungry, and annoyed, and probably about to anger another official who could order him killed with so much as a nod. At least it had been a clear night, and he'd always enjoyed gazing at the stars. His father used to say he was too much of a dreamer in that respect.

"You?" The headman was shocked to see him there. He quickly regained his composure, and went into a deep bow. "Apologies for my daughter disturbing you, noble samurai." Then he realized he probably wasn't showing enough deference to his better and began to grovel. "So many apologies for this inconvenience."

"Stop it. Just . . ." Kanemori waved his hand. "Stop all that." He'd never been much for etiquette or social niceties.

"It was not Iyo's place to—"

"She says you're about to get executed for not paying your taxes and you need help. This isn't any different than when you needed an extra man to drag that dumb ox out of the river. Today you're the ox. Where are these officials? I'll try and talk some sense into them."

"Thank you! Thank you, samurai!"

"I can't promise anything." Over the years he'd found that any given official's reasonableness and mercy was in direct proportionate opposition to their inflated sense of importance and level of corruption. Since they'd been assigned to administer a northern pig hole like this, he wasn't expecting much.

"The Kura-Bugyo should be here soon. I am willing to be executed. It is better they take out their wrath on me, than steal the last of our rice from the mouths of our children." Again, a good man was prepared to lay down his life for others. Too bad he was so poor nobody would bother to write a poem about it. He looked up, hopeful. "I would rather not die. They will listen to you."

"Maybe. More likely they'll still kill you, then take the rice anyway. Either way, that means you have time to make me breakfast first."

When I was young, they called me a dreamer. I suppose that is true. I imagined a world different from this one. Where a man could be free to do as he wanted, without legions of officials standing in his way. Where a man could own things without his superiors taking them away on a whim. A world where someone bold enough to make his own way could do so, and not be bound by the status of his birth. Where you could decide for yourself how to live, rather than be spent on a bloody field by a shogun.

I still imagine a world where a man could marry the woman he loved, rather than having her lord give her to another man for political expediency. A world where a samurai could protest this unfair decision, but not lose face and be condemned for his emotional outburst, and have to run away in shame . . . only to find out years later that she cut her own throat in protest, rather than be wed to a cruel, barbaric man instead of him.

These are silly ramblings. That is not the world we live in. Not at all.

The four men rode into the village not long after breakfast. Only Kanemori and the headman walked outside to meet them. The officials seemed amused that the rest of the peasants were hiding from them. Their haughty attitude was not so different from bandits.

Unfortunately, the Kura-Bugyo was a young man. An older, wiser official might have let the slight pass. The callousness of noble youth, coupled with the unrivaled arrogance of a tax collector, meant that Kanemori had his work cut out for him. The official also had three samurai escorting him, who were acting more like friends than guards. That was another bad sign. An official would feel no need to show off for soldiers, their opinions would be beneath contempt, but the same official would strut like a rooster to save face in front of his friends.

"Where is my rice, headman?" the official shouted, not bothering to give any introduction. "I said to have it waiting. There is a wagon not far behind. Why do you waste my time?" His friends snickered.

The headman bowed so hard he nearly buried himself in the snow. Kanemori was ashamed for him. This wasn't the emperor. This was probably some minor noble's third or fourth son, given a job intended for a clerk, probably to get him out from underfoot, but having power over these poor people had clearly gone to his head.

Only Kanemori had promised little Iyo that he would try, so he needed to speak up before the headman's blubbering caused this pack of dogs to get too riled up. When a deer ran, a dog's instincts were to chase it down. Likewise, a peasant's weakness would make a bully eager for violence.

"Greetings, honored officials." Kanemori gave a very proper bow, showing the right amount of deference, and for the correct amount of time. He hadn't slept through *every* lesson.

They didn't even bother to get off their horses. Sitting up there must have made them feel tall.

"Who are you supposed to be?" the tax collector sneered.

"I am Kanemori. I am merely a humble friend of this village, and have come to beg for leniency for them today."

The officials exchanged confused glances. "Who?"

"These kind people have called on me in the hopes that I might be able to appeal to your mercy. Their harvest this year was not very good, purely due to weather beyond their control and not from laziness, yet they still met their obligations. If you examine their stores, you will see that if they meet your new demands, they will not have enough food to survive the winter. They're already eating millet only fit for livestock."

"That's a sad story, only it isn't my problem," the tax collector said.

"But if these villagers sicken and die, then next year there will be no harvest at all." Thus far Kanemori had kept his face neutral and his voice polite, but he could feel that starting to slip. What was it with shortsighted fools? Officials who had nothing personal at stake could never see beyond their immediate gratification. "Please think of the next season, honored representative. Will your lord not be disappointed?"

"Next year I will have a better appointment."

"You talk like a samurai, but you wear no mon," said one of the young men. His own family signal was proudly embroidered on his sleeve with golden thread. "I think I've heard of this old man. He's that ronin hermit that lives up on the mountain."

"Ha! From his ratty clothing, I took him for another peasant!" said one of the other fine young examples of Bushido. "Have you been rolling around in the dirt to look like that?"

"He has dirt under his nails. He's more farmer than samurai."

"You are obviously a long way from home, old man. Step aside. You have no say here. Now where is my rice, headman?"

This was not his place. Kanemori had done all that he could. He had no further legal recourse. It was his duty to step aside. This was the world they lived in.

Enough.

They'd started calling him Kanemori the Defiant for a reason. Nobody had ever accused him of being Kanemori the Eloquent.

"It isn't *your* rice, boy."

"How dare you, old man?"

"Did you grow it? Did you harvest it? No. These people did. I didn't see your pampered ass sweating in the fields."

It was plain the bullies were not used to that kind of response.

"This land belongs to your lord, and he appointed you to administer and defend it. From the look of you songbirds, you've never defended a thing. The last few times these poor saps have been menaced by bandits, they didn't even bother calling for you. They came and got me instead. Your lord has already collected his taxes. This is about your greed. Spare me the sanctimony. I know how it works. That wagon coming down the road is probably some merchant paying you on the side."

"Such impudence! I'll burn this whole place down!" the tax collector bellowed.

The headman squeaked in fear, but the sound was still muffled by the snow. "Please no, young master! Have mercy." Kanemori had forgotten about him there.

"I was feeling merciful until you got some ronin fool involved. Now you will discover what happens when you disobey your betters."

Kanemori was old, tired, and too damned grouchy to get out of the way. His order-taking days were over. "The only difference between the government and bandits is that the bandits are at least honest about it."

"Kill him, Shingen," ordered the tax collector. One of them kicked his horse and it started forward. Kanemori watched him rapidly approach. It was obvious the young man wasn't a trained cavalryman, and that was certainly no war horse, but the animal seemed used to the idea of running down peasants.

Kanemori reached for his sword. Out of practice or not, a soldier kept his instincts, and not getting pulverized by hooves was among them. He drew his blade as he smoothly stepped aside, and the cut went very deep. The animal's front leg collapsed, the other hooves slipped, and the unseated rider flew over its head to land in the snow.

The tax collector was obviously shocked. This wasn't what normally happened when you rode down a peasant at all. His friend was thrashing about in the suddenly red snow, trying to figure out how he'd gotten there. The horse was screaming. The other horses began bucking, terrified at the sudden smell of hot blood, which just went to show the value of a horse properly trained for war.

There is nothing in the world quite so unnerving as the scream of a horse. Kanemori had killed a lot of men in his day, and none of them really kept him up at night, but the wide-eyed thrashing of a terrified wounded horse always bothered him, so he struck again. This time at the neck. *Clean.* It died quickly.

Worst-case scenario, once this was over, the hungry villagers could eat the horse. Peasants were efficient like that.

It was not so much a battle as a slaughter.

If any of those young samurai had a brain in his head, he would have stayed on his mount and ridden for help. The authorities would have come, and I would have died a criminal. But no. Fury made them dumb and pride demanded that they had to put me in my place. They were better than me. That's just how it was. That's how it always has been, and always must be. They don't understand any other way. That's how it is with these people. It's like they're compelled to meddle.

Such is the nature of man. We must join together to survive, but then somebody has to be in charge. Somebody always has to be in charge. And we let them. At first because we need them, but even when we really don't anymore, they're still there. And their power grows, and grows, and grows, until it consumes everything.

I dream of a world where a man can make his own way, but I suppose there will always be samurai and peasants.

I just wanted to be left alone.

The horse was the only clean death that morning. The rest were ugly. Damned ugly.

No honorable samurai would ever sink to the level of doing manual labor, but Kanemori had often lowered himself to help the local peasants, whether it was cutting trees, or dragging an obstinate ox from the river or, in this case, digging a shallow grave in the frozen ground.

"This must never be spoken of," the headman told the handful of peasants who were standing around their hastily filled hole. The ground was so hard that it had taken a long time, and they'd broken a few valuable shovels in the process, but if there was one thing peasants knew how to do, it was work. By the time the sun had gone down, there was no sign the tax collector, his friends, or their merchant crony had ever come to the village at all.

"If the governor was ever to discover what happened here today, our village would be razed, and every single one of us would be beheaded as criminals." The village headman really wanted to keep his. "We never saw our tax collector. He simply never arrived. Is that understood?"

All of the peasants agreed. Even though none of them had lifted a finger against the tax collector, those in power would never tolerate even the hint of rebellion. If there was something else peasants understood, it was how to keep a secret.

"It is unfortunate, but such things happen when there are so many bandits in these mountains," Kanemori stated flatly. "Perhaps they will send more officials to protect you better in the future."

Of the peasants, only young Iyo was truly glad he'd done what he had. To the rest, he'd simply complicated their already difficult lives. That's because, like him, Iyo was a dreamer. She was still naïve enough to think that one person could change things.

After the somber and terrified villagers returned to their huts,

Kanemori had remained standing by the grave. Men of such stature were due a proper funeral ceremony, and a small shrine. Instead, they got a shallow pit that no one would ever speak of. Some of the villagers had thanked Kanemori, but it had been a dishonest thanks. Those who were incapable of defending themselves were often frightened of those who fought on their behalf. He saw there was fear in their eyes, directed at him, and he did not like it one bit. If he had enjoyed such things, he probably would have made a fine tax collector.

It was time to move on, to find a new place, to try and make a new home again where he could just be left alone. Where he could be free.

But there was no place like that in this world.

Kanemori gazed up at the stars, and wished for another way.

Far up the hill, past an old hut, three villagers built a pyre for the body of an old man. The corpse had mummified, and the wiry muscles of the man underneath showed through the shrunken skin.

The youngest said, "Shouldn't we just put him in a hole? He was only an old hermit. This is costing the village money."

"No, we must do it this way."

"Why? He was a ronin."

"But his kami was that of a samurai. It deserves this. You do not know what he has done for us before."

The boy looked at the stone which was to become a discreet monument over the urn. "It's a lot of work."

"Just make the carving neat."

The inscription was simple.

The Defiant.

Even a ronin could fight with honor. Preventing peasants from being abused and starved was not a grand act, but it was still a great act. While she wished for more action, his life was a worthy one she was proud of.

She understood why she was hidden away. Peasants were not allowed swords, and the chief's daughter was no warrior. She waited in her saya, inside a silk case, in a trunk while time ebbed endlessly past. The samurai themselves faded away. That saddened her, and she hoped there would be another culture that respected her, not let her age away for naught. Eventually, the red blight of rust bloomed on her skin.

Then one day, she was taken from the trunk, and hands passed her to another.

INSTRUMENTS OF WAR

This novella was originally published by Skull Island Expeditions in 2013, edited by Scott Taylor and Doug Seacat. It is set in the universe of the Warmachine and Hordes tabletop war games. If I recall correctly, this is the first thing that I ever wrote set in someone else's already existing universe. It is the origin story of one of their main faction leaders in the game. However, anytime I write a story set in someone else's IP, I always try to do it in a way that everything is self-explanatory enough that you don't need to already be familiar with the setting in order to enjoy it. This is about a fantasy race of vicious desert warriors known as the Skorne, who are just so hard core and mean that I had a blast writing it. There were some challenges though, in that I had to take an alien culture based on dominance, slavery, and continual warfare, then make them the heroes of their story.

❖ PART ONE ❖

"WHAT IS IT that you whisper to yourself, child, when the pain becomes too much?"

Makeda wiped the blood from her split lip. Her head was spinning, and her body ached from the savage beating. "I recite the code."

"Why must a warrior recite the code of hoksune?" Archdominar Vaactash asked rhetorically.

"The code shows me the way to exaltation. Only through combat may one understand the way." She studied the blood on the back of her shaking hand as she spoke. All of it was hers . . . so far. She would have to remedy that. Akkad had beaten her mercilessly, but Makeda could still fight. The tremors slowed and then stopped. "Suffering cleanses the weakness from my being. Adhere to the code and I will become worthy."

"Correct. You have learned much for one so young," her grandfather stated without inflection. It was as close to a compliment as the archdominar had ever paid her. "Take up your swords, Makeda of House Balaash. Your lessons are not yet through today."

The practice swords lay in the sand near where she'd been thrown down. They were made of hard wood, their edges dented and cracked from hundreds of impacts, their hilts worn smooth by sweat and callus. She had begun learning their use as soon as she was strong enough to lift them. She may have been a child, but she was skorne, and thus she did not question, she endured. Makeda reached out and took the pair of wooden swords from where they had fallen. They mimicked the heft and balance of true Praetorian blades. They felt comfortable in her grip.

"Rise," Vaactash commanded.

Makeda struggled to her feet, muscles aching in protest. Her laminate armor had been crafted for an adult, and was far too big for her slim body, but it had kept her intact during Akkad's last merciless assault. She had yet to begin her studies in the art of mortitheurgy, but she did not need to be a master reader of the energy that dwelled within the blood and sinews to understand that her body was in danger of failing her. Her opponent was simply too strong.

Akkad was waiting for her to stand, obviously excited to prove his worth to their grandfather. There were only three present within the gigantic training arena of House Balaash, but one of them was Archdominar Vaactash himself, master of their house, and a warrior so great that he had already secured exaltation for his deeds. It did not matter that the stands were not filled with spectators, since the opinion of Vaactash alone mattered more than several cohorts of troops.

"What lesson would you have me teach her next, Archdominar?" Akkad asked. As the eldest of the two children of Telkesh, first son and heir of mighty Vaactash, Akkad would someday lead House Balaash. The code of hoksune dictated that the eldest, unless unfit for war, must lead. It was vital that Akkad display his martial superiority before his grandfather, and so far he had. "She is still but a tiny thing."

Vaactash's expression was unreadable. "Then why have you had to work so hard to defeat her?"

Makeda took some pleasure in seeing the anger flash across Akkad's face as he sputtered out a response. "I merely wished to provide you with an amusing show."

"Watching a paingiver flay a captured enemy is amusing," Vaactash snapped. "I am here to make sure my grandchildren are being properly prepared to bring glory to my house. Demonstrate to me that you are ready to fight in the name of Balaash."

Akkad dipped his head submissively. "Of course." Her brother was ten years older, far larger, and had already received advanced training under the tutelage of their father's veteran Cataphract. Akkad walked to the nearest rack of weapons and removed a war spear, the heavy pole arm of the Cetrati. It was longer than Makeda was tall, and even though the blade had been replaced with a block of shaped wood, she knew that it would still hit like a titan's tusk. Akkad tested the balance of the heavy weapon before grunting in approval. He spun it effortlessly before pointing it at Makeda's chest. "I will finish her swiftly this time."

"See that you do. Hold nothing back. Demonstrate your conviction."

For the skorne, life consisted of either making war or preparing for it. It was a harsh, brutal, and unyielding existence. That was especially true for those blessed enough to be born into House Balaash, the greatest of all houses. There was no doubt they would fight their hardest until physically unable to continue or were commanded to stop by their superior. Other, lesser houses may have done it differently, perhaps not risked the lives of their heirs so flagrantly, but that was why they were weak and House Balaash was strong.

Makeda welcomed the challenge. She crossed her swords and saluted her brother.

Their grandfather studied the combatants intently, his white eyes unblinking. Though bent with age, his mere presence seemed to fill the arena. This was a warrior who had led tens of thousands into battle and conquered more houses than any other dominar in several generations, earning himself the extremely rare title of archdominar. He was a master mortitheurge capable of commanding the mightiest beasts and rending unbelievable magic from the flesh. Makeda wished that she could have a fraction of his understanding, but promised herself that one day she would. Vaactash was the epitome of what it meant to be skorne.

After a long moment of consideration, Vaactash stepped aside, gathered up his red robes, and took a seat on the first tier of the training arena. He gestured dismissively. "Continue."

"Come, sister. Let us end this."

Akkad swung the spear in a wide arc. Makeda raised both blades to intercept, but the impact was so great that it nearly tore them from her grasp. Her arms were already exhausted and quivering. She grimaced and pushed back, but her boots slid through the sand of the arena as Akkad overpowered her. The pressure released, the heavy pole moved back, and Makeda lurched aside as Akkad stabbed at her. He followed, relentless, eyes narrowed, looking for an opportunity to finish her.

He was stronger, but she was faster. Stepping in to the threat, Makeda slashed at Akkad's face with her right, narrowly missing. *Show your foe one blade. Kill him with the other.* She stabbed with her left sword, and clipped the edge of his breastplate. Akkad didn't seem to notice. The spear hummed through the air again, and this time Makeda was unable to stop it.

She crashed hard against the arena wall.

The code of hoksune declared that the eldest was the default heir, but every child of the highest caste was a valuable war asset, and thus not to be wasted frivolously. Yet, when Makeda looked into Akkad's maddened eyes, she wondered if her brother really did intend to kill her. She narrowly rolled aside as the wall was pulverized into splinters. Vaactash said nothing.

Her brother was relentless. The war spear covered vast swaths of the arena with each attack. The muscles of Makeda's arms clenched in agony as her practice swords bounced harmlessly away. Sweat poured down the inside of her cursed, cumbersome armor. She was struck in the ribs, and then in the leg. Flesh bruised and swelling, Makeda continued fighting. She would fight until her archdominar said it was time to stop or she was dead, for that was the code. Another massive strike knocked one of her blades away. It spun through the air and landed in the stands with a clatter.

Makeda knew she was losing, but the words of the code played through her mind. *Only by conflict can the code be understood. Embrace your suffering and gain clarity.*

Time seemed to slow. His moves were too fierce, too uncontrollable. He had underestimated her resolve. Akkad lifted his spear high overhead before bringing it down in a crashing arc. Makeda barely moved aside in time. The mighty hit threw a cloud of sand into the air, but before Akkad could lift it, Makeda planted one boot on top of the war spear's blade. Though slight, the extra weight was enough to cause his grip to slip as he tried to tug the spear away. The momentary surprise was just enough to allow Makeda one clean strike.

"*Balaash!*"

The tip of her practice sword caught Akkad in the side of the head. Blood flew as skin split wide. The spear was pulled from beneath her boot and the siblings stumbled away from each other.

Makeda gathered herself, but there was a lull in the fighting. Akkad was glaring at her as if stunned, one gauntlet pressed to his head to staunch the flow of red. She had struck him hard. His ear appeared to be mangled, and the tip was broken and hanging by only a small bit of skin. Surely, he had felt that one.

"I have seen enough."

Gasping for breath, barely able to stand, Makeda looked to their archdominar. Vaactash nodded once. Her heart swelled.

"Both of you have improved since last I watched you spar. It pleases me that the blood of House Balaash does not run thin in this generation. One day I will die and your father, Telkesh, will lead my House, and you will serve him. In time, Akkad, you will take his place. When you learn to temper your ambition with wisdom, you will bring great honor to our house. Your sister will make a fine Tyrant in your service, and I have no doubt that multitudes will be conquered to feed our slave pits. Until then, you have much to learn."

"Yes, Archdominar."

"The more you bleed in training, the less you will bleed in war.

Learn from every fight, Akkad. Do you know why Makeda defeated you this time?"

"She did not defeat me!" Akkad snarled.

"Silence!" The entire arena seemed to flex at Vaactash's displeasure. That one stern word caused Akkad to fall to his knees and bow. "Do not ever disagree with the ruler of your house. If that had been an actual Praetorian blade, the contents of your thick skull would have been emptied into the sand. Fool. How dare you question my decree?"

The siblings shrank back. The archdominar's legendary temper was a thing only spoken of in hushed whispers.

"For that you will not have this wound repaired. Have the end cut off and cauterized. You will wear that scar as a reminder of your impertinence."

"Yes, Archdominar." Akkad kept his head down as droplets of blood painted a pattern in the sand. He was trying not to sound sullen. "It will be as you command."

"Again I ask, do you know why a tiny child capable of hiding in your shadow managed to beat you?"

"Forgive my ignorance. I . . . I do not know the answer, Grandfather." Akkad risked a quick glance toward Makeda. She could feel the malice in his gaze. Makeda did not gloat. She had merely done her best, as was required. "Please, enlighten me."

"You only understand the concept of victory. Makeda does not comprehend the concept of defeat."

A generation had passed, but the lessons of Vaactash would never leave her. His words were as ingrained into Makeda as the code of hoksune itself. It had been a year since her grandfather's death under the tusks of a great beast of the plains, but she still found herself calling upon his wisdom during times of struggle. She was a mature, yet unproven warrior now. The Swords of Balaash were sheathed at her side. Slivers of her grandfather's sacral stone were among those empowering the mighty blades, and though only an extoller could contact the exalted dead, Makeda always felt as though Vaactash was there to guide her with his wisdom.

Makeda would need that wisdom if she were to survive the day.

The atmosphere inside the command tent was as heated as the

drought-scourged plains. The officers of her decurium were in disagreement over what to do next.

"Tyrant Makeda, House Muzkaar's forces are nearly upon us."

"Akkad's reinforcements have not arrived yet. We are badly outnumbered. If we do not fall back now, we die here." Urkesh was the dakar of her taberna of Ventators. Of course a warrior who specialized in engaging the enemy from a distance with reiver fire would choose the pragmatic, if somewhat cowardly, approach.

"We have been commanded to hold this hill! So we dig in and hold!" Dakar Barkal was the leader of her Praetorian karax. Of course, the karax would choose to die like that, in a perfect xenka formation, each of their great shields being used to protect themselves and their fellow Praetorians at their side as they impaled their enemies on their long pikes. "Honor demands it."

"Muzkaar outnumbers us five to one," Urkesh insisted. "Your honor will not beat those odds."

"Do you question the strength of the karax?" Barkal shouted.

Makeda let them debate. She knew that they would follow her final decision, no matter what. Perhaps in the meantime one of them would surprise her with a solution.

"Your mighty shields won't matter when a wall of titans stampede over you." Venators were the lowest of the warrior caste, but Urkesh was young and hotheaded. Makeda doubted that he realized how close he was treading to simply having Barkal strike him down in anger. "We cannot hold anything if we are all dead and howling in the Void. I say we retreat from this trap, move to the plains, where we can maneuver and harass these Muzkaar dogs until Akkad's forces arrive."

Barkal looked to Makeda, his narrow face pinched with rage. She needed every warrior, even a Venator whose devotion to dying by the hoksune code was questionable at best. Makeda shook her head in the negative. She would approve no duels of slighted honor until after their battle was through. She could not spare any warriors. Deprived of his chance to gut Urkesh for his insolence, Barkal went back to defending his position. "Our duty requires us to hold," he snapped.

Deep in thought, Makeda listened to the words of her subordinates as they argued. She was glad to see that none of them feared death, only the possibility of failure. Skorne lived to serve and die, but there was no honor in dying pointlessly. This was her first command, and she would not lose it so easily.

Primus Zabalam stepped forward and placed his body between the two shouting warriors. Both dakars stepped back out of respect for their senior officer. "Regardless of which decision is best, we must give the order soon. We will be cut off by Tyrant Naram's beasts within the hour, and then it will not matter either way." It was the first time the veteran leader of her Praetorian swordsmen had spoken. Zabalam was the oldest warrior present, and had even served as one of Vaactash's personal guard. As usual, he spoke with the wisdom that could only be gained from countless battles. "Our commander must choose now, or the decision will be made for her."

The map was open on the table, but she was staring through it, rather than at it. The map was irrelevant. She had already memorized every brush stroke and line of ink. *Fail in their orders, retreat and live to rejoin the rest of the army, or hold their ground in the vain hope that her brother would arrive in time, and more than likely die as nothing more than a temporary distraction . . .* Ultimately, the choice was hers alone to make.

The situation was dire. The honor of House Balaash lay heavy on her shoulders. It was times like this that tested a warrior's dedication to the code.

Grandfather, what would you have me do?

Having only recently reached the age sufficient to go through the rites of passage necessary to be considered a full member of the warrior caste, this was the first time Makeda had led a cohort into battle on behalf of House Balaash. Archdominar Telkesh had ordered her to hold this position, a small hill on the plains south of Kalos, but no one had predicted this level of resistance. Their spies had reported that the bulk of the enemy had been camped much closer to the city, nowhere near here. So the main army of House Balaash was marching unopposed, while Makeda's cohort was badly outnumbered against the entirety of the forces of House Muzkaar.

If somehow she did live through the day, Makeda intended to have those spies tortured for a very long time.

That, however, did not solve her current dilemma. The enemy army was led by Naram, a Tyrant legendary for both his skill with beasts and the cruelty he used in breaking them. She had learned what she could of Naram's exploits, and had come to respect him for his brutal and unflinching victories. He was truly an adversary worthy of her father and his mighty army, not nearly as appropriate a foe for an inexperienced commander and one small cohort, but the ancestors had placed Naram against her, not her father. This battle was hers.

Makeda knew it was not her ever-increasing skills in the art of mortitheurgy, nor her considerable natural talent with the blade that made her valuable to her house. It was her certainty in the truthfulness of the code of hoksune. Her grandfather had recognized that. So as she always did, Makeda searched the code for an answer.

Combat favors the aggressor. There is a time for both defense and mobility, but every tactic is merely a tool enabling your inevitable attack. To draw with and kill your enemy is the true path toward exaltation.

She said a silent thank you to the shards of her grandfather's essence resting in her swords.

Makeda held up one hand. Her officers were immediately silent, waiting. "We will not retreat . . ." Regardless of whether they agreed or not, they immediately snapped to and began to move out to spread the word. "Nor will we hold this position."

The men froze, uncertain. They looked to each other, none daring to question their new commander. Though she was the youngest in the room, she was their superior both by birth and by appointment. Finally, Barkal of the karax dared speak. "What would you have us do then, Second Born?"

Makeda smiled. "We strike."

The sound of the reivers firing reminded Makeda of a swarm of angry buzzing insects, only this swarm was made up of thousands of razor-sharp projectiles. A House Muzkaar titan bellowed in agony as its hide was shredded. The gigantic warbeast took a few halting steps, showering bright blood from a plethora of wounds. Several Muzkaar beast handlers lashed the beast, urging it forward through the steel cloud. Driven mad with pain, the titan lumbered onward.

"Reload!" Urkesh shouted at his Venators. There was only a single datha of ten armigers, but they acted quickly, unscrewing the

spent gas cylinders from their awkward reiver weapons. Makeda
sized up the distances. The armigers were quick, but not quick
enough. The titan would trample right over Urkesh's warriors and
she would lose her ranged advantage.

House Muzkaar had brought no ranged capability of their own,
and dozens of Muzkaar corpses littered the road from where they
had been scythed down by her Venators while trying to cross.
Makeda did not wish to give up that advantage.

Makeda had few warbeasts of her own to spare. Since her cohort
had been marching quickly in order to seize their objective, she had
only been given a pair of cyclops savages. The tougher, but slower,
beasts had been left with Akkad. She reached out with her mind,
using her mortitheurge powers to find the lump of muscle and hate
that was the nearest cyclops. She took hold of its mind and steered
it into the path of the enemy titan.

The cyclops hoisted its great sword and stalked forward, towering
several feet over even the tallest warriors in its path. What the
cyclops lacked in intelligence it made up for in violent cunning. The
beast's single eye flicked back and forth, seeing the battlefield as only
a cyclops could, a few seconds into the future, and Makeda
wondered idly if the cyclops could see its own death coming.

The earth shook as the wounded titan charged. Each footfall was
like an earthquake. As large as the cyclops was, it was dwarfed by
the titan. Armored tusks crashed into the cyclops' armor with a
clang that could be heard over all the chaos of the battle. The cyclops
went rolling away, and the wounded titan followed, swinging wildly
with its massive gauntlets. Instinct demanded the cyclops flee, and
it screeched in protest as Makeda overcame its mind and forced it to
stand its ground.

Their weapons ready, Urkesh shouted at his taberna.
"Concentrate fire on that titan!" The Reivers rose from the ditch
they'd taken cover in, aimed, and let loose a stream of razor needles.
Hundreds of projectiles ricocheted off of armor plates and ivory
tusks, whining into the distance, but hundreds more found their
mark. Hide puckered and bled as the titan roared and crashed into
the dust.

Somehow, her cyclops had survived the mighty charge. Barely
alive, it was struggling to stand, using its sword to lever itself up.

Makeda used her magic, feeling the precious blood pumping out of the cyclops' damaged body, and then she reached deep within the beast and spurred its fury to whole new heights. The new anger gave her beast unnatural strength, and before the enemy could recover, Makeda's cyclops cleaved one of the titan's four arms off at the shoulder.

The titan's death bellow was like music across the plains. Its suffering would probably be heard all the way to the city of Kalos. Truly this was a great day for House Balaash.

The Muzkaar beast handlers that had been driving that titan were fleeing back across a ravine. "Urkesh." Makeda's voice was calm. "Make sure this is the last time those beast handlers annoy me."

The order was given, and the whine of razor needles filled the air, but Makeda had already moved on to survey the next part of the battle.

House Muzkaar had not expected her furious attack, and Makeda had stacked their corpses deep as a result. Tyrant Naram's army had been confident of their victory, but Makeda had struck so hard and so fast that House Muzkaar had been thrown into disarray. A wild charge by her swordsmen and karax had bloodied Muzkaar. They'd pushed back, but it had been disorganized, panicked, and it was only through their vastly superior numbers that Muzkaar had survived at all. She'd drawn most of her melee troops away, letting her karax set up a defensive line, allowing her Venators time to bleed the enemy. The proud swordsmen were eager to return to glory, but she ordered them to be patient. Let Muzkaar think they'd been used up . . .

As the sun had climbed and the hot morning had turned into blistering afternoon, House Muzkaar had counterattacked, and though it had been sloppy and hurried, Makeda was drastically outnumbered. She could not win a war of attrition against a Tyrant with a stable worth of titans.

Despite heavy casualties, the line of Praetorian karax was standing firm. They stood shoulder to shoulder, a wall of steel and wood, shields absorbing blows and their pikes thrusting continuously, spilling Muzkaar blood. The karax were methodical, plodding forward, always stabbing.

The code of hoksune taught that the purest combat was

individual, warrior on warrior. She could see now why it was so much more difficult for a member of the karax to gain exaltation than a swordsman. This was not the battle she knew, the calculation of offense and defense, and the sudden flash of a sword . . . this was mechanical. This was more like watching the lower castes harvest grain from the fields. The karax would stab, block, stab, block, and whenever Barkal saw an opening he would order an advance through the bloodstained plains, and then, as one, they would begin their harvest again. It was hypnotic to watch.

Zabalam was waiting for her at the ridge overlooking their remaining karax. His taberna of elite Praetorian swordsman were ready there, crouched in the tall golden grass, hidden, as per her orders, until the time was right.

"Second Born Makeda." Zabalam bowed.

"A fine afternoon for war, Primus," Makeda greeted him respectfully. Though she outranked him by birth and command, Zabalam had been her primary instructor in the art of the two swords. Truly, he was a credit to their house. She thanked the ancestors that her father had seen fit to send Zabalam with her cohort. "How goes it here?"

"The swordsmen chafe at being told to hide in the grass like mere Hestatians."

"They are elite warriors, proud . . ." Makeda noted. "It is understandable."

"They will do as they are told . . . I do not think your brother will relieve us in time."

"Akkad will come." Makeda had her doubts, but she did not speak them aloud.

"The karax have fought past the point of exhaustion. They will fall soon, and when they do, we will be overrun by these wretched Muzkaar *belek*."

"Good." A belek was a thick-skulled herd animal, strong but notorious for blundering stupidly into wallows and getting stuck. Makeda did not think Zabalam realized what a fitting insult that was.

"Good?" Since Zabalam's face had been split nearly in half with a sword many years before, only half of his mouth moved when he frowned. The other side was permanently frozen in a straight line. "I'm unsure how that is a good thing?"

"We cannot outlast a force this size. Our only hope to defeat them is by killing their Tyrant. Without Naram, Muzkaar will quickly fall. What do you know of Naram?"

"He is renowned for his skill, but your grandfather defeated him once and took many slaves from one of his cities."

"Yes. It is said he retains a rather passionate hatred of House Balaash, and he is still a warrior without peer. My ancestor shamed him, so he will come for revenge. He knows I am here, so Naram will want to give the killing blow himself."

"Or maybe he will capture you and turn you over to his Paingivers."

Makeda shrugged. "Either way, Naram is coming, and when he does, I will kill him first."

"You remind me of your grandfather sometimes . . . But what of the karax?"

"Hopefully Akkad's reinforcements will have an extoller with them." Only a member of the extoller caste or the much rarer ancestral guardians could save a warrior's spiritual essence in a sacral stone so they could live on as a revered companion to the exalted. "Look at how many they have slaughtered. Surely some of them will be worth saving."

"And if Akkad has none of their caste amongst his reinforcements?"

She thought it over for a moment. Though no extoller had arrived, the warriors below did not know that, so she signaled for a message runner. "Tell Dakar Barkal that I am personally observing the battle, watching for any who are worthy of exaltation. Tell him to spread the word to his troops." The messenger did not seem disturbed in the least that he was to relay something which would raise an impossible hope. He merely bowed and ran down the hill. Makeda turned back to Zabalam. "That will make them fight that much harder."

Zabalam's half face twisted up in the other direction. "You *definitely* remind me of your grandfather."

The temperature continued to climb as the sun beat down on her armor. Droplets of sweat rolled freely from under her helmet and into her eyes. Makeda welcomed the sting. The cries of the dead and dying were all around her. The cohort of House Muzkaar seemed to be an endless thing stretching across the plains. She passed the time mentally steering her cyclopes toward the weakest points of the Balaash lines. She stood there, her back banner whipping in the wind. Makeda wanted all of the enemy army to see her, defiant. Let them tell their Tyrant that a scion of House Balaash was waiting for him.

Makeda felt the pang of loss as the cyclops that had been injured earlier was dragged down and killed. She drained the last bits of vitality that had been dwelling in the cyclops tissues and gathered that strength to herself. She would need it shortly.

The line of karax faltered, broke, and were swept away before the swords of House Muzkaar. Their center had fallen.

A trumpet blew, and then another. A black banner was raised on the other side of the road and waved back and forth. The entire Muzkaar host seemed to hesitate, then their lines parted as a small escort of warriors and beasts advanced through the army.

"That is a lot of titans . . ." Zabalam muttered.

There were only two of the great grey beasts lumbering along behind Naram's personal banner, but one titan was a lot of titan.

"On my signal, rally your men and charge that banner. All that matters is that Naram dies. I shall use my power to give you speed," she ordered. Zabalam conveyed that order to his swordsmen who were waiting in cover. She mentally summoned her remaining cyclops closer. "Runner." Another messenger appeared at her side. "Tell Urkesh that when I draw my swords, his Venators must clear for me a path to that banner."

The knot of Muzkaar elite had advanced to the front of the army. The squat, powerfully built skorne in the lead had to be Naram. With a mighty spiked club resting on one shoulder, and his black armor gleaming in the sun, Naram appeared a formidable foe. She could sense his mortitheurge power, churning and hungry.

"I remember when you were teaching me the way of the two swords, Primus . . ." Makeda said.

"You were my finest student."

"I recall now one lesson in particular. Show your enemy one sword, and when they are focused upon that, kill them with the other. I am the first sword . . . Await my signal."

Makeda walked down the hill to where Naram and his army were waiting. She ran her hands across the tops of the thick grass. It was sharp enough to draw blood. The fury taken from her beasts was like a hot lump of power within her chest. She stepped through puddles of blood, and over the mangled bodies of her warriors.

Naram was striding toward her, with a great wall of titan muscle on each side. "Makeda of House Balaash!" he challenged. The two beasts were obviously well controlled, as they took a few extra steps forward to shield their master.

She stopped just within range of his voice. "Tyrant Naram." She placed her hands on the hilts of her sheathed swords. Part of her grandfather was within those swords. She would never let them fall into the hands of someone so unworthy. "It has been a fine battle so far. Have you come to surrender personally?"

The enemy Tyrant gave a hearty laugh. "I must admit, your tenacity impresses me. It has been a generation since I've seen someone so outnumbered account for themselves so well." He had to shout to be heard over the hot wind. "Order your remaining warriors to lay down their arms. Swear fealty to me, and you may retain your caste. There is room in House Muzkaar for such as you. A political marriage will be arranged to one of my sons. Your father will have to withdraw from Kalos, but this will be best for both our houses." Naram waved his free hand dismissively. "Or you can fight, and once you are defeated and shamed, you can join your men as slaves to my house. Choose quickly."

Naram's words, though certainly filled with truth, did not sway her. He did not understand just how powerful Makeda's mortitheurgy really was . . . Few among their people could. Their dark magic took decades of devotion to master, but no one was more devoted than a child of House Balaash. She closed her eyes and felt the world around her. Living tissue and pumping blood . . . She could sense Naram and his army before her, and then her few remaining warriors behind, each and every one of them reduced to their component bits of muscle, bone, and sinew, cloaked in steel and laminate armor, powered by blood and spirit, all of it there waiting to be manipulated by her superior will. Gathering up the energy she'd gleaned from her fallen beast, she awoke the power residing within Zabalam's waiting Praetorian swordsmen . . . In her mind's eye, their blood turned to molten, pulsing fire.

She opened her eyes. Zabalam's standard bearer rose from the grass and waved the flag of the Praetorian swordsmen. They leapt from their hiding place and moved with impossible speed. Makeda drew the twin swords and charged.

"So be it," Naram stated. His titans both took another great step forward, completely shielding him from view.

Urkesh had received her message, and his Venators fired. Makeda heard the high-pitched screech before she felt the passage through the air all around her, buzzing through the tops of the grass like angry bees. Razor needles exploded into the titans, and then Makeda was within the rain of blood.

The titan's leg was as big around as a tree, and the first sword of Balaash cleaved a chunk of meat sufficient for a feast from its thigh. She sidestepped as a massive gauntlet was swung past. Makeda was faster than any mortal had a right to be, and then she was behind the first titan. The second studied her, giant head tilting to the side in confusion, tiny black eyes blinking, before Naram drove it toward her like a great, flesh-covered weapon.

A hand, palm as big as Makeda's torso, reached for her, hoping to crush the life from her, but Makeda lashed out, the supernatural edge barely slowed, and the titan's thumb went flipping off into the grass. Makeda dove and rolled, armor clanking, and she came up behind the second titan before it could even begin to bellow in pain.

Naram was in front of her, surprised, but already invoking his own mortitheurgy.

But then they were surrounded in swordsmen, and most of them were not his.

The fight was brutal. It was a swirling mass of chaos as swordsmen clashed beneath the thunder of titan feet. She beheaded a Muzkaar swordsman that crossed her path. Naram crushed the skull of a Balaash warrior with his club. The two leaders met in the middle of the melee, and Makeda knew that this was the perfect moment spoken of in the code of hoksune.

Her blades met the spiked club. Naram was incredibly strong, surely driven by his own magic. She had to cross her swords and use both to block at once. The impact would have broken a normal blade, but the Swords of Balaash were anything but normal. Naram shoved her back, and Makeda moved gracefully away, ducking beneath a wild swing from a Muzkaar guard. She returned the favor by removing that swordsman's face.

As his essence fled, Makeda could feel herself growing stronger. *Let this dance continue forever, for surely, this is exaltation.* She had never felt so good.

The nearest titan picked up one of her swordsmen in two vast hands and pulled the screaming warrior in half. Then another barrage of reiver fire put out the titan's eyes. Makeda's remaining cyclops was chopping away at the other titan.

The Tyrant swung at her, but she was able to skip aside. Naram's mortitheurgy surged outward in a wave of force and swordsmen, both black and red clad, were knocked down. Makeda felt the hot energy pass over her, but she resisted it by sheer force of will, and leapt right back into the fray.

Naram looked down in surprise as the tip of a sword burst from his abdomen. He swung his club in a mighty back arc, and the Balaash swordsman that had struck the Tyrant from behind disappeared in spray of red. Naram grimaced and pressed one gauntlet to his stomach. The nearest titan roared in agony as Naram used his power to afflict the terrible wound onto the flesh of the beast in his stead.

Already severely injured, the titan toppled. Makeda jumped back as the beast blotted out the sun. She narrowly made it out of the way as the concussive impact blew the tall grass flat. Makeda found herself on her back. She rolled and sprang up, trying to get back into the fight, but then there was a black flash as Naram's club filled her vision.

She was falling. Turning through the air. The golden grass rushed up to meet her.

Much as Naram had a moment before, Makeda desperately called upon her power, instinctively seeking out her mental connection to her remaining warbeast. She could feel the damage, the all consuming agony, and the gasping blackness of the void, and instead of welcoming it, Makeda took all of that and shoved it off on her cyclops.

The cyclops absorbed all of the damage it could, snuffing out its life like a candle, but even then, that wasn't enough. The impact still left Makeda stunned and bleeding. The cyclops' body collapsed into the waiting arms of the Muzkaar titan, and not even realizing it was dead, the titan violently attacked the corpse, pummeling it beneath its great fists. Even disoriented, Makeda was far too practiced to let any vital life energy go to waste, and she instinctively gathered up the last of the cyclops' dying rage to fuel her magic.

The world was spinning. Makeda got to her hands and knees. All around her, the Balaash swordsmen were falling. Muzkaar soldiers were swarming in from every direction. Naram was walking toward her, spiked club dripping red.

Before he had died, Archdominar Vaactash had taught Makeda everything he knew about the thin line between life and death. Her people were a stubborn, hardy lot, and they did not give up their mortal shells easily. She was surrounded by the bodies of dead and dying members of House Balaash, but House Balaash still had need of their services. Makeda drew upon the well of power within her own blood. It was the greatest feat she had ever attempted, far beyond what she should have been able to accomplish as a novice mortitheurge.

She was a scion of House Balaash, granddaughter of the greatest warrior the world had ever known, and daughter of Archdominar Telkesh . . . Makeda did not comprehend defeat.

"You are not done yet. Rise and fight for House Balaash!"

Her power spun outward, blowing the tall grass almost as if another titan had fallen. Naram froze as he sensed the sudden shift in the battlefield. The wind died and the air hung unnaturally still. "What have you done?" the Tyrant of Muzkaar demanded.

And then the fallen soldiers of House Balaash stood up and returned to the fight.

"What have you done!" Blades pierced Naram's armor. His remaining titan bellowed and died, and then there were no beasts left for him to shift his wounds to. Hearts stopped, eyes blank, bodies broken, the spirits of the soldiers of House Balaash pushed onward. A sword took a piece of Naram's arm, another pierced his leg, and a third knocked his helmet off. "What have you done!" He clubbed them down, shattering limbs left and right.

Makeda was on her feet, striding forward, both swords raised. She called upon all the fury left inside and used it to give strength to her arms. Bleeding, barely standing, Naram turned to meet her . . .

But it was too late.

They were eye to eye. Naram's gaze slowly lowered toward his chest. Both of the Swords of Balaash had been driven cleanly through armor and between his ribs. Two separate shafts of red steel protruded from his back. The heavy club fell from nerveless fingers.

The army of House Muzkaar was frozen, staring at their Tyrant in shocked disbelief. They slowly lowered their weapons to their sides. The battlefield was strangely silent as the fallen swordsmen of Balaash sank back to the ground, their obligations fulfilled. Only a handful of Zabalam's swordsmen had survived, and all of them were painted red, panting, and exhausted.

"You are victorious?" Naram whispered.

Makeda nodded. "Yes." She could feel the strength leaving Naram's body. He was only still standing because he was leaning against her. Makeda knew the instant she removed her swords, Naram would perish. She slowly lowered him to the grass.

"Heh . . . Today was a good day. Best battle . . . in a very long time . . ." He trailed off, and Makeda could no longer hear his words. His eyes were wide, but not with fear. She pressed her ear in close. Makeda could feel his dying breath on her skin.

"The code shows me the way to exaltation. Only through combat may one understand the way." Naram gasped. "Suffering cleanses the weakness from my being . . . Adhere to the code . . . and I will become . . ."

"*Worthy*," she finished the verse.

What is it that you whisper to yourself, child, when the pain becomes too much?

This was a great and worthy leader of skorne. This one did not deserve to be lost in the Void. Makeda looked to the nearest Muzkaar soldier. "Do you have extollers amongst you?" The swordsman nodded quickly. "Summon one. Now."

They did not look the part of a victorious force as they marched along the road northward. There was no parade of slaves, no baggage train of looted treasure, no trophy heads raised on poles. No, Makeda thought to herself, they looked more like the losers. Only one third of her warriors had survived, and many of them were injured. They limped down the road, reeking of death, and covered in dried blood and bandages. They had no warbeasts. They'd been forced to leave their dead behind without ceremony. Their weapons and armor, much of it broken, was piled upon a wagon.

Yet, her single decurium had somehow defeated the combined might of a great house cohort.

This was not a pure victory however. Normally when a Tyrant is thrown down and a house conquered, then that house would be absorbed by the victors. That had not been an option here. Makeda was both relieved and bitter about the results. The Muzkaar army had them completely surrounded, and her ragged survivors would not have stood a chance. Akkad and his reinforcements had never arrived, because if they had, then all of House Muzkaar would have been in chains . . .

Instead, she had received a message from Naram's heir. It had simply read, *As you have spared the essence of my father, I will spare you.*

The sun was bloated and red as it set over the golden plains. Only two of her officers had lived through the battle. Dakar Urkesh, who stank of the caustic gasses used to drive his reivers, and the seemingly unkillable Primus Zabalam marched beside her. Dakar Barkal had perished, as had the vast majority of his karax.

"Tell me, Zabalam . . ." It was a sign of weakness, but she struggled to keep the weariness from her voice. "This was the first battle I have commanded. Does victory always taste so bitter?"

"Sometimes . . ." His ruined face was expressionless. "This was a great victory. Glory will be positively heaped upon your name when word gets back to our house."

She was unsure if Zabalam was capable of sarcasm. "Do you mock me, Primus?"

"I am incapable of mockery. If you believe I do so, say the word and I will cut out my own heart and hand it to you by way of apology." He looked her in the eye. "The bitterness is only because you were denied your rightful spoils."

"We should have crushed all of Muzkaar and looted Kalos, if only Akkad had brought his cohort like he was supposed to," Urkesh spat.

"That is what troubles me," Zabalam said.

An entire army had not troubled Zabalam earlier, why would the lack of one? "What disturbs you, Primus?"

"Just a feeling. Forgive an old swordsman for his nerves." Zabalam looked at the ground, not wanting to meet her gaze. "I am sure it is nothing."

"Where was One Ear anyway?" Urkesh muttered.

Makeda instantly backhanded the Venator in the mouth. The steel of her gauntlet split his lip. Urkesh crashed into the dirt, and before he could even begin to sit up, the tip of her blade was pressed against his throat. She twisted the hilt slightly, letting the edge of the sword of Balaash rest against the artery. Makeda could feel his pulse through the steel. All she had to do was relax a muscle and he would die.

Urkesh averted his eyes and did not speak. It was the not speaking that saved his life.

"Heed my words, Urkesh," Makeda hissed. "You killed many today. Your *taberna* was essential to achieve victory. You may prove useful for me again. For that reason, and that reason alone, I will spare your life. However, you will never speak ill of anyone above your caste again, or I will have the paingivers flay you. Do you understand?"

"Yes, Second Born."

"You do not truly understand hoksune. You kill from a distance. You have not looked into another warrior's eyes as they drown in their own blood. Hoksune is not real to you as it is to Akkad, who has felt a thousand deaths at his hands. Lay there in shame and think upon your transgression." She sheathed the sword in one quick motion and walked away. "Come with me, Zabalam."

The old Praetorian left the young Venator in the road and followed his commander. "What would you have of me?"

Makeda did not need deference, she needed honesty. "I have no patience for speaking around the truth. You know that. I never have."

Zabalam nodded. "Which is exactly why I asked to be assigned to your cohort rather than your brother's."

"So speak plainly and tell me what is on your mind, elder teacher."

"Our lack of reinforcements was suspicious. We should be dead." Zabalam took his time, choosing his words carefully. "Akkad has always desired glory. Abandoning you in a battle is as sure a murder as a knife in the back, and it is not unheard of for siblings to murder each other in order to rule a house."

Makeda shook her head. "But Akkad is the eldest. He is already Telkesh's heir. Ancient tradition declares that the eldest must rule." Despite any of her personal opinions about her brother, she would never go against the traditions of her caste, for to do otherwise would cause chaos and weaken their house. "The order of succession has been decreed. Telkesh rules and has declared it so. If I believed him unfit to lead, then I would declare a challenge. Anything else would be dishonorable."

"Ah, Makeda, but not everyone shares your devotion. They do not follow the old ways so closely. They merely talk of it while having no real devotion in their hearts. They assume all are like them. So they whisper and talk. They are not like us. They lurk in the shadows and play politics with their birthright." Zabalam spit on the ground. "Their words are like poison, and it would not surprise me if one such as that would whisper to your brother that you are a threat to his eventual rule."

There had to be another explanation. She knew that Akkad was extremely ambitious, and he was a fine warrior. She had no doubt he would made a decent archdominar when the time came. Violating the wishes of their father Telkesh was simply unimaginable, and she did not know which idea she found more disturbing: that her brother would leave her to die, or that anyone would doubt her honor so much.

"Incoming riders!" the shout went up along the column. "They fly the colors of Balaash."

Scouts for the army. They would be reunited soon enough. "Do not worry, Zabalam. I will speak to my father about today's events. I'm sure there is an explanation for Akkad's delay."

"As you wish." The Primus bowed.

She could see the cavalry now. The scouts tore down the road, heading straight for Makeda's tattered banner. The first rider came right up to Makeda, riding upon a ferox, one of the swiftest predators of the plains. The messenger wore the insignia of a dakar, and her mount foamed from the journey. The creature snarled at Makeda, so the rider punched it in the back of the head. It wheeled about and snapped at her legs with is long razor teeth, but she simply struck it again harder. Dominance established, that finally settled it down.

"Second Born Makeda," the messenger dipped her helmet. It was as close as could be approximated to a bow while on the back of an enraged ferox. "You are alive?"

"Obviously," she answered. "Where is the army?"

"Encamped a few miles to the north," the rider seemed rattled. "We were told your cohort had been destroyed by Tyrant Naram."

"He tried. It was an excellent battle, but Naram was the one who was destroyed. Who told you such lies?"

"Forgive me. It was all over the camp. Ancestors! You have not heard?"

"Spit it out, Praetorian!"

The rider was obviously terrified. Her mount sensed the unusual fear, and turned back curious and sniffing. "Your father—Archdominar Telkesh is dead."

The ferox was unbelievably swift. The powerfully muscled beast moved in great leaping bounds, its talons ripping up tufts of grass and dirt as they moved across the plains. A sudden plunge down a ravine forced Makeda to place one hand against the reptilian skin before her saddle. It was softer than expected. The ferox turned one curious eye back toward her. Perhaps, if it had been any other unfamiliar rider, the vicious thing may have attempted something, but it could sense the danger in Makeda, and simply did as it was told.

Her mount jumped high into the air, taking them over the edge of the ravine and into the open dusk. A large encampment stretched before them, hundreds of tents, all flying the proud banner of House Balaash. Housing thousands of soldiers, thousands of slaves, and dozens of beasts, it was more of a mobile city than an encampment. Makeda roughly kneed the ferox in the ribs, pointing it toward the nearest set of lanterns.

The guards rose immediately to challenge her approach. Just because she was flying the banner of Balaash did not necessarily make her an ally, especially here in Muzkaar land.

"Who goes there?"

"Makeda, Second Born of Telkesh."

The nearest guard shifted the grip on his spear. "Makeda is dead."

Makeda reached up and removed her helmet as the ferox padded closer to the lantern light. The sudden wind felt cool on her scalp. "Silence, imbecile. Take me to my father."

The guards were stunned. "She lives!" One of the soldiers, probably unfamiliar with the violent nature of the ferox, nearly lost a hand when he tried to gesture a direction. The beast snapped at him, and the daggerlike teeth missed his wrist by less than an inch.

A smarter guard pointed with his spear. "Forgive us. The archdominar's tent is over there."

Makeda looked at the tent. That was not her father's tent. That was Akkad's tent. There was a sudden pain in her heart, an altogether unfamiliar feeling. "Ha!" She kicked the ferox hard. It reached Akkad's tent within three bounds. Makeda slid off of the saddle and walked quickly inside. These soldiers recognized her and immediately bowed and moved out of her way.

Despite being a huge affair which needed several of its own pack animals to move anywhere, the inside of Akkad's tent was crowded with warriors of rank and lineage. Makeda recognized many of her father's advisors and officers. They all wore solemn expressions which turned to shock when they saw her. Whispers radiated outward as all eyes turned to see.

"Where is my father?" Makeda demanded, but already knowing the answer.

Heads were bowed. Feet were studied. A scribe hurried to the rear of the tent and disappeared beneath a flap into the sleeping quarters.

Abaish was the first to speak. He was of the paingiver caste, but was one of father's closest advisors. Only his narrow chin was visible beneath the traditional mask worn by all paingivers. "Forgive our surprise, Tyrant Makeda. We were told that your cohort had perished in battle today."

"Not today. Perhaps next time. Now where is my father?"

Abaish shook his head with exaggerated sorrow. "I am afraid mighty Telkesh is dead."

Makeda's knees turned to water. She tried not to let her emotions show. Telkesh had not been archdominar for long. Vaactash had only been dead a year. This was inconceivable. "How?"

"A sudden illness," said one of the Cataphract. "He was overcome with fever."

It seemed impossible, a skilled mortitheurge, a house leader with mastery over energies which controlled the flesh or could withstand death, to be taken by a simple fever.

"The chirurgeons could not find a cure in time," Abaish added apologetically. "For that failure, Akkad had them executed."

It was as if saying his name had summoned him, but it had more than likely been the scribe because the same flap opened and Akkad entered. Tall, broad and powerful of build, his features were sharp and strong, his eyes narrow and intelligent. When the artisan caste attempted to capture skorne perfection in a work of sculpture, it usually looked something like Akkad, except of course, for the one ruined stump of an ear.

He surveyed the room expectantly. All of the assembled officers and functionaries went to one knee and dipped their heads. The act should not have surprised her. Akkad was after all, now the archdominar of House Balaash.

"Sister," Akkad seemed as surprised to see her alive as she had been to find out their father was dead. However, he was better at concealing his emotions than she was. The paingiver Abaish rose from his knees and placed himself at Akkad's right hand. Akkad's smile seemed forced. "It is good to see you. My scouts had told me that your cohort had been surrounded and wiped out on the plains. It is good to see you escaped Naram."

"I did not escape Tyrant Naram, I killed him." The tent was suddenly filled with excited whispers, some more incredulous than others. She could not hear the words, but she could imagine them. *How did this inexperienced girl defeat the great Naram?* She would deal with them later. Yet many of the warrior caste seemed rather pleased. This news seemed to upset Akkad, but she could not dwell on that. "Please, Brother, tell me of Father."

"Yes. Poor Father. He fell ill during our march. Mighty Telkesh brought low by a disease only yesterday. I rushed to his side as soon as I heard. I was with him as he was consumed by fever."

"A tragedy." Abaish agreed.

"Indeed. He was in terrible pain, robbed of all his dignity. A death that was in no way fitting—"

"Wait!" Makeda could not help herself. She looked toward the council extoller. They were all watching her. All of their highly specialized caste ceremonially plucked out one of their mortal eyes and replaced it with a crystal that allowed them to see into the spirit realm. Her reflection was visible in the extoller's crystal oculus. "He did not die in battle . . . Are you saying his essence was not preserved?"

The extoller shook his head sadly.

Makeda gasped. "No." Telkesh had not been given the opportunity to be proven worthy. *Her father had been consigned to the Void.*

Akkad folded his arms as he studied his council. Abaish leaned over and whispered in Akkad's good ear, and it reminded her of Primus Zabalam and his warning about those that lurked in the shadows. Akkad frowned. "Why do you not bow before your archdominar, Makeda? Do you intend to disrespect me?"

Makeda was shaken from her thoughts by the accusation. "Why—"

"You are not kneeling. Why do you disrespect House Balaash by failing to honor your archdominar?"

And in that moment, Makeda knew . . .

Akkad had known Father was dying this morning. He had abandoned her entire cohort, knowing that Naram would kill them.

She could see the truth in the faces of many of the warriors in the room. They had figured it out as well.

"Kneel," Akkad commanded.

Her brother had consigned her to death. *Why?* Did he truly consider her a threat to his rule? Her mind was still fatigued from combat. Many of the warriors were staring at her expectantly. She could feel anger boiling up within her, yet the traditions of their caste were clear on this matter. It was the responsibility of the eldest to rule. Makeda forced the anger back, then went to one knee and lowered her head. "I am sorry . . . Archdominar."

Akkad had no idea that her sense of honor had just saved his life.

❖ PART TWO ❖

THE HALL OF ANCESTORS was a sacred place, and the only sound was their footfalls upon the stone. At this late hour the stonemasons of the worker caste were gone and only a few extollers scurried about in the shadows. Archdominar Vaactash lit their way with a single lantern. The pale light illuminated row upon row of statues as they passed. Makeda thought that the Ancestral Guardians towered over her, much as her grandfather did.

"Do not shrink before them, child. These are your exalted ancestors and their revered companions. They lived for House Balaash. We are the culmination of their great works," Vaactash said softly. "Each one of them has a story."

"Yes. Father ordered the servants to give us summaries," Makeda answered.

"And of course, when the summaries were not enough, you read everything in the library . . ." It was not a question.

Makeda was suddenly nervous. Was that why she had been summoned to the Hall? In a society based upon strength and born into a caste bred for war, scholarly pursuits were frowned upon. Time spent on lesser arts could easily have been spent on more important things. Yet one did not disagree with the archdominar. Akkad's missing half ear was a constant reminder of that fact. "Yes, Grandfather. I have read the histories. In truth, I find them . . ." she trailed off.

Vaactash paused. The lantern cast deep shadows around his gaunt features, his eyes nothing more than white dots in a black pit. "Finish your words."

"I have read all of the histories of my ancestors, and I am *inspired* by them."

"How?"

"I wish to emulate their successes . . ." She glanced at the statues. Inside each of them was a sacral stone, and within each of those stones rested the spiritual essence of a hero, fallen for the honor of House Balaash. She did not wish to give offense, but the truth was required. ". . . yet avoid their mistakes."

Vaactash nodded once, his expression unreadable. "This answer is acceptable." Then the light turned away and the old warrior continued on his way down the hall. Despite an ancient injury that had left Vaactash with a severe limp, Makeda had to hurry to keep up with her much shorter legs.

A moment later they came to the center of the Hall. Vaactash stopped before the largest statue of all. He turned back to her, the lantern again casting odd shadows on his features. "Do you know why this statue is special?"

Makeda nodded. "It is because there is not yet an essence stored within it." The stoneworkers had been toiling away on this project for years, for what seemed like most of her short life. It was the finest example of the artisan caste's craft in the entire Hall. It was a stylized rendition of her grandfather, only a much younger version, a version which she had never seen herself, and frankly had a difficult time imagining. "This is to be your exalted resting place, Grandfather."

Vaactash turned back to the statue and stared at it for a very long time. Makeda stood silently, still not knowing why she had been summoned in the middle of the night. "We are still so devout in our worship . . ." Vaactash spoke slowly, choosing each word carefully, "for a people who have no gods."

Makeda knew what the ancestral teachings said about the subject. "The skorne do not need gods. Through hardship we forged our own path. Only the weak need gods."

"So it is written . . . Where there was only a wasteland, we built our world. We forced crops from the sand, subjugated the beasts of the plains, and taught ourselves the power that dwells within blood and pain." The greatest living warrior remained fixated on his great statue. "And what happens to those of us who die without achieving exaltation?"

Was she being tested? "There is only the Void." It was a place of black infinity, a boundless eternal suffering that even the most creative of paingivers could never hope to emulate. Except for the exalted few or their revered companions, all skorne were destined for eternal torment.

"Long ago, there was no exaltation . . . All of us were consigned to the Void. It was only through the wisdom of Voskune, Ishoul, and Kaleed that we learned the way to preserve our essence. Rather than being cast into the Void, our spirits could be kept safe in a sacred stone. Our wisdom could be saved to be shared with our descendants, and in times of dire need, our honored ancestors could even return to fight for their house."

"It is a great blessing," Makeda agreed.

"Yet, even after the revelation, so very few could be saved.

Choices had to be made. Who would live on and who would be cast into the eternal death? There must be order. It was Dominar Vuxoris who would become the First Exalted. It was his teachings which would become hoksune, the code which governs the conduct of all warriors. Thus it was declared that only through adherence to the tenets of hoksune could we prove our worthiness. Only the greatest of warriors can earn exaltation. For everyone else, there is the Void."

"But, Grandfather, you have earned your place amongst our ancestors. In time, Father Telkesh will as well. I will do the same."

"When I'd heard you were neglecting your mortitheurgy in order to read the histories, I was angered—Balaash blood is not thin scholar's blood—but I can see now that there was no need. There is a place for such knowledge amongst the warrior caste."

It was a tremendous relief to finally know why she had been summoned, and even better to know that she had passed the archdominar's test. "My ancestors will guide me as I defeat the enemies of our house."

"And there must always be enemies . . . I do not think you yet understand the true burden of the warrior caste. You are old enough now. I will tell you a story." Vaactash leaned against his statue, taking the weight off of his crippled leg. It was a rare show of weakness from the aging archdominar. "Two generations ago, I visited the islands south of Kademe. That was the first time I have seen the sea. It is far bigger than Mirketh Lake. It seemed to stretch further than the eye could see, further even than the wastes."

That much water sounded inconceivable, but Makeda did not dare question the archdominar's truthfulness. She preferred her ears properly shaped and pointy, not mangled into scar tissue.

"There are mighty predators that live beneath the sea. Those that fished those deep waters spoke of a fearsome beast that would eat anything in its path, so I sought out one of the local beast handlers to learn more."

Makeda nodded. Of course, anyone skilled in the art of mortitheurgy would be interested in a fascinating new beast. Those that could be broken could be useful weapons or tools, and those that could not still provided useful lessons in anatomy.

"The beast handlers told me much about this mighty fish. It had more teeth than a ferox, and was the ultimate killer in its realm. It could sense the spilling of blood, even from miles away, and never hesitated to destroy the weak."

"It sounds wonderful."

"Indeed. Yet that was not what fascinated me the most. You see, this sea beast must constantly be in motion, hunting, seeking prey, or it will *die*. It cannot be restrained. It cannot stop, for to stop moving is to perish. It was not its might, or its savagery that impressed me. No . . . It was this constant need of struggle that reminded me so much of the warrior caste."

Makeda was perplexed. "I do not understand, Grandfather."

"Like the sea predator must perpetually hunt, so we must perpetually have strife. We are instruments of war. Only through war can we achieve exaltation. If that opportunity is removed, then we cease to be skorne."

"The houses would never stop fighting! That would be madness."

Vaactash chuckled. "Perhaps . . . Perhaps I am just an old warrior in his waning days and my mind tends to wander toward abstract thoughts. You have learned of *how* our ancestors fought, but now you must truly understand *why*." His voice grew dangerously low. "Only through conflict can we become pure, and only the pure can be exalted. This is why we fight. This is why we always *must* fight. Strife is our only opportunity to avoid being cast into the Void. Our entire society is based upon this."

Makeda bowed, thankful for the wisdom which had just been shared.

"Do you know what the foulest, most evil idea in the world is, Makeda?"

She shook her head. She had never heard her grandfather speak like this before.

"Peace." Vaactash spat the word out, as if it tasted foul on his tongue.

She knew the word, but peace was a difficult, abstract concept to her. "That is not our way."

"Correct, but it is a tempting one. I know you do not understand this now, but you may when you are older. Those of the lower castes can seldom achieve exaltation, so the ideal appeals to many of them. Sometimes, the idea of *peace* may even corrupt some of our own caste."

"I cannot conceive of this."

"Of course there are times when a house is not making war. There are consolations after conquest, or when a house bides its time waiting for a better opportunity to strike, and during those such, there is a lack of conflict, but it is certainly not *peace*. No. There is always another rising power, or a strong leader who becomes weak and must be cast down, or even the old being toppled by the young. You see, our caste must have something to strive against. It betters us. It completes us. Strife must be embraced."

He had never spoken so freely before, and Makeda tried her best to absorb her grandfather's wisdom.

"For every house I have imposed my dominion upon, I must constantly prove my worth, or I will be replaced by someone better. Ultimately, it is possible for a mighty enough conqueror to unite all of our caste beneath one banner. Even then, there would be strife among our caste, for we are like the great sea beast, and to cease striving is to perish."

"I understand, Grandfather."

"Do you, Makeda? Fools often mistake this tempting concept of peace with the similar concept of surrender. They would live without strife. There are many who feel as if being born into the warrior caste should be enough to earn exaltation. They would see an end to war so they could grow fat and soft, and yet still somehow escape the Void. So few of us can be exalted, it is vital that only the greatest achieve this."

"That is what the code dictates. It would not be right for anyone to achieve exaltation without sufficient struggle!" The blasphemous idea shocked Makeda and filled her with anger. "Why, then the weak would be saved while superior warriors would be cast into the Void!"

"Indeed. You must ponder on these things." Vaactash regarded her solemnly. "A warrior's thoughts must remain open to ideas beyond what they have been taught. Akkad is cunning, and his mind is quick, but it is dangerous to entertain new ideas without governing them against principles of honor. If only I could combine your adherence to hoksune with your brother's ambitious pragmatism, then House Balaash would be unstoppable. The mind reels at the possibilities."

"I will serve House Balaash, as the code dictates, and when he is archdominar, I will serve Akkad. I promise."

"A warrior does not need to promise, Makeda. The mere act of saying a thing will be done means that it will. To our caste, the act of saying and doing are the same. I have no doubt as to your loyalty to our house, and for that, I am glad that you were Second Born." Vaactash smiled. It was a rare expression. "Enough of an old warrior's ramblings. That will be all." He turned and went back to admiring his soon-to-be tomb. "You are dismissed."

"You are dismissed."

Makeda bowed low. "Yes, Archdominar Akkad."

She stood. Only a few of the warriors assembled in the great tent met her gaze, and those were warriors that she had trained with or who had served under her grandfather. There were far too many new faces already amongst the leaders of House Balaash. Makeda turned and walked quickly for the flap. More than anything, she wanted to be outside, away from the whispering nest of razor worms. Her brother seemed pleased at the show of subservience, but Makeda noted that Abaish of the paingivers was already whispering secrets into his ear before she had even made it outside.

The night was cool. Makeda took a deep breath and savored being alive.

Grandfather, what would you have me do?

The surviving remnants of her own decurium had not yet arrived. It would take them hours to catch up to the nimble ferox that had carried her here. Despite their great victory, she already knew there would be no conquerors' welcome for them. They had been a sacrifice sufficient to avoid suspicion, for why would an archdominar throw away troops? Surely, Akkad had meant for her and her token army to die on the plains, killed by Muzkaar hands and not of his treachery.

Her body still ached from the day's battle. Though she had been able to stave off serious injury by shoving it off to her cyclops, the pain remained. Makeda remembered her training and welcomed the pain. Morkaash, the first of the paingivers, had learned that suffering could lead to enlightenment. She accepted this truth. Once pain was understood, even welcomed, it could provide clarity of thought.

And Makeda needed clarity right then.

The night was far too quiet. The encampment was too somber. With thousands of warriors present, it was unnaturally still. The sudden, dishonorable death of Telkesh hung like a fog over the warriors. The only noise came from the nearby pens, as the enslaved warbeasts shuffled and grunted and fed. This encampment had been set up while she had been marching to her intended execution, so it took her a few minutes to find the tent of Telkesh. The archdominar's banners were missing, surely taken down sent to adorn Akkad's own. Telkesh's tent was dark.

A few of her father's long-time slaves were still there, kneeling in the sand, wailing and gnashing their teeth at the loss of their master. Makeda stepped around their prostrate forms. There was a great pile of ash where they had burned Telkesh and a few of his servants in a mighty funeral pyre.

"It is already done?" Makeda whispered.

One of the slaves looked up at the sound of her voice. He squinted in the dark. "Makeda lives?"

"It is I." She recognized the slave but had never bothered to learn the name of someone from such a low caste. "Why was my father burned so quickly?" she demanded.

The slave looked away in fear. "The new archdominar declared that the disease could spread through the camp."

Makeda gritted her teeth. This was an added insult to the memory of her ancestor. "Tell me of this mystery illness. What were the symptoms?"

"It was as sudden as lightning on the wastes. We had just broken camp and set out on the day's march when the master felt a pain in his stomach. It radiated out to his limbs and he complained of tingling and weakness. Soon, he was unable to march or even stay in a saddle. He was overcome with fever, and then madness and seizures. I was there. He twitched and jerked so much that I could not even get water past his lips."

The description reminded Makeda of something she had once read in the family histories . . . "And the chirurgeons?"

The slave pointed to a nearby pile of rocks that she had not before noticed. It was an accepted form of execution. Place the condemned beneath a board, and then slowly pile rocks upon it all day until they were eventually crushed flat. It was an agonizing and slow method of execution, and thus one of the favorites of her people. "Tormentor Abaish was displeased with their failure."

"I see. Did the chirurgeons speak with anyone before their execution? Did they speak with any of Father's retainers?"

"Besides Abaish and the new archdominar?" the slave shook his head. "A few, but all of them were given the honor of going into the fire to accompany Telkesh on his journey into the Void." He was trembling in fear. Makeda realized that she had unconsciously placed her hand on her sword as if she were about to draw it. She let go of the hilt.

"What is your name, slave?"

"Kuthsheth, personal servant of Telkesh, and Vaactash before him."

"Bring me the servants that prepared Telkesh's meal that morning."

"I'm sorry. I cannot. They too were cast into the fire."

Makeda's hands curled into fists. She remembered now exactly what she had read all of those years ago in the family histories about one particularly dishonorable ancestor, a Tyrant who had used poison to remove threats to his rule.

Murder was not unknown amongst her caste, but it was frowned upon. Being caught at it would bring shame to your house, but that did not mean that it did not happen anyway. A people that lived in a state of constant warfare had to find a balance between honor and the more pragmatic matters of house politics, but even then, a house lord deserved to die by the blade. It was possible Akkad had been impatient to assume his mantle and poisoned their father. However, Telkesh was of the warrior caste, and had already proven himself as a mighty Cataphract over and over again in Vaactash's armies. Poison was meant for sick animals and slaves who had ceased to be useful, not for house lords. Poison was a terrible, shameful way to die, and the most dishonorable way to kill.

Makeda had one final question, but it was not one that could be answered here.

"I speak out of turn, but your father will be missed." Kuthsheth said. "I was a soldier once. When Telkesh defeated my village and I was taken prisoner, I believed my life to be through, but Telkesh was an honorable master. I am consigned to whatever fate you would have of me, but I am thankful that my children will have the opportunity to rise to a higher caste in the greatest house of all—Balaash."

Telkesh had been a strict devotee of the code of hoksune. Surely, he had proven his worthiness, so why had he been robbed of his exaltation? Having no doubt that she was being watched by Akkad's spies, Makeda knelt as if she was paying her respects to the pile of ash. She kept her voice low. "Kuthsheth, I have two tasks of you. You will take word to my cohort. Seek out Primus Zabalam. Tell him my orders are to stop where they are now. They are not to enter this encampment. But first you will go now in secret and find the extoller Haradum. Tell her, and only her, that I have need of her, and that she will speak to no one about this. She must meet me . . ." Makeda needed someplace within in the camp where she would not be easily spotted or overheard. "Tell her to be at the beast pens at midnight."

The titans were nervous.

Something was in the air, and it was not just the stink of the massive warbeasts.

Makeda had wrapped herself in a cloak and was sitting in the shadows. The encampment's beast pens were a hurried affair of boards and serrated wire, in no way sufficient to hold an excited titan. But these beasts had been subjugated and broken. They would do as the barbed whips of the beast handlers demanded. The fences were mostly to keep a distracted beast from wandering too far. Titans were relatively smart animals, but they were still animals.

The titans were herbivores, and would often graze along the march, but it was too dangerous to let them graze on the open plains while in enemy territory. A titan was a considerable investment of a house's resources, so at night they were kept inside the encampments. Slaves had brought in tons of feed for the beasts, so Makeda had hidden herself between a haystack and the fence.

They did not look so dangerous without all of their armor, but Makeda knew better. In the distance, the camp's lone bronzeback scratched itself against a nearby post. The post was thick and had been set deep into the ground by slaves just for that purpose. The alpha titan's rough grey hide turned the post into splinters with in few minutes. Born in the wild, there was no such thing as a tame bronzeback, only one that was temporarily compliant because of an exhaustive regimen of carefully regulated abuse. There were paingivers watching it even now, because a single enraged bronzeback could cause unspeakable damage.

In the morning the beasts would be dressed in armor, and the pain compliance hooks would be driven into the most sensitive parts of their flesh, all in order to make them more efficient weapons and stores of mortitheurgeal energy. But for tonight, the itch finally satisfied, that particular beast lay down to sleep, surely to dream of grass and cows.

Makeda reached out and touched the great bronzeback's mind with her own. "Sleep well, great one. For tomorrow House Balaash may have need of your might."

A keening wail caused Makeda to shudder. The titans looked up from their chewing. A nearby Agonizer had begun its piteous mewling. Thankfully, it fell silent after a few moments, and the titans returned to their hay. That was lucky. Nobody wanted to listen to an Agonizer all night. She continued to scan for threats, but could see nothing. The occasional guard passed by, but she remained unseen.

Makeda had gone into Telkesh's tent and found a dark cloak. She had then slipped out the back. Hopefully, if Akkad was having her watched, then the spies would still be watching the tent. The warrior caste did not waste time mourning, but it was not unheard of to spend time meditating upon the deeds of the deceased.

However, Makeda needed to focus on the problems of the present, not dwell on the past.

Her stomach growled. Quite some time had passed since she had last eaten, but warriors were used to fasting. Makeda simply ignored it and went back to her vigil. She spotted a hunched form entering the beast area a short time later. There was a small glow coming from the other's hood, a sure sign of the extoller's crystal gaze. Haradum had arrived. Makeda had known that she would come, for it had been the elder Haradum that had taught her about the traditions of their people since Makeda had been but a small child.

The extoller caste was supposed to be separate and distinct from the politics of the houses. They were the isolated guardians of exaltation and the only ones who could communicate with the deceased. Haradum was utterly devoted to the extoller's path, and Makeda had no doubt that she could be trusted to be honest, but even then, Makeda watched for a time for any sign of a trap. When she was confident that Haradum was alone, Makeda rose.

Aptimus Haradum approached immediately. Of course she had seen Makeda hiding in the darkness. The crystal eye could discern the essence which was inside all living things. She was an ancient, alive for at least six generations, her face a mass of wrinkles and folds dangling loose over a skull. The only smooth part of Haradum was the crystal that had replaced her right eye.

"Second Born Makeda. It pleases me to no end to discover that you are still among us," the extoller wheezed. "I rejoice at this good fortune."

"Time is short, Elder." Makeda kept her voice low. Nobody would be able to hear them over the heavy breathing of the nearby titans. "I must know. Why was the spirit of Telkesh not preserved?"

Haradum did not seem moved by Makeda's intensity. "A difficult decision. It was not mine to make. Shuruppak was the extoller present at Telkesh's deathbed. I did not hear until afterward. I was busy working on my research. Did you know that beetles have a spiritual essence as well?"

Shuruppak had been raised as a warrior, and been a companion of Akkad's before deciding to pluck out his eye in order to join the extoller caste.

"Tiny, tiny, little things . . ." Haradum put her bony hands together at the wrist and quickly wiggled her fingers back and forth, like scurrying legs. "Yes. But their essence does not go to the Void, no. Are there beetle gods then, I wonder?"

Had Haradum's mind finally broken? It happened occasionally to the few among their people who managed to die of old age. "Telkesh has killed hundreds in battle. Like Vaactash before him, Telkesh was all that it means to be skorne. My father lived by the code. That cannot all be washed away by one day of fevered madness. Why would Shuruppak choose not to save him?"

The ancient extoller's mortal eye narrowed and she leaned in conspiratorially. "When a spirit is pulled, screaming, into the Void, it can tell no stories. So much knowledge is lost that way."

"Answer me, Haradum."

Haradum smiled. She had no teeth. "I just did. What stories would Telkesh have been able to tell, I wonder? Would he be able to tell of plots and lies? Would he be able to tell of conspiracies between houses? Perhaps of allegiances between castes which are supposed to remain neutral?"

"Tell me these stories, Elder."

"I would not know. I am nothing. I wish only to be left alone to continue my research. Yet, an extoller hears things . . . Yes, yes we do. It is easy sometimes to forget we are there, always watching, always judging. Telkesh judged too. He judged wisely. When presented with two paths by his advisors, he always chose the warrior's path, never the plotter's path. Perhaps those advisors tired of being denied? Maybe they decided they needed a new archdominar, someone willing to listen to their strange new ideas, one not so bound up in the traditions of old? Akkad would be such a one, yes?"

"He would," Makeda agreed. Akkad cared far more for personal glory than he did for tradition.

"These same plotters, after deciding to go so very far, would surely not risk having yet another honorable warrior of Balaash only a heartbeat away from becoming archdominar. Surely, once this honorable scion discovered the truth, she would raise an army from all of the honorable warriors of her house, and wage war against the plotters."

So there had been a conspiracy to kill Telkesh and replace him with her brother. Akkad's actions were cowardly, and depriving Telkesh of exaltation was blasphemous. "Thank you, Elder. But there will be no army raised. I will not weaken my house through civil war." Makeda placed a hand on Haradum's shoulder. She was surprised at how fragile the extoller felt beneath her robes. "Even if Akkad murdered my father . . . He is archdominar of House Balaash. The code declares that he is to rule. It is my place to serve, unless I believe he is a danger to the house, and then I must bring a formal challenge."

"We both know you are no match for Akkad in single combat. You will surely die."

"I cannot go against the traditions of my caste, Elder."

Haradum's laughter was like the rustle of dusty paper. "Child, those without honor assume that everyone is like them. There is no way he will ever accept a formal challenge to his rule. He will send assassins for you."

"How do you know this, Haradum?"

The crystal eye flickered across the beast pens. "Because they are already here."

Makeda spun in time to see the shapes running between the haystacks. There was a flash of crimson and steel and someone leapt effortlessly over a serrated fence only to disappear back into the darkness. *Bloodrunners!*

Bloodrunners were the elite killers of the paingiver caste, students of the magic released at the moment of death. Their presence confirmed the extoller's tale. "Flee, Haradum." The Swords of Balaash appeared in Makeda's hands. "Return to your beetles."

A titan startled and snorted as something brushed past one of its column-sized legs. There was movement all around them, a single careless footstep on gravel, the hiss of a dagger leaving its sheath, and then the bloodrunners attacked.

The first came seemingly out of nowhere, leading with a wickedly curved blade. Makeda deflected the attack with one sword, spun, and drove the second deep into the attacker's bowels. He gasped as she ripped the sword free, but did not cry out. She marveled at the mastery of pain, but only for a moment, because then she was fighting for her life.

A female stabbed at her throat, but Makeda ducked and slashed, cutting the bloodrunner nearly in half. They were all armed with the strange daggers, hooked and jagged, tools designed to incapacitate and torture. Makeda struck aside another attack, and then another. That bloodrunner had been a bit too slow, and a sword of Balaash removed his arm at the elbow. That one made no sound either, he merely stepped to the side, struggling to staunch the flow of blood.

The assassins were all around her, blades humming through the air. The clang of steel on steel caused the nearest titans to stir and grunt themselves awake. Those that had been eating looked up from their hay, confused and wondering if it was time for battle.

A handful of sand was thrown at her eyes, but she turned away just in time. Another kicked a cloud of straw between them, and feinted, all in an effort to distract her from another bloodrunner who was trying to stab her in the back. These assassins certainly did not follow hoksune, but Makeda relished a new challenge. She spun one sword, reversed her grip, and stabbed behind her, driving the point clean through the lightly armored torso of a bloodrunner. "Who sent you?" She sidestepped, and chopped another one to the ground. The spilled blood was fueling her strength. "Who?"

They did not answer. More of the assassins materialized from the shadows. Makeda was forced to dodge aside before she was completely surrounded. The terrain was not to her advantage. "Akkad?" A dagger clipped the edge of her armor. It stung and she felt the warmth of blood trickling out. Makeda circled around the nearest haystack. "Abaish? Who?"

Crack. There was a flash of pain as something hit her in the back. She turned to see another bloodrunner, this one was lifting a long, bone-studded whip for another swing. Makeda wheeled about, shrugging out of the cloak. *Crack.* The whip snapped through the fabric and was entangled. With a frustrated snarl, the bloodrunner shook his whip, trying to free it.

Two more attacks left Makeda with two more small cuts and two more dying bloodrunners. They were masters of anatomical precision, guiding their attacks past her armor. There were at least a dozen more assassins moving around the pens, and she would bleed to death long before she took them all. She kicked the knees out from under a bloodrunner and fell, impaling himself on his own blade. *I must escape.*

One of the slave's hayforks was hurled at her from out of the shadows. She knocked it aside, turned, and vaulted over the fence into the titan enclosure. Her boots slipped in the muck of the wallow, but she did not fall. Two bloodrunners were right behind. One dove between the wires, rolled, and came up standing. One simply leapt smoothly over the top in a rustle of cloth. She struck at them simultaneously, but they both parried with their daggers.

Agitated, the nearest titan opened its mouth and bellowed a challenge, bits of ground hay flying everywhere. Makeda had trained her entire life, learning how to master warbeasts and forcing them to obey her will, and she recognized an opportunity when it presented itself. It would take a second of concentration, but it was worth the risk. *I am your master. Obey me.*

The two bloodrunners pressed their attack as their brothers followed. The one with the whip appeared to be the leader. He was silently communicating through a series of rapid hand gestures at the bloodrunners still hidden in the shadows. An alarm horn blew as the Balaash guards overseeing the pens realized something was wrong.

Obey!

The titan blinked stupidly for a moment, but then its tiny black eyes narrowed in understanding.

Destroy.

Makeda parried another attack and kicked that bloodrunner hard in the stomach. His mouth twisted beneath his mask, but he remained focused on his mission. It only mattered for a split second though, since the titan's fist hit him so hard it left a pink cloud hanging suspended in the air.

The titan lifted itself to its full height and roared its battle cry. If the alarm horn hadn't already sounded, *that* would have certainly woken up the entire encampment. The second bloodrunner turned in surprise, so Makeda used the chance to slice his head off. It landed in the muck of the wallow at her feet, so Makeda kicked the severed head at the other remaining bloodrunners. "*Balaash*!"

The bloodrunners tried to avoid the titan, but it was too late. One had gotten caught on the barbwire of the fence, and the titan closed its hands around the assassin. This was the first one that had lost his composure and he started shouting. This seemed to annoy the titan, since it simply lifted the bloodrunner overhead and then hurled him screaming out into the night.

There were still bloodrunners everywhere, but they seemed to be fading back into the darkness, aware that their mission of a quiet assassination had failed. The titan easily stomped the fence flat and went after them. Light and shadows bounced along the fence posts nearby as the guards came running.

CRACK!

Makeda nearly blacked out as something wrapped hard around her neck. She was jerked from her feet and landed sprawled in the mud.

The one with the whip had not given up yet.

Her armor had saved her life, but bone shards had pierced her neck. The whip was pulled and the noose tightened. Makeda slid through the wet ooze. The cuts deepened, yet she was calm. *No arteries severed . . . yet.*

A quick slash of her sword cut the whip in half. The pressure ended and she could breathe again. The guards were closer and she could hear their angry cries over the ringing in her ears.

"Capture the traitor Makeda!"

"The archdominar says his sister has betrayed us!"

Curse you, Akkad. She did not need to be a mortitheurge to know that she was losing far too much blood. She would not be able to face the guards. She would be captured and executed as a traitor. Her name would be stricken from the histories.

The last bloodrunner was not content to let her die under a board and a pile of rocks however. He was intent on doing the job himself, and had dropped his ruined whip and drawn a paingiver's blade. He was charging across the pen, and Makeda knew she would not be able to stand in time.

He was upon her, dagger raised, mouth twisted into a snarl, but then the paingiver seemed to come *apart*. He jerked and spasmed as blood flew into the air, and then fell onto his face, forward momentum sliding him through the mud to stop at Makeda's feet, his back shredded so badly that she could see the white of his spine. He had been dead before Makeda had even heard the whine of the reiver.

A ferox landed next to her with a splash. She looked up to see that the predator was laboring under a pair of riders. Primus Zabalam and Dakar Urkesh both dismounted. She tried to speak, but no sounds would form in her damaged throat. "Makeda!" Zabalam grabbed her by the armor and hoisted her up with surprising strength while Urkesh loaded a fresh needle cone on his reiver.

"You must flee, Makeda," Zabalam hissed at her. "Akkad has declared you an outcast. Your life is forfeit. Go. Your cohort is waiting." The guards were almost upon them. The titan she'd enraged was still chasing bloodrunners and crushing tents underfoot. There was no time. Zabalam was right. She tried to climb into the saddle, but she was weaker than she thought, and struggled to do so. Zabalam pushed her roughly upward. The ferox shifted beneath her, but understood this was not the time to fight against its handlers.

There was a horrendous whine as Urkesh spotted another

bloodrunner and cut him to bits. Zabalam grabbed him by the arm. "Go with Makeda. I charge you to protect her." He drew his swords.

"What are you doing?" Urkesh shouted.

"This ferox can't run fast enough to get away if there are three of us on it. I'll buy you time. Protect her with your life. She is the future of Balaash, not that wretched dishonorable belek, Akkad." Zabalam looked to Makeda, the half of his damaged face that still worked turned up in a grin. "My apologies for insulting your family."

Makeda still could not speak. She put one bloody hand on Zabalam's head. It left a red print once she took it away. Urkesh climbed up behind her.

"You always were my best student. Now go!" He stuck the ferox on the rump with the hilt of a sword. The predator lurched away in an ungainly run.

Makeda looked back to see Zabalam striding toward the rushing host of guards, arms extended, displaying his swords proudly. "I am Primus Zabalam of the Praetorian, swordmaster of House Balaash, student of exalted Vaactash, and I fight to defend Makeda, the *true* heir of Telkesh! Who among you is stupid enough to contend with me?"

About half the guards froze, torn and unsure, but the other half attacked.

"Come then!" There was a flurry of motion as Zabalam struck back against overwhelming odds.

It was a single perfect moment of all that it meant to follow the code of hoksune, but then the ferox was around a tent and Zabalam was lost from sight.

"Ride! That way." Urkesh pointed with his reiver. The Venator had obviously never ridden a ferox before and was doing his best to hold on. Makeda kicked the predator in the ribs and turned it with her knees. There was a huge crash as the enraged titan slammed through a tent and appeared in front of them, a bloodrunner stuck on one of its tusks. Urkesh shouted in surprise right in her ear. The ferox bounded around the titan in two leaps, narrowly avoiding the desperate beast handlers who were trying to bring the titan under control.

More horns were sounding. Officers were standing at the corners, waving torches and repeating Akkad's proclamation that Makeda was a traitor to House Balaash and that she had to be captured. Yet as the ferox loped through the camp, many soldiers clearly saw her, but did not move to intercept. Enough others did, however, that escape did not look likely.

Cataphract moved ahead of her, war spears leveled. She struck the ferox and it turned, sliding through the grass, only seconds away from being impaled upon a wall of spears. A brief sprint and another corner took them into more swordsmen. One tried to stab the ferox, but it simply lunged forward, sank its huge teeth into a shoulder, and shook him to death. Another soldier came from behind but Urkesh shredded him with a reiver burst.

Soldiers loyal to Akkad were moving throughout the camp, shouting for the traitor Makeda's blood. "We're not going to make it," Urkesh stated.

The Venator was correct. They would be surrounded, cut off, and brought down. Unless . . .

The titan she'd bonded with was occupied, so Makeda reached out for the spirit of the great titan bronzeback she had connected with so briefly earlier. He was still there, snoring peacefully through the pandemonium now engulfing the encampment. The petty games of the skorne didn't matter to the mighty bronzeback. He existed only for the next challenge or the next cow. Makeda tapped into her power and awoke the bronzeback from its slumber. Bonding to such a potent beast, especially after such a fleeting contact, would be a great challenge. It took all of her effort, but Makeda pushed hard against his mind. His spirit was great, but simple, and she awoke its natural rage; in fact, she ignited it and set it free.

A terrible roar shook the entire encampment. Every skorne for miles all looked in the same direction at the same time. The ferox slid to a trembling halt. "What in the name of the ancestors was *that*?"

Our escape, Makeda thought, but it was still too difficult to speak.

The enraged bronzeback let its feelings be known by picking up another titan and throwing it across the encampment. The vast animal blotted out one of the moons for a moment as it passed overhead. The titan's landing shook the foundations of the world and nearly knocked over their ferox. Makeda did not even need to kick the ferox in order to make it run this time.

They bounded past Akkad's soldiers, knocking down a distracted Cataphract, as the bronzeback rampaged through the camp. Then they were out on the open plains and fleeing into the unknown.

The pain began in her ribs and then radiated out from there. At first it was a tingling in her nerves, and then a tightness of the muscles, and then an arcing lightning through the veins and arteries. Her mortitheurgy identified the cause quickly. The bloodrunners' daggers had been treated with some manner of strong poison, but she was overcome so quickly that there was nothing she could do but scream.

Every move of the ferox caused pain to ripple through her body. Every jolt and bounce caused joints to grind as if filled with broken glass. The air that filled her lungs was like bubbling acid, eating away at her flesh.

The midnight plains faded into complete darkness as she was robbed of her sight. She could no longer control their steed. Her limbs would not respond to her commands, and every effort at making them work merely caused the pain to grow.

This was not poison. This was a living thing, born only to cause suffering.

At one point she slipped from the saddle and crashed into the dirt. It was almost cushioned compared to the pain that was now cascading through her entire body, but even then, the poison discovered this small bit of cool relief and extinguished it. The ground seemed to become hotter and hotter until every bit of clinging dirt burned like lava. Urkesh had lifted her back onto the ferox. He was saying something about pursuers, but it was hard to hear over the hurricane in her ears. The pain was causing her to hallucinate and his fingers pierced her skin like the needles of his reiver.

The pain had gone on and on. Time lost all meaning. Reality was taken away and replaced with a world that was nothing but agony, and somehow Makeda knew that she was dangling by a thread over the Void. All she had to do was cut that tiny string of life and she could be plunged into the Void. It was cold in the Void, but the cold would extinguish the fire which was consuming her. She could see her father within the Void. The poison, the evil, sentient *thing* had done the same to him, until he had cut that thread and welcomed the nothing.

Somehow the pain became worse, and through it all, the only bit of the real world that remained with her was the presence of the Swords of Balaash, and the tiny sliver of her grandfather's spirit which powered them. Despite the agony, her exalted ancestors were still there. They helped her understand.

This poison was designed to kill mortitheurges, brewed to unravel bodies, corrupt wills, and break minds. Normal poison was useless against someone who could stall death or manipulate blood and tissue. How could she fight such an enemy? She reached for her power, but it was swept aside by the crashing waves of agony. The harder she tried, the more pain it inflicted on her as punishment. It whispered that only the cool Void could save her.

Suddenly a gigantic black stone statue was towering over her, offering a path away from the Void. The stylized face of Vaactash did not move as the thought hammered its way through her mind. "What is it that you whisper to yourself, child, when the pain becomes too much?"

And then the words were there.

Suffering cleanses the weakness from my being. Adhere to the code and I will become worthy.

The suffering was the key. She could not reach her power because she was weak.

Her power was still there, still ready to be utilized, she only needed to be strong enough to take it. She had to go through the pain, through the unraveling of mind and spirit. Let death come. Let her heart stop, but in that brief time while hurtling toward the Void, she would take what was rightfully hers.

Makeda welcomed the poison and told it to do its worst, for she was skorne, and she would *never* break.

The pain was gone. Now there was only the memory of pain.

Where am I?

The walls were made of rock, chipped and chiseled until it was in the semblance of a room. A single feeble lantern hung from a brass fitting sunk into the wall, leaving most of the space hidden in darkness.

Is this a dungeon? Have I been captured?

Yet when she moved, she discovered that she was not in chains. She felt the cold stone floor beneath her palm before realizing that her body was resting on a pile of dark furs. Her armor was missing and she was only wearing a thin grey robe. A bloodstained cloth was nearby, and resting upon it was a multitude of tools, tiny blades, pliers, hooks and barbs, needles and thread, bottles of potions, and bags of herbs. Though similar, these were not the injury-causing tools of a tormentor, but rather the injury-repairing tools of a chirurgeon. Bandages pulled as she tried to sit up. Clearly someone had tended to her many wounds.

Where are my swords? There was a brief flash of panic before she spotted them, sheathed and leaning against the wall. Makeda breathed a sigh of relief. Death was far preferable to losing her family swords. *Thank the ancestors.*

Something stirred in the darkness. There was a shape there, and it took Makeda a moment to make out the silhouette of a skorne in the light armor of the Venator, with a reiver resting on his lap.

Her throat ached. "Where am I?" The words came out so raspy that Makeda did not recognize her own voice. It did not feel like just the whip, but rather that her throat was raw and parched, as if she had been yelling for hours.

The warrior in the shadows stood quickly. "She is awake," he spoke loudly, his voice seeming to echo through the chamber. "Makeda is alive."

"I tire of hearing that said as if it is some sort of surprise." Speaking hurt. She welcomed the minor pain as it helped clear the sleep from her mind. She had seen real agony; from now on, minor pain would merely be another tool. "What is going on?" Makeda pushed herself up, but the effort made her head swim.

The figure in the dark had been Urkesh, and he rushed over to her side. "Do not struggle." He caught her by the shoulders and lowered her back to the furs. It was an insult to have someone of a lower caste touch her without permission, but it was obvious no offense was intended, plus she was not in any shape to do much about the slight regardless. "Those assassins' blades were poisoned. You nearly died."

Poison . . . a weapon of cowards and traitors. "Akkad. He poisoned Telkesh."

There were other voices inside the cavern. Armored footsteps echoed. More figures appeared. She should have been able to recognize them, but her vision seemed blurry, however they were wearing the colors of House Balaash. Some of them were bearing their own lanterns, and now she could see that the room was larger than expected, with windows covered in thick brown curtains. A small hunched figure moved between the much larger skorne. "They are aware. I told them. Most even believed."

Haradum? "So you survived the assassins, elder teacher. Good."

"I followed your cohort for days, even after Akkad's loyalists gave up the chase."

"Days?" Her body felt weak, but she did not feel like she had been asleep for days. "How long have I been ill?"

"Ten days and ten nights. I believe it was the same poison which felled mighty Telkesh. The others thought you had died." The old extoller came closer and placed one freezing-cold hand on Makeda's forehead. The crystal oculus stared down at her. "But I could see that your essence had not yet left your body. You would not allow death to claim you . . . it seems the last of the fever has passed. You must rest. The flesh needs time to heal."

"The flesh will do as I tell it to." Makeda rubbed her eyes. Her vision was improving. Now she could recognize many of the other figures as officers of her father's army. Their faces were grim, their white eyes reflective in the glow of the lanterns. "Where am I?"

"The Shroudfall Mountains," Urkesh answered. "We were fleeing Akkad's army and needed a place to hide."

"This is an old fortress. The mountain passes are extremely difficult to cross," stated one of the warriors, whom Makeda recognized as a veteran Cataphract of her father's cohort. "Your army is safe here until you decide it is time for us to mobilize."

My army? All that had remained of her small cohort had been a few battered taberna, and many wounded. This time Makeda focused through the dizziness and forced herself to sit up. Urkesh was there, ready to help, but she ignored him. She placed her hands on the stone and forced herself upright. Her knees nearly buckled, but she would not show weakness before these warriors. "What army do you speak of?"

The Cataphract nodded to the side. One of his soldiers rushed to the nearest curtain and drew it back. Cold night air flooded into the room. "While you were taken with the fever, they gathered."

Though curious, Makeda first walked slowly to the side and retrieved the Swords of Balaash. The scabbards felt good in her hands. Only then did she go to the window. Her steps were slow, unsteady. Her muscles quivered with weakness, but she would not show it. The cold air cut right through her thin robes and she began to shiver uncontrollably. She had lost a lot of weight and knew she had to look like a spirit that had escaped from the Void.

Outside the window was the ruined courtyard of a once great castle. They were so high in the mountains that the clouds had come down to gather around the towers like fog. Those clouds were glowing, reflecting the flickering light of hundreds of campfires.

"I do not understand . . ." Makeda whispered.

"We were few at first. Just your cohort and a handful of slaves," Urkesh said. "But then word spread of your sickness. Others had to come and see."

"It was a few individuals at first," the veteran Cataphract said. "Warriors loyal to Telkesh and Vaactash, then maddened cultists of Xaavaax, and even soldiers of proud vassal houses such as Bashek and Kophar. Akkad executed many as an example, but soon whole taberna and even decurium had deserted in order to come here and keep watch over you. More gather every day."

Makeda was stunned, her mind unable to estimate the number of troops assembled here. Even if there was but a single datha around each of those fires, it had to represent a mighty host, surely more warriors than most houses could boast, possibly even enough to rival Balaash's combined sabaoth.

One of the warriors saw her standing in the window. There was a shout, and then another and another, until the entire camp erupted in one long incomprehensible roar. It was a battle cry.

She was nearly overcome. "But I was sick with fever. I was helpless." The events in the encampment came rushing back. "I have been cast out of my house and declared a traitor. Why would they risk everything to follow such a weak leader?"

"It was anything but weakness." It was a new arrival who answered. Makeda turned to see a young paingiver whom she had never met before. "When I heard of these events, I had to come and see for myself. This poison is an extraordinary invention, a curse that would make even great Morkaash proud. It is a marvel of the paingiver's art. Never before have I seen a mixture capable of causing such pure agony and suffering. It felled even the great Telkesh and drove him insane within a single day. Even as strong as he was, his flesh could not withstand that level of purification before it broke his mind."

The pain. It was only half recalled, like a bad dream. Yet, she had not broken. She did not follow the way of the paingivers so she did not feel as if she had reached any sort of enlightenment, but she had endured. That was what mattered.

"Your cohort told others of this terrible agony you were experiencing," Haradum said. "So they had to come to hear for themselves."

"Hear what, elder teacher?" Makeda rasped. "Hear me descend into gibbering madness?"

"No," the paingiver answered. "Despite being rent apart by the most delicious agonies possible, you rose above it. As your body was wracked with unfathomable pain and seizures, you transcended it all. These warriors came to hear the way to enlightenment."

Haradum sounded reverent, "Every day for ten days and every night for ten nights, you recited the entirety of the code of hoksune."

As if of one mind, every warrior in the room went to their knees and bowed.

❖ PART THREE ❖

THE TWIN SWORDS OF BALAASH had been placed reverently on the stone floor before her as Makeda had knelt in meditation. At times she was envious of the extollers and their ability to commune with the exalted dead, because the swords were silent to her ears. Hours had passed, but still the answers eluded her. If only she could truly know the wisdom of her ancestors, perhaps then, choosing between the demands of honor and the potential future of her house would not be so difficult.

They were high in the Shroudfall Mountains, and the air in the uppermost chamber of the tallest tower of the old fortress seemed permanently chilled. Makeda's measured breathing left clouds of steam in the air. The sun would rise soon, and when it did, her army would need direction.

There was a sound from behind her, a shuffling and wheezing on the stairs. Makeda did not need to look to know that it was Aptimus Haradum. The aged extoller had made it a habit to check on her. "Archdomina Makeda?" she called out.

"That is not my title, Haradum."

"Your warriors seem to think it is."

Makeda stared at her swords. "They believe me to be more than I am."

Haradum wheezed and shuffled her way into the upper chamber. "*So* many stairs, and it is so cold here. This place must have been built by nihilators wishing to suffer. I am lucky our young dakar with the reiver allowed me to pass. I believe he has appointed himself to be your personal guard."

"Urkesh?" Makeda asked. She had not been aware that the Venator had been following.

"Yes, yes. He took the final order of Primus Zabalam most seriously. I collected Zabalam's soul by the way. He killed twenty warriors before catching a spear in the throat." She patted a glowing stone chained to her apron. "He will make a fine revered companion to Vaactash."

Makeda was surprised by the sudden feeling in her chest. She hid the physical reaction, and merely nodded in approval. "A wise choice."

"As for the young Venator, after you were overcome with poison, he lost control of the ferox. Wily beasts have no patience for untrained masters. He carried you on his back for miles until reaching your decurium. He never left your side the entire time you were consumed with fever."

"I was unaware." Urkesh's commitment to duty was commendable. Perhaps it was possible to honor hoksune even without looking into a warrior's eyes as you killed them.

"What troubles you, Makeda?"

"I have a decision to make, but the code does not provide me with clarity on this issue. I do not like being uncertain."

"You always were one for clarity. As Vaactash used to say, when a titan is chasing, do not dither, pick a direction and run!"

That really did not sound like something her grandfather would have said at all. "I would ask a favor of you, Aptimus."

"I am already aware of what you seek, and I already have an answer for you. While you were battling the fever, I attempted to commune with the essence of your grandfather's spirit which dwells within your swords. Such a task is onerous and difficult, and sometimes our exalted ancestors do not deign to answer. Sometimes they know that the living must seek out wisdom for themselves. There was only the briefest communication."

"What did he say?"

"*The true heir of House Balaash has already won.*"

Makeda was not surprised. It was not like Vaactash to provide an easy way out. "Akkad is the eldest, thus it is his legal right to rule. However, should an heir be deemed unfit, and I believe his dishonorable and cowardly murders—"

"Do not forget the blasphemy!"

"Of course." Makeda had to suppress a small smile. "That too. These things prove he is unworthy to lead House Balaash. So it falls to me to issue a challenge. It is my duty to defeat him in single combat and assume the mantle of archdomina."

"Assuming of course you could defeat the finest warrior of his generation in a duel, but that doesn't matter now, does it?"

"Akkad will ignore my challenge and merely have me killed. Someone so dishonorable will not risk his throne. Akkad declared me an outcast. Officially, I am of lower status than a newly captured slave."

"Most slaves do not have their own armies."

"Yes. And if I march this army south, then somewhere on the plains north of Halaak we will clash against the rest of House Balaash. Thousands upon thousands will die."

"It will be glorious." Haradum shook one of her bony fists in the air. "To war! To war! The blood will flow like rivers!"

Makeda sighed. "The problem with a civil war is that whoever wins, House Balaash loses. Akkad or I, the victor is irrelevant. We will rule over a house that is weakened and ripe to be conquered by our neighbors. House Balaash has far too many enemies to gut our army and expect to survive."

"Yes, yes." Haradum was nodding along. "Perhaps you should accept your title of outcast and wander the wastes the rest of your days. I hear the Abyss is quite the sight to see." Haradum's laugh sounded like old bones being shaken in a dried-out leather bag.

"My fate does not matter, Aptimus, only that of my house. Is it better that a blasphemous fiend rule than I start a war that ends House Balaash? Will my house rot under the rule of a dishonorable archdominar? I am of the warrior caste. I must fight for the good of my house."

"Is that why you fight?"

Makeda paused. It was such a simple question with such a complicated answer. Why did she fight? Why did the skorne have to fight? She thought back to the very first time in her life when she had come to understand the reasoning behind that question, in a hall filled with silent ancestors . . .

And then Makeda had her answer. *Thank you, Grandfather.*

"Do you know what the foulest of all words is, Haradum?"

"Surely something involving rhinodons. They are obnoxious things with disgusting reproductive habits!"

"The foulest of all words is *peace*." Makeda took up her swords and rose. "Come. I must prepare the warriors. We march."

The ancient extoller squealed with delight. "Many will be exalted, I am sure!" Haradum cackled and patted one of the many empty sacral stones she wore like jewelry, knowing that it would soon be filled. "To war! To war!"

During the journey south, her body healed, but her mind was at turmoil. At night, sleep would not come, and when it did, it brought uneasy dreams of disapproving ancestors and House Balaash in flames.

Her cohort grew. New warriors joined her daily. From simple Hestatians from the plains wearing basic armor stitched together from titan hide, to proud Cataphract so large of stature and wearing so much steel and laminate armor that they looked more like ancestral guardians than mortals, to nihilators obsessed with death and with barbed pain hooks embedded in their flesh, to Venators armed with nothing more than slings and vials filled with corrosive acid, to other rich and powerful tyrants with their own stables of warbeasts.

Veterans knelt before her. Great leaders presented their swords or their mortitheurgy and swore to fight in her name. She formed new datha and taberna, and promoted warriors to lead them, gave battle orders, and saw to their logistical needs. They travelled fast and lean, often making do with innate toughness rather than sufficient rations. By day Makeda had to learn to balance the politics, bickering, and petty ambitions of so many competing warriors, and by night she dreamed of war.

The warriors came for various reasons. Some because of old loyalties to Telkesh, or belief in the code, or disgust over the dishonor of losing an archdominar to poison, or vassals who decided to support one heir over another, to others who simply wished for a battle worthy of their skills. But whatever the reason, they continued to join, and the further south they went, the stronger her army became.

Within a week of leaving the Shroudfall, her army had grown large enough to pose a real threat to House Balaash. She estimated that nearly a quarter of House Balaash's total sabaoth was under her command. A host so numerous, in fact, that even if they were to go down in defeat, it would be a great enough battle that it would surely ruin the entire army of House Balaash in the process.

And for one of the only times in her life, Makeda understood what it was to fear.

She feared not for herself. If she was to be found wanting, let her be cast into the Void with the rest of the failures. That did not matter. Makeda feared only for the future of her house.

Ancestors, if I am to be defeated, let it happen swiftly, so that my house may be spared.

Each night she would counsel with her officers and listen as the tacticians made their plans. Far too many of those plans ended with a slaughter that would lead to the eventual destruction of her house. She spoke with each of the officers individually, searching for ideas that would accomplish her mission, yet leave the great army of Balaash relatively intact.

Yet it was not one of the mighty war leaders that had finally proposed a possible solution to her dilemma.

It had been a slave.

❖ ❖ ❖

"I do not see Akkad's personal banner among the horde," Urkesh said as he slowly moved his eyes from side to side, searching carefully for targets. "He did not bother to come himself."

The Venator had proven to have the most acute vision of any of her officers so Makeda was inclined to believe him. "I should not be surprised." It was difficult to keep the disgust from her voice. "But I am disappointed."

The morning mist had risen from the lake and a low fog hung over the plains. Makeda had spent most of her life in this region. She knew it well. Within a few hours the sun would rise enough to cut through the kneehigh fog, but until then the air would be still. To the east was what seemed like a never-ending sea of red and gold marching through the churning grey. The majority of the great army of House Balaash was arrayed before her, thousands strong. A few miles behind that army was House Balaash itself, once her home, and now her target. At her back was a much smaller army, made up of warriors who still believed that honor meant something. To their north was the long crystal-blue expanse of Mirketh Lake. To the south was nothing but miles of open plains until the great city of Halaak.

It was a fine place for a civil war.

Makeda and Urkesh had stopped on top of a small rise to survey the opposition. The rest of her command staff was making their way up the hill for a hasty council before the battle commenced. It had taken a month to march south from the Shroudfall Mountains. During that time they had been met by a few small cohorts of Akkad's loyalists, but had faced no serious combat. Judging by the great force waiting for them, that was all about to change.

It did not matter. Makeda had looked upon these officers and judged them worthy. The warriors of House Balaash who believed in hoksune and the traditions of their ancestors had flocked to her banner. Despite being outnumbered three to one, victory would be hers. The real question was whether House Balaash would survive for long after the slaughter necessary to achieve such a victory.

It was the potential fall of her house which had kept her awake each night during the journey. "I was afraid of this. I had hoped he would show himself. Curse Akkad. This complicates matters, Urkesh."

"I understand."

"Do you?" Makeda glanced at her subordinate. The Venator had barely left her side since their march had begun. "You assume much, Dakar. I know what I must do, but in order to succeed, I fear I must behave as dishonorably as my brother."

"A Venator spends so much time looking at targets in the distance that often we cannot focus on things that are near." Urkesh studied her for a moment. "I know what vexes you. The burden can be seen in your countenance, Archdomina."

"That is not yet my title."

"It would not be my place to disagree with you, but if it was, I would tell you that you are wrong. You are nothing like your brother. He would burn your house in order to rule it, but you would kill yourself in order to save it. This army follows you because to them you embody the code of hoksune. You are more the true heir of House Balaash than your brother could ever hope to be, and these warriors know it."

Her caste did not display their emotions openly, so Makeda gave the Venator a small, respectful nod. "They follow me because they follow the code. So why are you here, Urkesh?"

He shrugged. "The code means different things to different warriors. Just because I am not good at it, doesn't mean that I don't believe it."

"You are wiser than you look."

"Thank you, Archdomina." Urkesh went back to surveying the opposing army. "Now where are you hiding, One Ear?" Urkesh looked over at her and grinned. "I didn't think you would mind me calling him that now."

Makeda sighed. "Do not tempt me. Beheading you could still boost morale."

The incorrigible Venator chuckled. The other officers had reached them, so Urkesh put on a much more serious face. "Since Akkad is telling everyone that our army is only a minor rebellion that needs to be squashed, apparently he decided we're not nearly worthy of his attentions, and has failed to honor us with his presence."

Her officers took in the great horde awaiting them. "Leading from the rear? That is not how Akkad was taught," muttered Primus

Tushhan of the Cataphract. "I served Telkesh and Vaactash before him. They would never have done such a cowardly thing."

Aptimus Haradum had shuffled her way up the hill along with the officers. "Not cowardly—cunning," she interjected. "Akkad is a shrewd one. He knows that his sister will take the honorable and direct path, thus his absence is the most politically expedient choice." At times Makeda suspected that the ancient extoller was not nearly as mad as she liked everyone to think, but then she cackled with glee and removed all doubt. "House Balaash will be emptied of blood before you crack him from that shell. Extollers will have gathered from all across the land! So many will die! Everyone will die! It will be *glorious*!"

Makeda ignored the crazed extoller and addressed her officers. "I cannot challenge Akkad if he's not present. If he were here, he would either have to accept and risk potential defeat, or decline and be dishonored. I was hoping he had retained enough honor to come out and face me."

The gigantic young Cataphract from the vassal house of Kophar had a deep, hearty laugh. "Be careful what you wish for. I have trained against Akkad. He is a mighty warrior, the finest of our generation. I do not mean to question your skill with the blade and offer no offence, but know that Akkad is one of the greatest combatants I have ever seen."

There were solemn nods of agreement from every officer who had ever served with Akkad in combat. Even her most loyal warriors understood that honor alone would not carry her through that duel, yet they followed anyway.

"Not that I wouldn't enjoy watching you two duel," Only a small contingent of House Kophar volunteers had jointed her forces, but they were renowned for their size, ferocity, and strength. "But I did not come all the way from Halaak to leave without a proper battle."

"Do not worry, First Born Xerxis. You will get your fight, but it is better to spill my own blood than leave our house without an army to defend it. I intend to finish this quickly." The time had come to share her plan. It would be controversial, but it was necessary. "Tell me, noble Cataphract. Does your house still speak of how my grandfather conquered you?"

Xerxis frowned, obviously not liking having to admit his family

268   *Target Rich Environment: Volume 2*

had ever been bested. "Of course we do. Each of us studies the battles in great detail." He folded his thick arms. "There is no dishonor in losing against the greatest tactician of all time."

"Of course not. When Vaactash went to war against House Kophar, your warriors impressed him greatly, so much in fact that he decided it was a waste to kill them. I remember him telling me the story, *Why kill these warriors who would be able to fight so capably in my name?* So instead Vaactash concentrated his strength against your dominar, defeated him, and added the proud Cataphracts of Kophar to his own army, strengthening us all."

That seemed to placate the heir of Kophar. The rest of her officers were nodding. "What do you propose then?" Xerxis asked.

"There was great wisdom in what Vaactash did to House Kophar. I will not see House Balaash destroyed. I will not satisfy my honor only to see House Muzkaar or Telarr sitting upon our throne within a year. As Vaactash said, 'Why kill those who would be able to fight so capably in my name?' Yes, you will fight here today, but seek your exaltation quickly, because you will only fight long enough for me to reach Akkad."

"There is the matter of a very large army standing between the two of you," Tushhan pointed out.

"Indeed, but Haradum spoke the truth. Akkad will expect me to do the honorable and direct thing. He knows that honor demands that my place be here, leading this cohort. Yet, I remember the lessons of my sword master. Show your foe one blade, and kill him with the other." Makeda looked toward the waters of Mirketh Lake. "Today you will be the first sword. I will be the second."

Ancestors communed with, blades sharpened, and armor readied, the battle of House Balaash commenced. Hundreds of eager extollers looked on, seeking those worthy of exaltation from the masses.

It began simply enough, as affairs of such historical magnitude often did, but every veteran on the field knew that by the time the sun crawled to the middle of the sky, thousands upon thousands of House Balaash's warriors would be dead.

Venator catapults hurled balls packed with explosives and steel shards high into the air to hurtle down into the opposing ranks. The mechanical whine of millions of needles filled the plains as thousands of reivers fired simultaneously. Beasts bellowed and shrieked, whipped into frenzies by the beast handlers, before being released on paths of destruction.

And despite this great conflict, the army of Makeda fought on, completely unaware that their leader was not even there.

If only I could combine your adherence to hoksune with your brother's ambitious pragmatism, then House Balaash would be unstoppable. The mind reels at the possibilities.

The words of Vaactash gave her hope. Makeda's hand was resting on the hilt of one of the Swords of Balaash. If victory required her to be pragmatic, then she would do so, no matter how much it pained her. She knew that her grandfather was watching over her now, but she could only hope that he approved of her decisions.

Kuthsheth the slave worked the oars, and the small rowboat made steady progress along the shores of Mirketh Lake. The morning fog had not yet burned off, and it still provided some measure of cover.

Makeda could not see the battle begin, but she could hear it. The clash of sword and spear, the whine of reivers, the thud of catapults, the screams as acid ate flesh, and the thunder as warbeasts clashed. It was the sound of two forces testing each other. Soon the melee would become general. Her army would fight and die all without her there to lead it, and Makeda cursed fate and begged her ancestors to forgive her dereliction of duty.

She wore a rough cloak of woven hair, ratty and filthy. The garb of a slave hid her proud armor. Her banner, bearing the noble glyph of House Balaash, had been left flying with the army she had abandoned. It was not even the indignity of it all that bothered her, it was that she was being robbed of her chance to lead her warriors into glorious combat. Perhaps if she was lucky, one of the great underwater beasts of Mirketh Lake would do everyone a favor, rise from the depths, and devour her to hide the dishonor.

Makeda had never truly hated Akkad before. She had merely done her duty as honor dictated. She was warrior caste and thus lived only to bring glory to her house. However, now as the great battle commenced without her, Makeda understood what it was to hate. She despised Akkad.

And she pitied him as well. How empty would a life be without hoksune to fill it?

"We are nearly there," Kuthsheth said. "The docks are not—" He cringed as a black shadow passed overhead. The massive beating of leathery wings rocked the tiny boat with blasts of wind, but then the Archidon was past. The flying warbeast paid no attention to their tiny boat. It had been summoned to the battle by some powerful mortitheurge. It roared, and dove, plunging out of sight behind the dunes along the shore.

"The docks are what, Kuthsheth?" Makeda asked calmly.

"They are not well guarded. The slaves use the docks mostly to bring fish to the kitchens. There are always a few warriors, but I am certain they will be the most inexperienced."

Of course. The most capable would have gotten themselves placed into the battle. No capable warrior would volunteer to guard a dock when such a great opportunity for exaltation presented itself. At worst they would be facing Hestatians, little more than militia. "The problem will be Akkad's personal guard. They are all veteran Cataphract."

"Also the bloodrunners who prowl the corridors," Kuthsheth said, and seemed surprised when Makeda did not appear to understand what he was speaking of. "Noble Telkesh kept a few on retainer to watch out for assassination attempts against his heirs. They skulk about the house, answering only to Tormentor Abaish."

"I was not aware of them."

"That is because they are very good at skulking . . ."

Makeda had learned that there was much she had not known about the inner workings of her household. There was a world beneath the surface, populated entirely by workers, slaves and servants, members of the lower castes which she had never bothered to pay attention to. The warriors and leaders of a great house did not wish to look upon their lesser all day, so they remained hidden as they fulfilled their purpose, hurrying through their world of mazes.

Kuthsheth was laboring against the oars, but he still did his best to compose himself. "Once I get you into the central keep, I believe I can distract the bloodrunners. They pay no attention to mere house slaves. I have overheard them speaking about what they perceive to be vulnerabilities. Once you are inside the servant's tunnels, I will cause a disturbance in Abaish's laboratory. That should attract the bloodrunners like a moth to a flame."

"What do you intend to do?"

"Make lots of flames."

To attract the attention of the bloodrunners was to die. "Why do you do this?"

"Because I was a warrior once, a swordsman of the Praetorian, long ago before my village was taken. As is our way, I lost my caste and was placed among the slaves of House Balaash. Because Telkesh was an honorable master, my children will be given the chance to be warriors. If not them, then their children, or their children's children will have a chance at achieving exaltation. That is the way."

It had been this particular slave who had broached this idea to her during their march south. He had overheard her speaking with her officers, and had later spoken on the subject of this little-known passage through the great fortress that was House Balaash. At first she had been annoyed by Kuthsheth's impertinence, but the more she had thought about it, the more she could see the possibilities. If Akkad was trying to avoid their duel, then she would simply bring the duel to Akkad.

There was an explosion in the distance. Makeda turned to see the ball of fire rolling into the sky. The battle had truly been joined.

"We are nearly there. Do not worry, Archdomina."

Makeda did not correct the slave's terminology.

The last dying warrior fell into Mirketh Lake with a splash. The water billowed red around him, and then he sank from view. Makeda lowered the Swords of Balaash and let them disappear beneath the slave cloak. The docks were clear. She had eliminated all of the guards before the alarm could be raised. "Come, Kuthsheth. Show me these tunnels of yours."

The slave finished rolling the last corpse into the lake before rushing past her, his sandals slapping against the weathered wood. They passed barrels of salted fish and sacks of grain. In all the years she had lived here, Makeda had never seen this part of her great house. Kuthsheth opened a door and led her inside.

There were a few slaves there, working away, chopping fish with cleavers, blissfully unaware that they were being invaded. What did it matter to a slave if they were being invaded? The work would continue regardless of who was their master tomorrow.

Kuthsheth knew right where to go, so she followed, keeping her head down and her face covered. He took a lantern from the wall to light their path. They went up a flight of stairs, down a long tunnel, and then up another circle of stairs. Kuthsheth took her through a multitude of passages and alcoves. The great house had been grown and added to for twenty generations, until the interior truly was a warren that would confound any invader, but her guide knew these passages well. The stone around her began to feel familiar and comfortable. The lantern oil smelled of home.

They entered a hall that Makeda knew well. She had gazed from these windows, admired this artwork. Her sleeping quarters were not far away. It was an odd sensation, being an invader in your own home. "We are nearly there." Kuthsheth rounded a corner and disappeared from view.

"You, slave! Where are you going?" a voice demanded. "Did you not heed your overseer?"

"Forgive me, Praetorian. I meant no—"

"Silence!" There was the sound of a gauntlet striking flesh. "This area is off limits while the council meets."

Makeda walked around the corner. A swordsman stood over the fallen Kuthsheth. He looked up at Makeda and snarled. "You slaves will get the lash for—" and then his head went bouncing down the hall. Makeda had time to wipe her sword clean with the slave cloak before his body realized it was dead and fell, dumping blood down the polished floor. She frowned. Killing an honorable Praetorian was such a waste . . .

Kuthsheth stood, rubbing the spreading bruise on his cheek. "Thank you, Archdomina." He pointed at a nearby tapestry detailing the life of Vuxoris. "Behind that is a passage which will lead you directly to the council chambers. Please allow me a few minutes to set fire to Abaish's laboratory, otherwise you will surely encounter bloodrunners on the way."

"One moment, Kuthsheth. If you are to die for me, then you should do it as a member of the caste you were born into." The headless Praetorian was bleeding on her boots. Makeda reached down and picked up the dead warrior's swords. She presented them, hilt first toward the slave. "I hereby proclaim you to be of the warrior caste of House Balaash. Here are your swords, Praetorian."

"My lady . . . I . . . I . . ." His eyes were wide, his mouth agape.

"Wield these in my name."

Kuthsheth took the swords from her with trembling hands. "I will." Now armed, Kuthsheth moved like a changed skorne. With renewed purpose, he quickly lifted the tapestry, revealing the passage. "There is an alcove around the first corner. You should be able to see when the bloodrunners leave, but they should not be able to see you. Go straight on after that, up three more levels of stairs, and you will come out near the council room."

Makeda had spent many hours in the council room, watching and learning as her grandfather, and then her father had ruled over their house. It would be a fitting place to face Akkad.

"I have been a slave of your family for two generations now. I know the soul of Vaactash favors you." Kuthsheth, still reeling from Makeda's generosity, bowed with great humility. "May he guide your steel."

Makeda threw off the slave's cloak and entered the passage.

There had been six guards in the hall leading to the council chamber, but they had not mattered. The last of them crashed through the double doors of the council chambers and rolled down the stairs in a clanking, bloody heap.

The assembled leadership of House Balaash leapt to their feet and reached for their weapons. Akkad was standing at the great window which looked toward the west, watching the distant battle. He turned to see the guard spill out the last of his life down the marble stairs. "What is the meaning of this?"

Makeda paused in the doorway and surveyed the council chambers. The room had always reminded her of the arena, only this sunken floor was meant to be occupied by house leaders rather than gladiators, and the stone benches were filled with those petitioning the council as opposed to bloodthirsty spectators.

There were thirty present: assorted leaders of House Balaash and their vassal houses, as well as representative of other castes, such as the extoller Shuruppak, the wretch who had denied her father's exaltation, and of course, Abaish, who represented the paingivers, and then many scribes and scholars. There were gasps or curses from all present. Akkad's personal guard lowered their spears and rushed forward in a rattling armored mass to place themselves between their lord and the threat.

Makeda turned slowly, looking everyone present in the eye. Many shirked and looked away, others met her gaze, surely knowing that a reckoning had come. Those were the ones torn between honor and duty. They retained some measure of her respect. *Excellent.* She needed witnesses. She would kill all of the others later, and she made careful note of who fell on each side.

"I am Makeda of House Balaash." She kept her voice cold and level. "Second Born of murdered Telkesh, granddaughter of mighty Vaactash, and I have come to take back what is mine."

Akkad seemed speechless, but Tormentor Abaish rose from where he had been seated at his left hand. "How dare you enter this house! You are an outcast, a criminal! You have been exiled!"

"So now the whispering servant finds his voice? Do not worry, Paingiver. I will get to you." Makeda stated. Abaish seemed to shrink and tried to hide behind her brother. "So, Akkad, why did you bother to wear your armor if you are too much of a coward to lead your army?"

Her brother's lip curled back in a snarl. "I am afraid of no one."

"You should be . . ."

"Kill the traitor!" Abaish shrieked. "Kill her!"

The elite Cataphract of Akkad's personal guard hesitated. The order had not come from their archdominar, and for this Makeda was thankful. She would not be able to fight an entire datha of Cataphract. "Only a coward would send his warriors to do something he lacked the spine to do himself." She pointed the Swords of Balaash at Akkad's heart. "Akkad murdered Archdominar Telkesh with poison, denying him a proper warrior's death. Akkad is a coward and a usurper. His dishonorable behavior has brought shame to House Balaash. Shuruppak of the extoller caste is a heretic, denying murdered Telkesh his rightful exaltation in order to hide Akkad's blasphemous crimes."

"Lies!" Abaish was desperate. Even if Makeda was to be killed, the words had been spoken, the accusation made, and it could never be taken back. "No more of your lies."

"Search your hearts and know I tell the truth." Makeda looked about the crowd as she walked down the stairs. "You are the leaders of House Balaash. I am disgusted that the honorable few among you would tolerate this filth in your midst. You would have a coward take up space in our Hall of Ancestors?"

More eyes were averted. Makeda vowed that those would weep bitter, repentant tears before this day was through.

Akkad pushed between his Cataphracts, roughly shoving them aside. "You dare threaten the archdominar with his own family's blades?" One of his retainers ran forward, presenting the archdominar with his personal war spear. It was a mighty weapon that also bore slivers of their ancestors' souls, and its wicked blade glowed with a pale light. "I will not tolerate this insolence. Surrender *my* family's swords, and I will have you executed painlessly. Resist and you will suffer—"

Makeda laughed hard. "You think to threaten me with pain, brother? I know pain."

"You know *nothing*!" Akkad bellowed.

"I survived the same poison you used to kill Father. Tell me what I don't know then, Brother, because I would like to understand this treachery of yours before I send you into the Void."

"You threaten me? For half a generation I fought for Vaactash. I won battle after battle in his name. I crushed our enemies and drove them before me. I burned cities and took hundreds of slaves. Yet they never listened to me. For a year I fought for Father, but he preferred you. I was the heir! Me! You are a child. You play at war. You speak of lessons that no longer matter and stories of dead heroes, but they are not your words. You have not earned them! You are weak, pathetic, tiny!"

"My lord! Say no more, please." Abaish cried out.

She continued slowly down the stairs until she reached the sunken floor. "Is that all? Because while you talk, our army kills itself. Think of the future of our house."

"You don't understand that it doesn't matter. Just like Telkesh, you lack vision."

"Enough," Makeda ordered. The council chamber was suddenly

deadly silent. "Stand aside," she ordered the Cataphract, and shockingly enough, they did.

Now it was only brother and sister, nothing between them but two philosophies that could never be reconciled. The glyph of House Balaash had been engraved deep into the marble beneath their feet. Akkad stood at the top. Makeda stood at the base.

"You speak of dangerous new ways. They are not *our* way. Demonstrate your conviction, Akkad. I challenge you to a trial of individual combat."

"To the death." Akkad lifted the war spear and spun it effortlessly. "Come, Sister. Let us end this."

They met in the center of the glyph.

The war spear hissed through the air in a blur. Makeda blocked with one sword. The impact sent electricity through her joints. She slashed with the other sword, but Akkad spun and knocked it aside with the shaft. Specks of light, like dust motes in the sun, floated as the two magical weapons hammered against each other.

Akkad moved with frightening speed. He was still bigger, still stronger, and Makeda barely danced aside as the war spear tore a chunk of stone from the floor. He lunged, stabbing, and Makeda rolled aside at the last instant. The spear pierced the chest of a scribe. Akkad lifted the screaming worker and flung him off the blade. The lesser caste members pushed back, scrambling over each other to get to the higher seats. Contemptuous warriors shoved them aside so they could better watch the duel.

Makeda attacked, furious, her blades descended, hacking away, one after the other. One would strike while the other rose in a continuous rain of soul-hardened steel. Akkad retreated smoothly, the massive war spear effortlessly diverting every attack. He backed against the far wall, but then placed one boot against it and launched himself at her.

She was able to avoid the blade, but his armored shoulder caught her in the chest and knocked her back. Ribs cracked. Akkad swung the war spear along the ground, but she was able to jump over it. Akkad quickly followed, extending one hand and pointing at her. Makeda was unprepared for the bolt of power which leapt between them. It hit her in the side. Sickening energy crackled through her bones, causing her muscles to contract in clenching agony. She was flung back, but managed to stay on her feet. *His mortitheurgy is strong.*

Akkad rushed forward, eager to finish her, but Makeda focused through the crackling pain, and forced her arms to respond. The dark powers were gathered up from her body, channeled through her, and pushed away. Akkad gasped as his spell was broken. Makeda quickly counterattacked. One sword diverted his spear, while the other one struck armor, then flesh, and finally bone.

They separated, the full length of the Balaash glyph between them. Akkad glanced down at the strap severed and dangling loose below his shoulder plate, and then blood began to drip slowly down his armor. He pressed one hand against the wound, and grimaced as he probed the hole. It was not fatal, not nearly so, but the message had been sent, and Akkad had felt the sting of Balaash steel.

Makeda stood, waiting, her armored breastplate scorched and smoking. Akkad's attack had hurt her, but this pain was *nothing.*

Wary now, Akkad took his bloody hand from the wound and placed it upon the shaft of his spear. He shifted slowly, his boots sliding across the marble as he took up a ready stance, the spear point angled low toward the floor, ready to sweep up and eviscerate. Makeda lifted her swords, one protectively before her, the other low and ready at her side, in a stance taught to her long ago by Primus Zabalam.

They waited, unmoving, studying each other, watching for any sign of weakness, any opportunity to strike. Two warriors, both masters of their respective martial traditions were coiled, ready.

A minute passed. Another.

No one in the council chambers made a noise. All knew that a single movement would end the duel and decided the fate of House Balaash.

The loudest noise in the room was the *drip-drip-drip* of Akkad's blood sluggishly decorating the floor.

It was that splattering of life that would force Akkad to move first. Such was the danger of having such an understanding of the anatomy and the power that dwelled within. Time was no longer on his side, and every heartbeat that passed would leave him that much weaker. Makeda shifted, ever so slightly, and her grip tightened on her sword. The tiniest bit of a smile split her face.

The siblings struck.

They looked into each other's eyes. This should have been one of those moments of perfect enlightenment spoken of in the code, only achievable at that razor-sharp moment between life and death, but as Makeda saw into Akkad's soul, she saw only the turmoil, the lack of conviction, the doubt in the true ways of their people, of their family . . .

She judged him unworthy.

The spear blade had grazed her, barely turned away by one sword as she'd stepped inside her brother's reach. The tip of her other sword was *in* Akkad's neck.

Makeda spoke slowly to her dying brother. "I would have followed you. It was your place to rule. I would have done whatever duty required of me. I would have followed you into the Void if necessary."

Akkad tried to speak, but sound would not form through the blood running down his throat. She could tell he still understood her words though, and that was what mattered.

"But you thought I was weak, malleable like you. You misjudged me. So now you must go into the Void alone." Makeda twisted the sword and drove it upward, deep into Akkad's brain.

The true heir of House Balaash has already won.

The new archdomina of House Balaash pulled her sword from her brother's skull and stepped away from the falling corpse. Akkad collapsed, and lay there in a crumpled heap, deprived of all his glory, his blood slowly coloring the crevices of the house glyph engraved in the floor.

Makeda looked up from the body and around the council chambers. None dared question. She would deal with the traitors soon enough, but there were more pressing matters at hand. She turned to the nearest military officer. "Order the cohorts to stand down. Tell them that Makeda rules House Balaash now and has declared this battle to be through. No more of my soldiers will be wasted today." Several warriors ran up the stairs to spread the word. One of the Cataphract opened the great window to the west, while another brought forth a green signal flag, the color which would order a full halt. He shoved it out into the wind, and began waving it side to side.

Extoller Shuruppak gathered up his voluminous robes and rushed down the steps, grasping wildly for an empty sacral stone at his belt. Makeda looked at the extoller with mild disbelief as he knelt next to Akkad. "What are you doing?"

"Akkad was one of the greatest warriors of his generation. I must keep his soul—"

"Silence." Reaching down, Makeda gathered up a handful of the extoller's robes. "You would betray the ideals of your caste?" She hauled Shuruppak roughly to his feet. Makeda raised her voice, but she was no longer addressing the extoller. "Let the dishonorable name of Akkad never be spoken again in the halls of House Balaash."

"But Akkad was—"

"I must have not made myself clear." Makeda dragged the extoller past the Cataphract with the signal flag, and hurled Shuruppak out the window. His scream could be heard for several seconds, but they were too high up to hear the impact.

Turning back to the council, Makeda raised her voice. "My brother's name will be stricken from all of the histories." Several scribes immediately opened their scrolls, inked their quills, and began furiously blotting out names. "And as for his fellow conspirators . . ." Makeda glanced at Abaish, who was crouched fearfully on a stone bench, looking like he might be contemplating jumping out the window himself. "Fetch *my* tormentors. Fetch *all* of my tormentors. They are going to be very busy."

Makeda went to the window. In the distance, horns were sounding. The green flag had been seen. The fighting would cease, and hopefully before enough of Balaash blood had been spilled to leave them weakened before the other great houses.

Smoke rose in pillars across the battlefield. From this great distance individuals were nothing more than tiny specks of movement; only mighty warbeasts could be distinguished as what they really were. It was nothing more than a swirling mass of color, red and gold, death and life, all beneath a spreading tower of black.

She watched the smoke climb into the clear sky and wondered if she could see as the extollers did with their crystal eye . . . would the flow of souls into the Void look at all like that smoke drifting into nothingness? When the worker caste refined the impurities from metal, they had to torture it with fire. The weakness was burned away, but what was left was refined.

Saved.

"This is why I fight," the Archdomina of House Balaash whispered to herself.

Grandfather said a warrior did not promise. House Balaash would not fall today, nor would it fall as long as she lived, and as long as House Balaash stood as the greatest of all houses, the skorne would continue as unceasing instruments of war.

Archdominar Vaactash had imparted great wisdom to the child Makeda that night in the Hall of Ancestors. He had taught her, even praised her for her devotion to hoksune, and cautioned her as to her place within the hierarchy of their house. It had been a blessed evening, one that she would always remember, and now she had been dismissed.

Makeda stood perfectly still, unsure, staring up at the seemingly giant Vaactash and the even bigger statue behind him. She was not quite ready to navigate her way back through the darkened Hall of Ancestors, and there remained one thing that the archdominar had mentioned which she had always wondered about. She built up her courage to speak. "Grandfather, I have a question."

Vaactash turned away from the great statue that would someday hold his soul, and toward her, seemingly curious as to why she had not simply fled when given the chance. "Yes. I will allow this question. Speak."

"Tell me about the gods we don't have?"

The greatest warrior of their people folded his arms. "You ask difficult questions, child."

"Yes."

"Lyoss had gods . . ." Vaactash stroked his long chin as he contemplated his answer. "There are lands beyond that sea, lands beyond the Abyss, beyond the Stormlands, even lands past where the giants dwell. We live in a land free of meddling gods, but are there still gods in those other dark lands? I do not know. And if there are gods there, do they have people who worship them still?"

"Only exiles have gone beyond those places, Grandfather. They are a mystery to us." It was an odd thought, but she was clever enough to see it through to a logical conclusion. "But if there are others, and they still had their own gods, then they would be soft, probably used to relying on divine help. Not like the skorne at all."

"Indeed. Ponder on this then, child. We must always make war because our salvation depends on it . . . But should the opportunity present itself, what if we could make war on *someone else*?"

Makeda mulled it over carefully, and the sudden answer struck her like a war spear to the heart. "If there was a foreign house, we could have a whole new adversary. There would be no need for our people to make war on each other. Making war against a new enemy would surely provide opportunities for exaltation to all our houses!" The idea nearly stole her breath away.

"This idea is only a fantasy, but imagine it with me, Makeda. All skorne, all of the warrior caste, all of the houses, united in one glorious conquest. It is *beautiful* . . . May your dreams be of war, Makeda."

"May your dreams be of war, Grandfather."

Two generations had passed, but the lessons of Vaactash would never leave her. His words were as ingrained into Makeda as the code itself. It had been ten years since her grandfather's death under the tusks of a great beast of the plains, but she still found herself calling upon his wisdom during times of struggle. She was the archdomina now and had led her house through countless battles. The Swords of Balaash were sheathed at her side. Slivers of her grandfather's sacral stone were among those empowering the mighty blades, and though only an extoller could contact the exalted dead, Makeda always felt as though Vaactash was there to guide her with his wisdom.

"Archdomina, I fear the news is grim. Three more western houses have fallen before the invader from the west. Two of the southern houses have bent their knee and offered fealty rather than fight. The ranks of the invader's army have swollen with troops."

"The invader is like nothing we have ever seen before. He has crushed every cohort that has stood in his way."

The council chamber of House Balaash was silent as the words sunk in. Makeda walked away from her advisors and across the Balaash glyph that adorned the floor. The stain had been scrubbed clean over a generation before, but she could still sense a chill on the spot where her nameless brother had died so long before.

The word from the western tors had been troubling, but this new information was even worse. The divided houses were being systematically conquered. It was as Vaactash had spoken of so long ago: there were lands beyond theirs, and now a warrior of incomprehensible power had come from those lands, and was systematically subjugating her people.

"We are the last great house standing in his way . . ." one of her Tyrants said.

And should we fall, all our people will be dominated.

"What is the name of this *conqueror*?"

"They say he is called Vinter Raelthorne."

Walking slowly, Makeda went to the window and looked toward the west. Ominous clouds had gathered over the plains. The honor of House Balaash—the honor of all skorne—lay heavy on her shoulders. It was times like this that tested a warrior's dedication to the code.

Grandfather, what would you have me do?

A MURDER OF MANATEES
The Further Adventures of Tom Stranger, Interdimensional Insurance Agent

This is the first time this story has appeared in print. It was originally an Audible exclusive audiobook in 2018, narrated by Adam Baldwin, and edited by Steve Feldberg.

The Adventures of Tom Stranger are a comedy series about an Interdimensional Insurance Agent and his bumbling intern. Adam Baldwin (Firefly, Chuck) is so talented that every single character has a distinct voice. Since this was originally written for audio, there are going to be a few parts where you see something like INSERT X NOISE here. Being able to add sound effects is a nice perk.

❖ CHAPTER ONE ❖
Tom's 8 AM Customer Service Response Panel

Miami, Florida
Earth #984-A-3256

IT WAS TIME FOR THE PRESS CONFERENCE to begin. Tom Stranger—an unremarkable-looking man in an unremarkable-looking suit—walked onto the stage and surveyed the audience. The room was crowded with reporters and concerned citizens from across the Multiverse. Once again Tom's company had been embroiled in controversy and its good name besmirched. He knew from experience the best way to deal with spurious allegations was to meet them head on, with honesty, integrity, and superior customer service.

"Hello, I am Tom Stranger, of Stranger & Stranger Insurance. As an Interdimensional Insurance Agent I often travel across the multiverse caring for my clients' needs. My job takes me to many alternate realities, where I deal with a variety of insurance-related, sometime apocalyptic crises. Many would consider this . . ." Tom paused to make quote marks with his finger ". . . *adventure.* However, what unaugmented beings think of as adventure is merely a normal day here at Stranger & Stranger. I do not understand why anyone would chronicle such mundane events, but recently I was informed that a client of mine documented one of my average work days and created an *'audiobook'* about it. For those of you perplexed by this term, on some worlds that is a *book that you listen to.* Though this 'audiobook' about my life has been extremely popular on Earth #169-J-00561, the customer satisfaction rating for this product has averaged less than four and a half stars out of five. I always strive for perfect scores in customer service. That half a star is . . . *troubling.* Thus I have called upon this panel of experts so that we may address these customers' legitimate concerns."

"We're number one! Whooo!" somebody shouted from off stage. "Bestselling audiobook in the world, baby!"

"Correction, Jimmy. *The Adventures of Tom Stranger, Interdimensional Insurance Agent*, written by Larry Correia and narrated by Adam Baldwin, was briefly number one on one particular world. On most civilized worlds it came in a distant second place after the eighth *Game of Thrones* novel."

"Whatever, dude! Number one! Hear that, Mr. Chang? *Number one!*"

"Who is Mr. Chang?" asked one of the reporters.

"Please, let us hold questions until the end."

But Jimmy the Intern answered anyway. "My high school guidance counselor, man. He said I'd never amount to anything. Suck it, Mr. Chang! I starred in the number one audiobook in the world! Woot woot!"

"Calm your wooting, young Intern." Tom Stranger shook his head sadly at Jimmy's display of wanton unprofessionalism. "Such frivolity is an example of why I arranged this Customer Service Response Panel."

"Sorry, Mr. Stranger."

"You might as well come out now. Allow me to introduce our panelists. You have already heard from my intern, Jimmy, whom I brought along today because he was present during the chronicled events."

"S'up, homies." Since today was such an important day, Tom had asked Jimmy to act and look his best. So Jimmy was less unkempt than usual, only partially hungover—a remarkable achievement—and was wearing a shirt and tie instead of one of his usual Chico State T-shirts. However, since Jimmy's default state was *disheveled mess,* he had already dropped a salsa-covered breakfast burrito down his shirt during the drive to the press conference.

"Also joining us is Larry Correia of Earth #169-J-00561, who authored the work in question."

"Hi." Larry the Author waved as he came out on stage and took his seat. There was a little bit of sporadic, polite clapping from the audience.

"And last, but certainly not least, a very special guest, representing one of Stranger & Stranger's most-valued clients, renowned expert on customer relations, Wendell T. Manatee, Chief Financial Officer of CorreiaTech, the most powerful megacorporation in the Multiverse."

A giant fish tank was rolled out on a dolly. Wendell the Manatee floated peacefully inside. "Mehwooooo," Wendell shook his ponderous bulk in greeting. The audience immediately went wild, cheering and chanting his name. *Wendell. Wendell. Wendell.* A woman even threw her panties at Wendell's tank.

Tom waited until the enthusiastic standing ovation for the popular manatee tapered off. Having a public figure of such eloquence and gravitas on his side was certain to help his case. Wendell had agreed to appear as a personal favor. They had picked this location because it was Wendell's home reality, and only one hyperspace jump from Home Office World.

"Let us begin. Mr. Correia, as an accountant—it is good you have retained those skills by the way, in case this writing thing does not work out for you—do you have the statistics?"

"Yes, Tom. We currently have 4,237 five-star reviews on Audible.com, where *The Adventures of Tom Stranger, Interdimensional Insurance Agent* can still be downloaded."

"Of course. The consumers of your home reality would be fools not to purchase this fine entertainment product. But that is not why we are here. How many one-star reviews are there?"

Larry the Author hung his head in shame. "Two hundred seventy-three."

"Tsk, tsk. I always strive for tens on all customer satisfaction surveys. Or fives, when a world's rating system is based upon stars, smiley faces, or stickers. Now, we shall address these customer complaints directly."

Larry the Author had a stack of 3x5 cards with all the negative reviews written on them. He began flipping through. "Okay, let's see . . . 'I'm offended,' 'I'm offended,' 'I'm super offended,' 'This was offensive.' It's about ten 'That was funny' to every one 'I'm offended,' but that guy is *really* offended."

"I see. I believe I know what the problem is," Tom nodded thoughtfully. He turned to address the audience directly. "I accept full responsibility for causing this offense. At this time, I would like to issue a formal apology to all of those whom I inadvertently upset. Humor can be subjective, and what one person finds amusing, others may not. However some things are *never okay* to joke about. So, at this time, I would like to offer my sincerest apology . . . to dolphins."

"Wait. What?"

"Yes, Mr. Correia. During the events chronicled in the previous audiobook, I referred to aquatic mammals as 'flippant.' I inadvertently implied that dolphins were not meticulous about paying their insurance premiums or filling out their claim paperwork on time. That is a hurtful negative stereotype, and for that I am truly sorry to the dolphin people."

"Actually, Tom, I'm pretty sure these were mostly humans, offended that I poked fun at their political beliefs, and they took it personal."

Tom scowled. "That makes no sense. Does your world not have *Saturday Night Live*, stand-up comedy, skit shows, *South Park*, Jon Stewart, Tina Fey, Seth Rogan, John Oliver, *That's My Bush*, Judd Apatow movies, the rest of Comedy Central's programming, Patton Oswalt, Bill Maher, Lewis Black, Stephen Colbert, Janeane Garofalo, or any episodes of *The Simpsons* featuring Lisa?"

"Flooooooo," Wendell explained.

"You are telling me that on Larry the Author's home planet it is only acceptable to make fun of *some* beliefs, yet the predominant belief system held within their entertainment industry is sacrosanct?" Tom thought the manatee had to be pulling his leg. "Good one, Wendell. No. It has to be dolphins. Moving on to our next complaint."

Larry the Author read from the next card. "'It was vulgar.'"

"All things considered, I found R. Lee Ermey to be remarkably restrained," Tom stated.

"Fleeeeeeerrp," Wendell agreed. He was a huge *Full Metal Jacket* fan and could practically recite the opening boot camp scene from memory. The manatee showed them his War Face. "Hoooon."

"A fantastic impersonation, Wendell. Regardless, I will pass this concern onto Secretary of Defense Ermey. Next card."

"Some of the humor was dated, and made jokes relating to pop culture as far back in ancient history as the 1980s."

"Hope that dude never watches *Family Guy*," Jimmy muttered.

"Silence, Jimmy. The customer is always right, even when they are being absurd. Also, he will want to skip the *Guardians of the Galaxy* movies. Next card, Mr. Correia."

"'There was too much profanity.' Now this one is interesting, Tom, and I've got the numbers here. We used no F-bombs. Twice we used the word **BEEP**." Larry paused, confused. "Is the panel being bleeped if we use bad words now?"

"Yes. I thought it best not to cause further customer anguish. Do not worry. I will shut it off after the conclusion of this press conference."

"Hang on. I gotta test this," Jimmy interjected. **"BEEP BEEP** mother**BEEP BEEP** sheep dip! Man, that was awesome!"

Larry the Author looked at his cards. "That's going to make reading these complaints a challenge. Okay, we used **BEEP** six times, uh . . . That's the naughty word for a butt."

"What kind of lame**BEEP BEEP** is that?" Jimmy asked.

"We used crap eleven times . . . Wait, no beep? Okay, apparently crap is cool. H E double hockey sticks, a whopping *seventeen* times, but in our defense that was an actual geographic location in the story. There you go, Tom."

"You must explain this one, Mr. Correia. Your sad customer service failings are not upon my head this time."

"Well, as a writer, language is art, and words are your tools. You choose the best tool based upon the impact you are trying to achieve. Sometimes bad words are funny." There was a scattering of half-hearted applause from a few members of the audience.

"Meewhoo**BEEP**ooo**BEEP**eeeer**BEEPBEEP**floooo**BEEP**"

The audience laughed uproariously at Wendell's profanity-laced, George Carlin-like rant. The manatee was killing it.

"There you have it. I don't think anyone can argue with such keen observational humor. Next one-star complaint."

"Well, Tom, there's accusations that you are some sort of *idealized libertarian superman.*"

"Preposterous. As an insurance agent, I am above petty partisan politics and only care about providing quality customer service. You must be mistaken. That customer was probably referring to President Adam Baldwin."

"Yeah, that guy is pretty awesome," Jimmy agreed.

"Fleeeeeerp," Wendell added, because he mostly knew Adam Baldwin as Animal Mother. "Mooo."

"You heard the manatee, Mr. Correia. Next card."

The author had a perplexed look on his face as he read from the stack. "It is apparent that Larry Correia hates people like me. I'm triggered."

"Sheesh, friggin' dolphins," Jimmy said. "Let it go, already! You guys need to chillax."

"Okay, this one is a direct quote: *The story lacks in every dimension.*"

"Hmmm . . ." Tom was puzzled. "Do you think they meant that literally, or was it an attempt at humor regarding the existence of multiple dimensions? Regardless, the customer is always right. Bad writer. Bad."

"Sorry, Tom. Up next, we have a few about what awful ego-stroking it is for an author to insert himself into a story. That's kind of a funny one since I didn't exactly cover myself in glory back there. I spent most of my time getting my **BEEP** kicked."

"It does not matter. The customer has spoken. An author putting himself into the narrative is never okay. In the future you should strive to be more professional, like Stephen King or Clive Cussler. Is that all of the negative comments?"

"It appears so, Tom."

"Well, there you have it, news media and gentlecustomers. Thank you for attending this Customer Service Response Panel. Are there any questions? Yes . . . there in the back."

"This question is for Larry the Author. Despite your virulent anti-dolphin hatemongery, do you intend to write about any more of the adventures of Tom Stranger?"

"Okay, first off, I don't even know any dolphins."

"That just makes it worse, sir."

"Second, sure. I'd be up to writing another story about Tom and company."

Because of Larry's ham-fisted, clumsy, pulpy writing style, it meant Tom probably had more of these awkward press conferences to look forward to in the future. "Next question, please."

"This question is for Mr. Manatee. Would you care to comment about your megacorporation's controversial move to perform a hostile takeover of many of the most evil companies in the Multiverse, thus creating one super giant megacorp legion of doom ensuring galactic domination?"

There were murmurs from the audience. Tom had not even been aware of these events, and he read the Drudge Report.

"Floorp." And when Wendell the Manatee put his flipper down and said no further questions, he meant it. His handlers immediately came out and wheeled his tank off stage.

"Well, I am afraid that is all the time we have today. We apologize for this utter failure of customer service, and I will personally endeavor to make up that half a star in the future. Thank you for coming."

❖ CHAPTER TWO ❖
Stranger & Stanger's Quarterly Employee Evaluations

Home Office World

After the press conference Tom had returned to the office, looking forward to another productive workday. There was a Multiverse in constant turmoil, clients in need, and quality customer service wouldn't supply itself. Plus, it was nice to turn off that annoying profanity beeper.

The Stranger & Stranger Home Office was a bustling, upbeat place, where the finest office staff in the Multiverse efficiently processed claims and sold policies using the most advanced technology available from a hundred worlds. Tom's personal executive office was very plain and businesslike. There were no personal mementos or knickknacks to distract him from his duties. It was his happy place.

And today was a very important day on Home Office World.

An Interdimensional Insurance Agent was only as good as his team, so it was company policy that every quarter Tom would assess his Junior Associates to make sure that they were operating as a well-honed insurance unit should. Each member would be tested in a variety of grueling simulations, pushing their mental and physical limits to the ragged edge, and then Tom would personally grade their performances.

Interns came from many different realities, but only a handful survived long enough to make the leap to Junior Associate. That position required genius intellect, Olympian physicality, and a courageous dedication to customer satisfaction. After years of experience, the greatest among them would step into the Insurance Crucible and overcome the Final Claim in order to be certified a full-fledged Interdimensional Insurance Agent. Those elite few would get their own franchises and the circle of life would continue.

Until his employees faced the Crucible, it was Tom's solemn duty to mentor them in the Path of Customer Service. Luckily, as the evaluations came in, it turned out that most of his staff was excellent as usual. Tom only had one evaluation left to go over, and he *had* been putting it off for last. He did not rejoice in the failure of others, and it was with heavy hearts that Tom ever let anyone go. Alas, Tom could procrastinate no more, so he pushed a button on his desk.

"Ms. Wappler, could you bring me Jimmy the Intern's evaluation, please?"

His secretary entered a moment later, loudly chewing her gum. Muffy "Sparkles" Wappler was part Jersey girl, part android killing machine, and all insurance professional.

"I kinda been dreading this one too, Mr. Stranger. I know you've taken Jimmy under your wing and all, but . . . Well, here you go. See for yourself."

Tom looked over Jimmy's performance records. The results were not pretty, like anal polyps-level *not pretty*. "This is possibly the most dismal score I have ever seen from anyone in the Interdimensional Insurance Business."

Muffy had blown a rather magnificent pink bubble while he'd been reading. She popped it and went back to chewing. "Yeah, I thought so, too, so I checked with the Licensing Board to see if scores that low were some sort of record. Like an anti-achievement. I thought no way could Jimmy be the worst intern ever. Remember, there was that period back in the nineties where some other companies tried to save money by hiring sign language gorillas."

"At least Jimmy is not last place then."

"Sorry. I didn't mean to imply Jimmy beat out the gorilla. That Amy could really hustle. For the record, Jimmy isn't dead last. Just the lowest-scoring carbon-based life form. One year Conundrum & Company hired a See 'n Say as a customer service rep. You know the toy you pull the string and the little arrow spins and *the cow goes moo*? It was close, but Jimmy edged it out."

"That is . . . something." Tom had been doing his best to help Jimmy discover his inner insurance agent, but they had faced some serious hurdles. "We must remember that Jimmy is from a very backwards Earth. It's the one reality so statistically improbable that their Cubs actually won their World Series."

"Also, I think that's one of those weirdo oddball universes where Donald Trump got elected president, Mr. Stranger. Back on my planet, that guy owns a chain of all-you-can-eat buffets slash strip clubs."

"Before my home planet was obliterated, our Donald Trump was a professional wrestling villain. Jimmy's home reality is truly an oddity," Tom agreed. "By the way, who won the recent presidential election on your home world?"

"Adam Baldwin's two magnificent terms were up, but the Libertarian Space Cowboy Revolution Party won it again, and former Labor Secretary Mike Rowe is president now."

"It's a dirty job, but someone has to do it." That was enough workplace-appropriate small talk. "Now, back to Jimmy's evaluation. Test scores are valuable, but real world performance is where it counts. How has he been integrating with our corporate culture?"

Muffy shrugged. "Jimmy's the reason I had to send out that employee newsletter about why licking toads is a terrible idea. He routinely burns popcorn in the break room microwave. That new sign on the copier saying that it is not okay to photocopy your own butt? Jimmy."

"Surely there is some way to get him up to speed." Tom's body had been extensively enhanced and genetically modified with every groundbreaking combat and customer service-related technology possible. Muffy's robot arm could bench-press a truck. "Perhaps we could have him cybernetically augmented?"

"We tried implanting an infolink chip directly into his brain so he could automatically access the Galactic Data Sphere. But then I had to disconnect it a few days later because Jimmy was downloading so much that he was eating up all the company's bandwidth."

"Let me guess. Pornography?"

"Surprisingly, no. It was something called Ozzy Man Reviews."

"I see." Though providing quality customer service to their existing clients was an Interdimensional Insurance Agent's greatest calling, it was always important to find new clients. The thought of some poor potential customer out there somewhere in the Multiverse, insufficiently insured, was a terrible one. "How does Jimmy do at developing new business?"

"To put it bluntly," which went without saying because that was the only manner Muffy ever put anything, "Jimmy kinda sucks at selling policies, too."

"That is most unfortunate, but let us remember that we all struggled with sales at first." Back when he'd been an intern at Mifune & Eastwood, Tom had once been submerged in acid by an enraged Burgundian Hive Queen for forgetting to give her a free rate quote. It had been a teachable moment. *Good times.*

"Seriously, just in case you think I'm exaggerating, Mr. Stranger, watch this."

She transmitted a file to Tom's desktop holo projector. The image showed a very nervous Jimmy seated in their conference room, and resting on the table in front of him was what appeared to be an ordinary head of cabbage.

"Hmmm . . . curious. Why is Jimmy speaking to a leafy vegetable, Ms. Wappler?"

"I didn't trust him not to scare off any real prospective paying customers, and I was cleaning out the break room fridge and found that. It had gone a little wilty. I didn't think whoever brought it in would miss it. So I told Jimmy that it came from a universe run by sentient vegetables."

"And Jimmy believed this ludicrous ruse?"

"Sir, Jimmy still believes all the spambots sending him friend requests on Facebook really are lonely beautiful women. He answers every email from Nigerian princes trying to move money out of the country. Jimmy didn't even question it when I introduced him to Cabgar, Chief Ambassador of Cabbage Land."

Muffy hit play.

"*So insurance, you know? Well, Mr. Cabgar, 'round here that's like our dealio. It's where you pay money for stuff that hasn't happened yet, so when it happens we fix it and you don't get screwed. Because there's like this thing, where there's these different dimensions, but what's normal on one planet isn't normal on another planet. And sometimes they bump into each other, and like stuff happens, and then more stuff. Cool, right? No way. Sometimes it's totally uncool. Anyways, that's what we're here for.*"

Tom winced. "At least he is enthusiastic."

"Oh, don't worry. It gets worse." Muffy fast-forwarded through Jimmy's rambling, incoherent sales pitch.

Jimmy's tie was now undone and he was looking rather flustered. "*So, uh, you're like the strong silent type. Fine, whatever, dude. If you don't want insurance, that's on you, man. Don't come crying to us when a portal opens and vegetarians attack and make your planet into a salad bar! And you're all like ahhh nooo I'm getting chewed! Some dude's eating my face!*"

"Not the most diplomatic approach, but young Jimmy does raise a valid concern." Militant Space Vegans really were a terrible menace, so gassy and self-righteous, as they roamed the galaxy in their eco-friendly battle cruisers.

"There's more," Muffy assured him.

When the hologram returned to normal speed, giant sweat rings had appeared in the armpits of Jimmy's dress shirt. He had taken his necktie off and was wearing it as a bandana as he shouted at the hapless cabbage. *"You just keep staring at me! Why you got to be so judgmental, man? You think because you're all full of vitamins and minerals and antioxidants and shit you're better than me? Huh? Well you're not! You're not!"*

"Ah, I think I see your point, Ms. Wappler."

"Uh-huh." Muffy just nodded as she skipped forward again. Now Jimmy was out of view of the camera, but it was obvious from the sound that he was beneath the table, crying.

"It would appear that Ambassador Cabgar won that round."

"That whole video was only four and a half minutes long, Mr. Stranger. Look, I know you like the kid because he took a bullet for you, and I'm not saying that he's *totally* useless, just mostly useless."

"What use *would* you suggest for him then?"

"Uh . . ." Muffy was temporarily stumped, but like a true insurance professional she always managed to find the bright side of every situation. "Some planets still use Soylent Green. Jimmy is mostly made out of valuable proteins and fats."

He had been hoping Jimmy had some prospects better than being rendered down into an edible paste. "Thank you, Ms. Wappler. That will be all."

"Sorry to be the bearer of bad tidings, Mr. Stranger." Muffy got up to leave.

Normally, anyone who was enough of a warrior and scholar to survive an Interdimensional Insurance Internship would be offered a Junior Associate position upon graduation. Despite Tom's initial assessment that Jimmy would be a miserable failure—for heaven's sake, he was getting a degree in *Gender Studies*—Tom had still hoped the young man would make the cut. Miraculously, Jimmy had survived for a bit, but in so doing he had brought dishonor upon their company. Unfortunately, in a business where the smallest error could lead to horrifying painful death or, worse, dissatisfied customers, there was no room for a Jimmy.

"Would you please send Jimmy in to speak with me? I'm afraid I'm going to have to make some cuts."

Muffy clapped her hands gleefully. "Yes, sir! Should I fetch your decapitating axe and a tarp?"

"What? Why?"

"To protect the new carpet obviously."

"Oh." That failure of clear office communication was upon Tom. Jimmy's use of slang had rubbed off on him. Yet another example of reckless unprofessionalism. The intern was a force of chaos. "Sorry, I meant I was going to terminate him. His employment I mean . . . Not his life. That would probably be wrong."

"Well, shucks." Muffy seemed a little dejected. "I'll go get Jimmy."

When Muffy told him that Mr. Stranger needed to speak with him in private, Jimmy was super pumped. He'd been totally rocking it as the new hotness at Stranger & Stranger. He was probably going to get an epic raise, probably a promotion too, a big office with windows, and his own giant fighting robot.

"S'up, Mr. Stranger?"

"What is that thing on your head?"

"Oh, this?" Jimmy touched the awesome bundle of hair he'd tied up on top. "It's called a *man bun*. It's the hot new look on my planet. Pretty badass, huh?"

Jimmy saw Mr. Stranger pause, scowling as he checked the internet thingy implanted in his brain. "Apparently the latest 'hipster' fashion trends on your home world require looking like an effeminate lumberjack in a romper. *What an odd dimension . . .* Please, have a seat, Jimmy." He gestured at the chair in front of his desk. "We need to talk about your future with the company."

"Cool." Jimmy sat down. As usual, Mr. Stranger's desk was super organized. There was a cup with pencils in it and they were all exactly the same length and uniformly sharp. Even the papers in his inbox were perfectly lined up. "When I get my own giant fighting robot, I want it to look like a ninja turtle. Not Donatello though. Who wants a friggin' pole? But everybody always wants to be Leonardo with the sword. That's cliché. So I'm thinking nunchucks."

"I'm afraid discussing the relative merits of various turtle-based weapon systems is not why I have summoned you. Now please, I am attempting to show an appropriate amount of sensitivity. Because you once saved my life—"

"I sure did! That Jeff Conundrum guy is such a douche! He's like the worst insurance agent ever, like how way back he let your home planet get blown up. He's our competition but his company is a total rip-off. It was pretty awesome how you left him trapped in Hell."

"Indeed. That was rewarding. Now please, stop interrupting . . ." Mr. Stranger cleared his throat and tried again. "I had high hopes that you would develop the skills necessary to provide quality customer service. With this internship completed, you will be graduating soon—"

"With a degree in Gender Studies I'll be making the big bucks!"

His boss sighed. "Yes . . . *Gender Studies.*"

"I just got to say, Mr. Stranger, these last few months have been the best time of my whole life. I've gotten to fly around outer space, blow up monsters with lasers, and meet all sorts of hot alien chicks, and they're all like, whoa, *you're with Tom Stranger? Whaaaaat?* And I'm all like, yeah baby, I'm his right-hand man. And they're all swooning and stuff. You know what I'm saying?"

"As usual, not really."

"Before this internship I didn't really know what to do with my life, man. You can only go to so many protests before you get tired of catching scabies, and all the ladies are bossy with dreadlocks and smell funny, and blocking freeway traffic with your body isn't nearly as fun as it sounds. Insurance is James Bond super cool. I love being an insurance agent. This job is like the best thing ever!"

Tom Stranger took a deep breath. "Then I'm afraid that I have some unfortunate news. It is with great sadness that I must inform you that you are being term—"

Suddenly the Claim Alarm sounded. "AWWWWOOOOOGA! CODE RED! CODE RED! ALL ASSOCIATES ON DECK! THIS IS NOT A DRILL!"

The announcement was so loud that Jimmy fell backwards in his chair. With catlike reflexes honed over months of hard core insurancing, Jimmy rolled to the side and tried to take cover behind a potted plant.

"What's going on, man?" he screamed, trying to be heard over the shrieking noise.

Mr. Stranger had leapt to his feet. "That alert only sounds when one of our Premium Comprehensive Platinum Policy holders files a Level Ten Claim."

"That sounds bad! Is that bad?"

"Exceedingly." Mr. Stranger calmly walked to a big case mounted on the wall, which read *In Case of Armageddon Break Glass,* and shattered it with his fist. He reached inside and pulled out an unremarkable leather briefcase. "I must get to the conference room."

It was crazy out in the office. The lights were flashing red. Junior Associates were ducking and covering beneath their desks. Someone had taken a bunch of files, dumped them into a wastepaper basket, and set it on fire. Jimmy had never seen his coworkers wig out like this before. Another intern ran by wearing nothing but football pads with spikes on them.

"I'm scared!"

"That's just the customary dress of Fred's people. I should have never allowed the implementation of *Casual Friday.* That decision also allowed such travesties as your *man bun,*" Mr. Stranger explained as they hurried down the hallway. "Oh, wait, you are remarking upon the general atmosphere of pandemonium and terror. That is to be expected with a Level Ten Claim. The last time we had one of these, hundreds died."

That totally sucked, but from what Jimmy knew about Interdimensional Insurance, that sort of thing happened all the time. "Compared to whole planets blowing up, hundreds doesn't seem too bad."

"I meant hundreds *in this office*. The death toll across the Multiverse was incalculable. Many brave Junior Associates gave their lives. It was a dark day for insurance. Our entire HR department was vaporized. We even had to replace the carpet."

"Whoa. So what were you about to tell me when that siren went off, Mr. Stranger?"

"It will have to wait. If we do not all perish, we will speak again later."

"Cool, cool." Mr. Stranger was a busy dude, he'd get around to Jimmy's promotion later. They had reached the conference room and it was filled with nervous employees loading guns and checking spreadsheets. Jimmy would just have to wait until after this Level Ten thingy was cleared up before he got his fat raise and some sweet nunchucks.

Tom had dealt with several Level Ten claims over his career and he knew that they always required the utmost care. To qualify as a Level Ten, the potential damages had to be staggering, the likely outcomes catastrophic. Previous events of such magnitude had caused the fall of empires, the extinction of species, the destruction of worlds, and a great deal of customer dissatisfaction.

Muffy had already prepared the conference room, put a pot of coffee on, and even had time to apply her war paint. She had gone with a festive blue *Braveheart* theme. "We're all ready, Mr. Stranger."

"Excellent. Which Platinum Policy is it, Ms. Wappler?"

"The *big one*," she whispered.

"CorreiaTech Prime?"

"The Interdimensional Lord of Hate *himself* is on the line."

The room fell deadly silent. A few of the weaker-willed Junior Associates fainted.

Not only was this their biggest account, but this particular claim was coming from the merciless CEO of the most powerful megacorporation in the Multiverse, a man whose hobbies included collecting vintage antique atomic bombs, who subsisted on a diet of endangered unicorn steaks, who was so rich that when he shot trap and skeet, he used Fabergé eggs instead of clay pigeons.

That guy . . .

"Put him through, Ms. Wappler."

The ruggedly handsome, totally ripped CEO appeared on the screen, smoking a cigar.

"Greetings, sir. How can we serve your insurance needs today?"

The Interdimensional Lord of Hate ran one massive hand through his thick, luxurious, heavy metal-quality hair in a very frustrated manner. "Damn it, Tom! Where's my manatee?"

"I do not understand."

"Wendell volunteered to help you at that panel thing this morning, with you, your idiot sidekick—"

"Hey!"

Tom shushed Jimmy.

"And that bald fat clone version of me who writes fantasy books or some crap."

"Technically, the author is not a clone, merely another version of you from an alternative reality, who is, comparatively speaking, an utter failure."

"Lame. Whatever. Anyways, my CFO went missing after your presser. I'd leave it up to my private army, but our scans show another dimension was involved, so his abduction should be covered."

There were gasps from the Junior Associates. Wendell the Manatee had been kidnapped! This was terrible news.

"That is most unfortunate. I can assure you that Stranger & Stranger will not rest until we find him and your claim is settled."

"That's what I'm paying you for, Tom. I don't know who took him, but you'd better shake the trees until something falls out, or there's gonna be hell to pay."

Tom made a solemn vow. "I will not rest until Wendell sleeps with the fishes."

Only Jimmy was confused. "We're going to kill him in a mob hit?"

"What is *wrong* with you?" Muffy whispered.

"What?" Now it was Tom's turn to be puzzled. "No, Jimmy. He lives in the ocean. We are going to return him to his home."

"Oh, okay. But I still don't get what's so important about one manatee?"

All of the other Junior Associates stared at Jimmy like he was insane. Then they quickly stepped away from him, clearing a circle like he was about to get struck by lightning. Which he probably was, since the Interdimensional Lord of Hate had snarled and raised his mighty finger and thumb, poised to snap.

"Please forgive him, your Hateyness. Jimmy is but a lowly intern, ignorant in the ways of the Multiverse. I assume you are aiming a satellite death ray or some such device at him as we speak. I would politely ask you to refrain from disintegrating any of my staff."

"Fine." The Interdimensional Lord of Hate lowered his fingers. "But I'll elaborate for your village's idiot. Wendell may be my accountant, and we've roped him into playing the cleric in our monthly company D&D night, but it isn't me you have to worry about. When his people find out, they're going to be torqued. They will call for a *hooning.*"

Tom was proficient in six hundred and eighty-five languages so he explained it for his staff who weren't as knowledgeable. "The word is rather nuanced, but *hoon* is the battle cry of the Manatee. They are slow to anger, but when it comes, it is terrible to behold."

"Damned skippy. There isn't anything scarier than a herd of vigilante sea cows on a rampage. They tend to nuke first and ask questions later."

It was a race against time. "Understood, sir. Consider it done."

"Good. Contrary to what my critics might say, I don't like when whole planets get slaughtered. Losing that many customers sucks. CorreiaTech Prime out." The screen went dark.

"Okay, am I the only one who is really super confused?" Jimmy asked. "The manatees on my Earth are pretty chill."

"That's what they want you to think!" Muffy said. "Does your home world have legends of the sunken continent of Atlantis?"

"Yeah, sure, I think so."

"Who do you think sunk it?"

"Enough," Tom ordered. "Muffy is correct. Manatees are known for two things: their fiscal responsibility, and their unrelenting thirst for vengeance once provoked. Wendell is a hero to his herd. His kidnapping will surely rouse their fiery Florida-Man tempers. Their justice will be swift, unflinching, and indiscriminate. If we do not retrieve him quickly, the Multiverse will face *a murder of manatees.*"

❖ CHAPTER THREE ❖
The Big 10 AM Shakedown

Miami, Florida
Earth #984-A-3256

FOR CLAIMS LIKE THIS, Tom knew it was best to start at the scene of the incident. He quickly assembled a crack team of forensic insurance investigators and they traveled through the Thorne Gate

back to the press conference center. The parking lot was quickly
filled with Stranger & Stranger battlemechs and hover tanks from
across the Multiverse.

After interviewing the witnesses and watching the security
camera video, Tom had a good idea what had happened. After
concluding the panel, Wendell's handlers had wheeled his giant fish
tank back to his signature monster truck. Of course, Wendell had
been given the VIP parking space. While loading they had been set
upon by invisible attackers (good invisibility cloaks, too, genuine
Predator brand, not the chintzy knock-off invisibility cloaks you
could pick up at Walmart on any half-decent world).

The handlers had been stunned with phasers and had not seen a
thing. Wendell was a fearsome warrior, usually armed with several
advanced CorreiaTech weapons but, alas, had been distracted
looking at his phone, having a political debate on Twitter (where the
popular manatee had more than ten billion followers) and had never
seen them coming. His fish tank had been shot with a freeze ray,
instantly solidifying the water and placing the noble sea cow into
cryostasis. Then the whole thing had been rolled into a suspicious
black van with out-of-universe plates which had been waiting
nearby. The kidnappers were gone in seconds.

This was the work of professionals. The only DNA found at the
scene was aquatic mammal. The kidnappers had left no tracks, and
according to Miss Cleo, no psychic residue. They were well trained,
well armed, and highly motivated. This was shaping up to be quite
the challenge.

"All right, listen up Junior Associates, our manatee has been missing
for 90 minutes. Average rocket-boost-assisted hover van speed is
400,000 miles an hour. That gives us a radius of 600,000 miles. What I
want from each and every one of you is a hard-target search of every gas
station, residence, warehouse, farmhouse, henhouse, outhouse, and
doghouse in that area. Checkpoints go up at the edge of the solar system.
Your manatee's name is Wendell. Go get him."

"Whoa! I love that movie too, Mr. Stranger!"

"What movie?" Tom was momentarily puzzled why Jimmy the
Former Intern was present at all, but then he remembered that in
the heat of the moment he had neglected to finish firing him. "Oh,
I'm sorry, Jimmy. I forgot to tell you that you're fired."

It took Jimmy a moment to process that. "Huh?"

"Fired. Terminated. You are no longer employed by Stranger & Stranger. It was due to your terrible performance review. I should have told you back at the office and saved you the drive. I would be happy to discuss this with you later so that you may learn from your mistakes, but right now I must focus on staving off the Sea Cow Apocalypse."

Tom did not enjoy rudeness, but he had no choice but to leave Jimmy befuddled and stammering in the parking lot. He had much work to do. The rest of his team were running back to their vehicles. There was a series of sonic booms as mechs blasted off. He found that Muffy was busy consulting the Galactic Data Sphere, searching for any individual or group which might hold a grudge against the manatee, either professional or personal. Professionally, the Chief Financial Officer of an ultra-powerful, Multiverse-spanning megacorporation tended to make enemies. The personal list was far longer, but mostly because Wendell tended to talk a lot of trash while playing Call of Duty online multiplayer.

"Ms. Wappler, this morning a reporter asked a pointed question about a hostile takeover. Do you have any further information concerning that?"

"I sure do. CorreiaTech wants to merge a whole bunch of super evil companies together, and really corner the market on evil products."

"Sounds evil, yet efficient. Do you have a list?"

"A bunch of our clients are already on there: Weyland-Yutani, Cyberdyne Systems, LexCorp, Umbrella, Kentucky Fried Velociraptor, and United Airlines." Muffy sent the data directly to his infolink. "You got a hunch, Mr. Stranger?"

"A good agent must follow his instincts," Tom said as he picked up his Doomsday Briefcase and headed for his mech.

As Tom strapped into the pilot's seat and prepared for takeoff, he noticed poor Jimmy still wandering the parking lot, lost and forlorn, dreams shattered, forever deprived of the opportunity to provide quality customer service. Perhaps Muffy had been right, and it would have been more merciful to put him out of his misery. Just not on the new carpet.

❖ ❖ ❖

"This sucks," Jimmy muttered as the last of the groovy space tanks and giant robots blasted off, leaving him all by himself. There was a conveniently located can for him to angrily kick down the road.

It wasn't fair. Jimmy had been awesome as an insurance intern. He'd made copies, fetched coffee, and only ate an appropriate amount of doughnuts when Muffy brought them in. Where did Mr. Stranger get off with his fancy *evaluations*? That cabbage dude had been stone cold. Nobody could have sold that heartless bastard insurance.

He had never really been good at much. Sure, he had a whole bunch of participation trophies, but now he was beginning to suspect those weren't as meaningful as he'd always thought. But he'd worked super hard to get good at insurance, harder than he'd ever worked before. He'd even been pumping iron. Heck, he'd gone from a .07 on the Grylls Survivability Scale to a .09. A 1.0 was how much trauma it took to kill a single Bear Grylls, and Jimmy had a ways to go before that, but he'd started out equivalent to a standard Earth chicken, and now the GSS ranked him as survivable as a ficus plant. Though Jimmy didn't know what a ficus plant was, he was certain it had to be pretty badass.

He'd come too far to give up now! He was going to show Mr. Stranger that he had what it took to be an insurance agent! He knew he could do it if he believed in himself hard enough. Only, unlike college, Mr. Stranger had standards. Begging wouldn't work. Mr. Stranger only cared about customer service and results.

That gave Jimmy an idea. Everybody else was out trying to find their missing client, but if Jimmy could find that manatee first, he'd be golden. He wouldn't just get his job back, he'd be Employee of the Month! All he had to do was figure out the Crime of the Century before all of the trained, competent people did.

Only he had something those guys didn't. Most Junior Associates came from super tough worlds, where every day was a fight for survival, so they didn't watch a lot of TV, but Jimmy had mastered the art of binge streaming and most of that had been cop shows. He'd had to keep his love of cop shows a dirty little secret from the other Gender Studies majors because they mostly watched *Girls* on HBO and if they found out, they would've yelled at him about *cisnormative fascism* or some other big words he didn't really understand.

If all those cop shows had taught Jimmy anything, it was that it was always the rogue, loose-cannon detective who didn't give a damn about "authority" and "rules" who got the job done. That sounded like Jimmy to a T because, let's face it, Jimmy knew he was pretty much a real-life cross between Luther and Raylan Givens.

Sure, the average Junior Associate at Stranger & Stranger had been a Navy SEAL Astronaut Lawyer or something before getting into insurance, but right now they'd be bogged down with "logic" and "facts" while Jimmy was going to follow his gut. And on TV cop shows, whenever they didn't know what to do next, they would go roust some shady characters until somebody talked, and somebody always talked.

This version of Florida was way more high-tech and swoopy than Jimmy's home world, but it also had kind of a cool cyberpunk *Blade Runner* vibe. That meant there was bound to be a seedy criminal underworld.

Since he had tankpooled over to the conference center and his Prius was back on Home Office World, Jimmy had to call for an Uber. He told the driver to take him to the sleaziest cesspool of shifty lying dirtbags on the whole planet. But, sadly, by the time they got to London it would be after work hours so there wouldn't be anybody at *The Guardian* to shake down. It was those newspaper dorks' lucky day.

So they picked the next best sleazy local thing.

The Faceless Mook Bar & Grill was supposed to be a wretched hive of scum and villainy. Jimmy's driver said this was where all the bad dudes hung out. Not the top tier really bad guys, but more like the low- and mid-level threatenable bad guys who would rat out their bosses. Man, Uber drivers were super helpful in this dimension!

The bouncer at the door was a five-hundred-pound cyborg gorilla. "Greetings. Human females drink free on Fridays."

"Sweet. Maybe I'll meet some ladies."

The gorilla looked at Jimmy's ID. "Oh, my bad. You are a human male."

"Whoa." He'd heard about this all the time in Gender Studies but had never had it happen to him personally before. "Did you just assume my *gender*?"

"Yes. You are very puny with delicate bones." The gorilla plucked a tick from his own pelt and ate it.

"I can't wait to post about this on Tumblr!" Misgendering was worth like ten thousand victim points!

"I must warn you, frail human. Inside this establishment the sick and weak are usually killed and eaten. But you are over twenty-one, so go on in." The gorilla opened the door.

On the other side was truly the scariest bar Jimmy had ever seen. It was all bikers, roughnecks, Yakuza, killer robots, pirates—both space and the old-fashioned, time-travelling kind—and assorted monstrous aliens from across the Multiverse. He'd heard Wendell's home Earth was truly cosmopolitan, which was a word they'd used a lot in college though Jimmy wasn't sure what three-flavored ice cream had to do with anything. All he knew was this place was so nasty Patrick Swayze from *Road House* would have walked in, took one look around, and said, nope, screw this, I'm out of here.

Jimmy swallowed hard, called upon his inner insurance agent, and stepped inside. The music was so loud it punched him in the ear holes. It was a good thing they'd shut off that profanity filter, because otherwise the gangster rap soundtrack would be nothing but a string of beeps. Jimmy thought because he'd watched every episode of *Burn Notice* and *Dexter* he would be prepared for the Miami criminal underworld, but this was a bit overwhelming. There were exotic dancers in cages suspended from the ceiling, several burly men were engaged in a bloody knife fight, and Jon Taffer from *Bar Rescue* was loudly berating the owner about how the buffalo wings had not been cooked to a safe temperature in order to prevent salmonella.

He went up to the bar. The bartender looked suspiciously like Danny Trejo. Jimmy ordered a mojito because that seemed a very Miami thing to do. This place wasn't messing around, and it came out in a Super Big Gulp-sized cup, which Jimmy immediately chugged. Then he thought better of it, and ordered four more, because his courage could use a little boost.

"You think you can handle all that, little man?"

Jimmy snorted. He might not be as skilled as some of the other interns, but he'd gone to Chico State. Jimmy could function with a blood alcohol level of *half.* "Just keep 'em coming, Machete."

"Okay, but don't blame me for your poor life choices. What brings you here anyway?"

Jimmy leaned over the bar and looked on the other side, just in case there was a manatee tied up behind it. *Nope.* That would've been super convenient.

"I'm looking for information."

"You a cop?"

"Do I look like a cop?"

"Not really. They've usually got some department-mandated physical fitness and grooming standards. What is going on with your hair?"

"It's my man bun."

"So you're like a special-needs samurai or something?"

"Nope." He pulled out a business card and slid it across the grimy bar. "Jimmy Duquesne, Interdimensional Insurance Agent . . . Intern . . . Former. Whatever. Maybe you've heard of me?"

"No way, homeboy!" The bartender stared at the card in shock. "You're *the* Jimmy the Intern?"

"Wait . . . Seriously. You have heard of me?"

"Sure. We all loved that audiobook, *esè*! Adam Baldwin is the bomb!" the bartender shouted so everyone could hear. "Guys, guys, it's Jimmy the Intern!"

Suddenly Jimmy was surrounded by a crowd of terrifying meat heads, asking things like, "Is Muffy super hot?," "Can I get your autograph?" and "What's Tom Stranger really like?"

Jimmy was starting to feel his 64-ounce mojito so he answered truthfully. "Muffy looks like the movie version of Harley Quinn, only less slutty, more classy. Sure, I'll sign stuff. And Mr. Stranger is super badass at customer service, but he can be kind of insensitive. He fired me today!"

There was a chorus of "No way, man!" and "That's bullshit!"

"I know, right? Us interns have feelings too!"

The room of hoodlums seemed moved by his plight. "Yeah, nobody ever stops to think about how us minor supporting villains feel. We're always getting beaten up and we never get no credit!"

"John Wick shot me seventeen times," one giant with a

handlebar mustache sniffed, "and my boss didn't even send me a get-well card."

This was going way better than expected. "Groovy. So like I'm here to kick some ass until somebody tells me who kidnapped Wendell so I can get my job back. So consider this a shakedown!"

"Yay!" Thugs loved a good shakedown.

Jimmy downed his third mojito. It was getting a little blurry since he couldn't remember drinking the second one. "Okay then!" He stood up on his stool. "I need information and I ain't leaving until somebody talks! So how do we do this? Do I just like grab a pool cue and start whacking dudes over the head or what?"

Immediately, several of the patrons shattered their beer bottles so they could stab Jimmy with the pointy ends.

"Damn it! I have to clean this place!" the bartender shouted.

"Sorry. Reflex," said an embarrassed thug.

"Every night I've got to spend an hour sweeping up broken glass and eyeballs and nobody ever says so much as a thank you. Now listen, Jimmy, you don't have to solve all your problems with violence. I suppose you could just ask nicely."

It turned out stereotypical criminal bar bartenders really were wise. "That works too, I guess. Okay, help me out guys, what kind of sick bastard would steal a manatee?"

The thugs pondered on it for a moment and then began shouting answers.

"Sea World!"

"Manatee collectors!"

"No! You can't just guess! Somebody has to know the right answer so I can get to the bad guys and file a claim before Mr. Stranger does. Think!"

"Uh . . . Petco?"

"Not helping!" Jimmy was getting frustrated. And also a little dizzy, so he got down off the stool before he fell off.

"Psst . . ." The bartender leaned in conspiratorially. "I think I know which *pendejos* stole your famous manatee. They're the baddest of the bad. They hang out at this rival bar down on the waterfront. It's even meaner and tougher than this place."

Well, knowing that would have saved him a bunch of time! "Damn it, Uber!" Jimmy shook his fist at the ceiling. "Sorry, everybody, but it looks like I've got to take my shakedown business elsewhere!"

The assorted scumbags were all like "awwww, man . . ." and "bummer, dude."

"Hey, everybody, I know what to do!" the bartender shouted. "Let's go riot and burn things to help Jimmy the Intern get his manatee back!" *That was a great idea*! The rest of them immediately began to cheer as they pulled out a wide assortment of guns and knives.

Jimmy led his newly formed angry mob out into the street. This was gonna be sweet! As Mr. Stranger would say, things were going *splendidly*.

❖ CHAPTER FOUR ❖
Tom's 11:00 AM March for Science

Louisville, Kentucky
Earth #587-F-2288

THINGS WERE NOT GOING SPLENDIDLY for Tom Stranger at all. It looked like he would have to work through his lunch hour again *and* he was being pursued through the jungle by a pack of vicious, genetically-modified, plus-size velociraptors.

A velociraptor leapt from the shadows. Tom slugged it in the teeth, sending the eight-foot-tall dinosaur flying back through the leaves.

"Bad dinosaur. Stay." Only like most husky velociraptors it was exceedingly disobedient, so it hopped back up and tried to disembowel him with its deadly hook toe. Dodging aside in a blur, Tom let the superefficient predator pass by, and then grabbed it in a choke hold.

It began rolling and crashing through the underbrush, trying to dislodge him. This was not the first time that he'd had to choke out a dinosaur—this week—but their colorful feathers got all over his suit, which was a very unprofessional look, and he'd left his lint brush back in his office. Tree trunks shattered into splinters as his body was driven into them, but Tom held on as its struggles gradually became weaker.

Once he had rendered the dinosaur unconscious, Tom got up and tried to dust off his charcoal three-button Men's Wearhouse suit only to discover there were feathers stuck to him *everywhere*. "Tsk tsk." Then he realized that he had been surrounded by the rest of the pack, and they were creeping slowly forward in order to rip him into pieces. Tom was opposed to being devoured by hungry dinosaurs on general principle, but getting killed while he was trying to take care of an important claim was especially vexing.

"I really do not have time for this nonsense." Tom drew the ultra-lethal CorreiaTech Combat Wombat from the holster on his belt and declared, "Unless you wish me to obliterate your entire flock, show yourself, Colonel."

Someone blew a whistle. Immediately all the velociraptors fled in terror. A moment later Tom heard the high-pitched whine of a jet pack as a portly, white-haired gentleman in a white suit descended through the treetop canopy. The Colonel stopped and hovered above the clearing. "Surprise! So what did you think of our exciting new dining experience?"

"I'm not sure I see the appeal, sir," Tom said as he holstered his Combat Wombat.

"Great googly moogly, Tom, the adrenaline rush makes the meat taste better!"

"The customer's meat or the dinosaur's?"

"Both! Don't you get it? It's man versus his dinner! Only the strong will survive. It's primal supper!"

"Hmmm . . . I believe I will stick with original recipe."

"That's because you're a traditional sort. Popeyes came along and then everybody wanted spicy! Well I'll show them spicy! There's nothing spicier than fighting your food to the death. Will the tables turn? Will the hunter become the hunted? I call it the Most Dangerous Meal Deal. We drop you off in the jungle with nothing but a sharpened spork and a bucket of mashed potatoes, biscuits, and a medium soda for $7.99. It's even all-you-can-eat, if you're man enough."

"That does sound like an excellent value."

"And the best part, so many customers will get eaten, I'll save a bundle on velociraptor feed. I'll still come out ahead!"

It was unfortunate when his clients descended into murderous insanity, but Tom did not discriminate. As long as the Colonel's premiums were paid on time, Tom would continue to render the finest customer service possible.

"If I may be so bold as to offer a suggestion, Colonel, if you will be advertising this *meal deal* across dimensions, have them sign a waiver first. It will prevent many claims. In most realities dinosaurs went extinct."

"They're so finger-licking good those poor saps don't even know what they're missing. I do declare I was surprised to see you show up here, Tom. I saw the news. I figured you'd be keeping your head down because of all those angry dolphin protestors."

"That was all a misunderstanding, Colonel. I hold no animosity toward dolphins and was wrong to use a hurtful stereotype."

"*Sure,*" the Colonel said as he gave a big obvious wink.

Tom sighed.

The Colonel paused to wipe his brow with a handkerchief. It was very humid in the primordial jungles of Kentucky. "Anyways, what brings you all the way out to my dimension?"

"There are rumors that CorreiaTech is attempting to take over all of the . . . I will call them *alignment challenged* companies in the Multiverse. You are among their number. I was curious if you knew if any in particular would go after Wendell."

"That sea cow is a financial genius. Without him the whole deal falls apart. So any of them might want him dead. I'd have taken him myself and fed him to my flock, but manatees are fatty, and raptors get sluggish after a big meal like that."

"Fortunately, I believe you." If it turned out the claim was against another one of his clients, it would require some finesse to come to an equitable solution. He'd never be voted Number One in Customer Service for the fourth year in a row if he started shooting his own clients. "Do any of them in particular stand out to you?"

"Now that you mention it, there's one shady type who holds a grudge. Personally, I'd check out Bill Nye."

"The Science Guy?"

"More like the megalomaniacal science jerk."

Tom knew of him, and did not care for Bill Nye at all. As a children's television show host, he had been okay once, but he'd been driven mad with power, and now he was giving all bow tie wearers a bad name. "I did not think Bill Nye would be into Grand Theft Manatee."

"Those two got into a heated argument recently. Bill Nye hates rising sea levels. Manatees think they're great. Really opens up new real estate opportunities for them. They went at it on Twitter, until Bill blocked him because Wendell made fun of his song *My Sex Junk*."

"To be fair, *My Sex Junk* is quite possibly, literally, the worst thing ever made."

"I'd agree, Tom, and if this encounter was ever recorded into another one of those newfangled audiobooks of yours, I'd encourage listeners to go plug *Bill Nye My Sex Junk* into YouTube and listen themselves to see that we ain't exaggerating." The Colonel gestured at the unconscious velociraptor. "Anyways, you want that I should fry this one up for you?"

Tom still had important business to attend to, but it was rather difficult to provide excellent customer service on an empty stomach. "Thank you, Colonel. Please make it a to-go bucket."

The Colonel waited until Tom Stranger's mech had disappeared into the atmosphere before speaking aloud.

"Alrighty then, Tom's gone. You can come out now."

There was a weird twisting of light as an invisible kidnapper floated through the jungle. As suspected, the nefarious beings had been watching the whole exchange to make sure the Colonel honored their deal.

"I did just like you asked and sent Tom off on a wild goose chase. I said the same thing to those manatee bounty hunters that came by earlier. Now pay up." A little bottle appeared as the invisible creature tossed it to him. The Colonel caught it and greedily read the label. "Ah, the rarest of my eleven herbs and spices, all the way from Arrakis." Ground-up sand worm kept the meat so tender and juicy it warped the very fabric of space and time.

Chuckling, the Colonel dropped the spice into his pocket. "Pleasure doing business with you fellows—" But suddenly another invisible creature materialized behind him and ripped a spark plug wire out of his jet pack. The engine sputtered and he fell into a giant fern. "Hey!"

The kidnappers laughed at him as they levitated away.

"You good-for-nothing, double-crossing scallywags!" the Colonel shouted. Realizing he'd been had, he pulled out the spice bottle, unscrewed the cap, and sniffed. "What? This is just *paprika*! Come back here! Nobody bamboozles the Colonel! Nobody! Mark my words, you seedy ruffians, you'll pay for this!"

Except they were already gone. Grumbling thoughts of revenge upon the tricksters, the Colonel got up, only to trail off as he realized he was surrounded by deadly velociraptors. "Stay. Bad dinosaurs." He reached for his anti-raptor whistle, only to discover the kidnappers had snagged that too. "Well, ain't this a pickle."

The Most Dangerous Meal Deal pounced.

Washington D.C.
Earth #169-J-00561

TOM STRANGER had been to this particular dimension a lot recently. It contained Jimmy's home planet, a place so odd and statistically unpredictable that it made Tom a little uncomfortable. But it was also the home of Bill Nye, alleged manatee kidnapper. On most planets Nye would merely be considered an engineer who had gotten a TV show, but apparently on this strange world that meant he had been crowned Science Pope.

On most civilized worlds science was a process involving observable data and testable hypotheses, not a religion based on feeling superior toward anyone with differing political beliefs. So it was with a great dealt of trepidation that Tom attempted to infiltrate the so-called March for Science to search for his target.

It was an exceedingly smug, yet festive event. Tom did not understand the strange local customs, so when he found an oddly shaped pink knit hat which had been recently discarded, he put it on in order to blend in better. Most of the other marchers were carrying colorful, grammatically incorrect signage having something to do with Cheetos, or pithy sayings that always boiled down to how anyone who disagreed with them were stupid idiots who could be safely dismissed without thought, analysis, or debate. This didn't seem particularly scientific to Tom, but what did he know? He was only a man with eleven advanced degrees who flew around the galaxy in a space ship. It wasn't like he knew "science."

There was no time to scan the entire crowd of self-righteous marchers, so Tom would need to gather human intel directly. Luckily he had been trained on how to build rapport with backwards, superstitious civilizations. He approached some marchers who were having a conversation.

"I read on this movie star's blog that a good juice cleanse can remove vaccines that cause autism, because I think I'm like totally allergic to gluten."

"Me, too! I just need to align my chakras so my healing crystals will fight off GMOs better."

"I'm so glad that we're smart and believe in science, unlike those nasty Republicans!"

Tom smoothly tried to mingle. "Greetings, fellow citizens of Earth 169-J-00561. I, too, pound sign f'ing love science."

One of the Science Marchers glared at Tom suspiciously. Despite Tom's new pink hat, she must have suspected he was not really of their tribe. "I wish Medicare would cover goat milk therapy, don't you?"

From his extensive knowledge of anthropology, Tom could tell this was some manner of test. He would have to tread carefully in order to be accepted as one of them. "Obviously." They did not immediately attack, so Tom pushed onward. He needed to build a relationship of trust. She was carrying a sign that said REPUBLICANS R FLAT TEH EARTH SOCIETY. "I have been to the Flat Earth. It was mostly a tourist trap with a very underwhelming gift shop."

"Triggered!" She hissed and pointed. "Republican nazi fascist sexist!"

"Seize the climate denier!" someone else shouted.

This was not going well at all. Before Tom could be seized by the mob and burned at the stake for heresy against their unquestionable science gods, he threw down a ninja smoke bomb and escaped in the confusion.

After several more failed interactions, Tom found himself wishing that Jimmy was still employed with the firm, because at least he would be able to communicate in the mangled gibberish of made-up buzz words this particular tribe spoke. Many of these humans were also sporting man buns. Tom began wondering if perhaps he had been too harsh on the lad . . .

Then Tom caught a break. Through the meandering crowd he spotted another bow tie wearer. It was Bill Nye! *Finally*. And since Nye wasn't a client, Tom was free to deal with him however he wanted, up to and including merciless beatings. Tom was looking forward to getting this claim filed so he could return to a sensible reality. He began pushing his way through the marchers.

Only that was when Tom realized he wasn't the only one heading directly toward The Science Guy.

Like Tom, the pair of manatee bounty hunters were doing their best to blend in with the Science Marchers. They had both put on 8XL *I'm With Her* T-shirts over their power armor. One manatee was holding a sign that he'd found which boldly declared HANDS OFF MY UTERUS, only he was holding it upside down because he had probably never bothered to learn English. The other had stretched one of the odd pink hats over the glass dome of his helmet. Their disguises were perfect. Though the anti-grav propulsion units in the suits made it so that their tails were hovering inches off of the ground, none of the marchers seemed to notice. Manatees were sleek infiltrators that way.

One bounty hunter stuck a flipper beneath his Hillary shirt— probably stolen for this mission, since manatees were such big supporters of free market economics they'd never vote Democrat— and pulled out a Combat Wombat.

That was a bad sign. There was no *Less Lethal* setting on a Combat Wombat. In fact, they were advertised as *More Than Lethal*, because sometimes they even killed ghosts. CorreiaTech was so philosophically opposed to Less Than Lethal weapons that they'd once made a version that shot bean bag rounds, only the bean bags were made of depleted uranium.

So these manatees really weren't messing around.

"Hmmm." Tom was in a bit of a quandary. Even though the bounty hunters were from a different dimension, Nye wasn't one of his clients, so technically this wasn't his problem. However, if they obliterated Nye before Tom confirmed he was the kidnapper then he'd never know where to send the claim paperwork. So he pushed onward. "Excuse me. Pardon me."

Before Tom could reach The Science Guy, he received a priority call from Muffy. "I am really rather busy right now, Ms. Wappler."

"*I figured, Mr. Stranger, but it'll only take a second. Remember how those initial DNA tests from the seawater spilled at the scene came back as Aquatic Mammal? Well, it wasn't Wendell's tank water at all. I'll send you over the detailed results right now.*"

"Very well." Tom viewed the report over his infolink as he continued to shove hippies out of the way. He was very good at multitasking. He gasped when he got to the DNA match. This wasn't just terrible news, it was the worst outcome possible! The repercussions would be awful. He'd never hear the end of it. Also, it meant that he had been set up.

"The kidnapper isn't Bill Nye after all."

"*That guy who made* My Sex Junk?"

"Yes. And he's about to be destroyed by manatees for a crime he didn't commit."

"*Ugh. Let them. That song was so bad it's like sound barfed in my ears.*"

"Indeed."

"*Photons that touched the* My Sex Junk *video touched my eyes, Mr. Stranger. My eyes! I had to pay to grow new eyeballs in a vat and get a transplant it was so bad.*"

The manatee was dramatically screwing a silencer onto the muzzle of his Combat Wombat. "Please forgive me for interrupting your tirade, Ms. Wappler, but I will have to call you back."

Bill Nye was giving a long-winded speech to his adoring worshippers. "So then Neil DeGrasse Tyson said nobody could make science more boring and pedantic than he could, so I said challenge accepted! Ha ha ha!" He noticed Tom. "Oh, hello my child, have you come to hear about how our Lord and Master Science has declared nuclear power is scary bad?"

"Everyone on this planet is insane, but no." In fact, Tom had three nuclear reactors on his body at that moment, and he used one to activate his personal energy shield because the manatees were closing fast. "Get behind me, Science Man."

"Witchcraft!" Bill Nye shrieked when he saw Tom's flickering energy shield materialize.

The manatee fired his Combat Wombat. The hypervelocity round exploded against the shield. Tom immediately responded by spin-kicking the pistol from the manatee's flipper. Though incredibly fearsome, their lack of opposable thumbs could be a real detriment in close combat.

The bounty hunters seemed surprised to see an Interdimensional Insurance Agent here, and hesitated before launching their rampage. Tom took advantage of their momentary confusion.

"Stand down, noble manatees. Though sanctimonious and annoying, this human is not your enemy."

The bounty hunters exchanged a glance. They did not give up so easily, but they knew Tom Stranger had a reputation for integrity. "*Fleeerp?*"

"Correct. Bill Nye has, as you put it, *jumped the shark,* but we have been lied to. In the colloquial terms your people are so fond of, he is a *red herring.*"

"The red herring is endangered because of fracking," Bill Nye suddenly declared. "Impeach Trump or the red herring will go extinct. Science has spoken!"

"Science has spoken!" chanted all the marchers, even though that hypothesis had not been tested, and no data had been collected or analyzed. "We are more smarter!"

"May clean energy be upon you, my children."

"I stand in awe of how absurd this planet is." Tom turned back to the bounty hunters, because at least they were rational. "Please spare these pathetic land mammals. I will go settle this claim, and retrieve your leader."

"*Hoooon,*" said the other manatee.

"What do you mean you two are just tying up loose ends because your herd has already dispatched an armada to wage unrelenting total war across the Multiverse?"

He spread his flippers apologetically, like *whoops, shit happens.* Then since his mission was already compromised, the manatee took his ridiculous pink hat off in order to retain what little dignity he had left.

"Oh, no," Bill Nye cried once their clever disguise was revealed. "Behold! As was prophesized in my scholarly Netflix show, these peaceful sea creatures have been driven from their habitat by global warming! Hurry, my children! Roll them back into the water. They're dying!"

The marchers immediately mobbed the manatees. The bounty

hunter began beating people with his UTERUS sign. It turned into a giant wrestling match between the cultists and the manatees who really didn't want to get rolled anywhere. Tom figured they could work it out without him, so he began running to his mech. He had to get back to Wendell's home world before the manatee armada indiscriminately pulverized every Florida in existence.

❖ CHAPTER FIVE ❖
Tom's 12:00 Noon Reminder
To Have Muffy Schedule Some Training
On Non-Violent Conflict Resolution

Miami, Florida
Earth #984-A-3256

THEY HAD ASSEMBLED a crack team of insurance professionals in the abandoned warehouse across the street from the building where they believed the kidnappers were holding Wendell. When Tom arrived, Muffy was already briefing the Junior Associates.

"Okay, kiddos, time is of the essence. The manatee armada is on its way to blow up this Florida as we speak. However, we can't just barge in willy-nilly and start wrecking the place."

One of the Junior Associates raised his hand. "How come?"

"Because this has potential public relations nightmare written all over it. Duh. You all saw Mr. Stranger's press conference this morning. This is super sensitive. The last thing this company needs is more controversy. One screw-up and this is going to be all over social media. The details are in your handouts . . . Oh, hey, the boss is here. It's all yours, Mr. Stranger."

"Thank you, Ms. Wappler." Tom took his place in front of his team.

They were the elite, the best of the best, the finest Junior Associates in the Multiverse, perched like falcons, ready to swoop in and deliver the finest-quality customer service possible. They all came from harsh, tough worlds. Before getting into the far more challenging field of Interdimensional Insurance, each of them had developed a respectable resume. Rip Face-Punch had been an elite hostage rescue team leader, brain surgeon, and children's book illustrator. Dirk Hardsack had been a matador, Shaolin monk, and inventor of the Fidget Spinner. And last but not least, there was professional polar bear wrangler, Iditarod champion, and cosmonaut, Beardly McSpetsnaz.

"Gentle-agents, we will strike in exactly five minutes and forty-seven seconds. I have downloaded detailed maps of the target directly to your infolinks. Using my years of experience I have formulated an exacting plan, accounting for every possible danger, which you will memorize, and then execute to the second. This will be a surgical strike."

Tom pointed at each Junior Associate as he gave their assignments. "Face-Punch, you are on over watch. McSpetsnaz, crowd control, and remember when you hand out business cards to let them know about our free rate quote. Wappler, heavy weapons."

Muffy pumped her fist in the air. "Yes!"

"And Hardsack, claims paperwork."

"Aww . . . but I brought my nunchucks."

"Do not forget the photo documentation this time. This claim could go to Arbitration and Chuck Norris has no patience for sloppy paperwork. Now, as Ms. Wappler has already so aptly explained, discretion is everything; the reputation of our company, and also the future of this Florida, are at stake. Due to the sensitive nature of the individuals involved, this could go very badly for us. We must keep this quiet. So I reiterate . . . *discretion* is of the utmost importance."

"Sir, there might be a problem." Face-Punch interrupted the briefing, but he was at the window on lookout duty, so it had to be important. "I don't think Jimmy the Intern got the memo."

"I fired Jimmy this morning. Of course, I did not CC him on the email."

Face-Punch peered through the scope of his Sniper Wombat to confirm. "Well, Jimmy's blundering down the middle of the street directly toward the target building at the head of what appears to be an angry mob."

Well, there went that plan.

Jimmy was having a great time. "Man, this is awesome!"

The bartender looked over their small army as they flipped over cars and broke windows, and nodded approvingly. "You were right, Jimmy. Taking the time to stop by Home Depot for torches and pitchforks first really set the ambiance."

Mr. Stranger was always talking about the value of being *proactive*. He was going to be so impressed that Jimmy was sure to get his old job back. Sure, there might have been *some* inadvertent property damage to the city on their way over, but it was a small price to pay for customer service or whatever.

"This is the place," the bartender declared.

It was a rough neighborhood down by the docks. There was lots of trash, stray dogs, and graffiti everywhere. The cars had already been flipped over so Jimmy's mob flipped them back right-side up.

"Where?"

The bartender pointed. "That one."

The building was extra sketchy, cinder blocks, bars over the windows, razor wire over the bars, and featuring gaudy neon signs which declared the establishment was named Bottlenose Jack's.

The mob paused because it was a little intimidating. This place had a rep.

"You sure about this, Jimmy? These guys are the baddest gang in town. There's no shame in backing down now."

"No way, man. Insurance is counting on me!" Jimmy boldly walked right up to the entrance.

A five-hundred-pound cyborg gorilla was working the door. "Hit the bricks, human."

"Hey, aren't you the same gorilla from that other bar?"

"Do I know you?"

"Dude, we talked like a couple hours ago!"

The gorilla shrugged. "You puny Homo sapiens all look the same to me. But sure, the way the economy is now, I need two jobs just to put peanut butter and grubs on the table. Not all of us gorillas can get fancy insurance jobs like Amy. Some of us got to work for a living."

"Yeah, tough story, bro."

The bartender joined them. "What's taking so long? Oh, hey, Harambe."

"'Sup, Danny."

"Second job, huh? Me, too. I teach interpretive dance at the community college."

Fascinating as this was, Jimmy really didn't have time for dicking around. That checkout line at Home Depot had taken *forever*. "Anyways, same deal. I've got to go in and rough these guys up for information. So, step aside."

"No can do, buddy." The gorilla jerked one massive thumb toward another sign. This one read DOLPHINS ONLY. "No bipeds allowed. Trust me, you don't want to go in there anyway. It's all porpoise strippers eating fish. Real snooty."

"Wait . . . This is a *dolphin bar*? Like literally dolphins? Like those humorless, easily-offended reviewers who are all angry at Mr. Stranger?"

"Dude, Jimmy, I told you on the riot over this was a dolphin bar."

"Yeah, but I thought you meant like Miami Dolphins, like the NFL team."

The gorilla snorted. "There's a football team called the Dolphins? How lame is your universe?"

"I'm a Miami Manatees fan," the bartender proclaimed. "I've even got season tickets."

"So jealous," said the gorilla.

Jimmy started freaking out. He'd read all those one-star reviews. Dolphins seemed hypersensitive and perpetually offended. After the controversy around that audiobook, Muffy had sent out a memo warning everybody to be super careful not to offend any more dolphins. If he went in there and started kicking porpoise butt, Mr. Stranger would get even more bad reviews! Jimmy would never get his job back. He'd be like . . . *extra fired*.

"Oh crap. Oh crap. What've I done? We gotta go."

Only, while Jimmy had been distracted talking to the bouncer, his mob had grown restless, stolen a city bus, and were in the process of driving it toward the front door really fast.

"Stop! Stop!" Jimmy jumped up and down, waving his arms. "Noooo!"

Only the driver couldn't hear him over the roar of the engine. "This is for you, Jimmy the Intern! *To Valhalla shiny and chrome!*"

Luckily, the gorilla had reflexes befitting a mighty silverback, and he scooped up Jimmy and the bartender, and leapt out of the way right before impact. The cinderblock wall exploded into fragments as the bus flipped end over end through the dolphin bar. The mob ran through the smoking breach, eager to put boot to blowhole.

The gorilla bouncer lifted his head as debris rained down around them. "Aw, come on!"

"Trust me, dude, the version of you on my home planet got it way worse," Jimmy said.

The gorilla groaned. "I am soooo gonna get fired for this."

"You and me both!" Though, technically, he was already fired. Causing an interdimensional incident was like the cherry on top of today's poop sundae. However, Wendell was still missing, so Jimmy still had a job to do. Did rogue TV detectives ever give up just because they accidentally caused a post-apocalyptic maniac to steal a bus and crash it through a bar full of dolphins? Not that he knew of! To hell with the consequences!

"Cover me! I'm going in!" Jimmy sprang to his feet and ran for the hole.

"Cover you from what?" the bartender shouted back.

"I don't know! That's just what they always yell in the movies!"

Since these were animals who lived in the ocean, Jimmy had kind of expected the place to be filled with water. Instead, the interior of the bar was all strobe lights and techno music, conveniently perfect for a fight scene. It turned out that when dolphins wanted to party on land, all they needed to do was turn up a humidifier and it was all good.

Jimmy's army was slugging it out with a whole bunch of rowdy dolphins. It had already turned into a giant rumble. Dudes were getting tossed into mirrors, lots of kung fu, that sort of thing. Dolphins might be a bunch of easily offended prima donnas on the Internet, but it turned out in real life they could *throw down*.

He narrowly dodged a flipper. Then a tail swept his legs out from under him. Jimmy got up, only to have another dolphin shatter a chair over his head. "That was a dick move!"

But that dolphin was fresh out of pity, and it grabbed Jimmy by the shirt collar, picked him up, and slid him down the bar. Jimmy crashed face first through a bunch of bottles and fish sticks before flying off the end and onto the floor.

"I'm not leaving until somebody tells me where Wendell is!"

Jimmy struggled back to his feet, only to get nailed in the head by another chair. "Oooof! What is up with all the friggin' chairs! You dudes can't even sit!"

The dolphin held up one flipper and dramatically twirled open a butterfly knife.

"Whoa, easy there! You don't want to do something you'll regret."

The dolphin looked over incredulously at the upside-down bus in the middle of their dance floor, then back to Jimmy, as if to say *are you shitting me, human?* Then it lunged for him.

Jimmy scurried back, and then grabbed a butter knife off the bar. He held it out defensively. "I'm warning you, I've played a whole lot of Fruit Ninja!"

Only before the dolphin could gut Jimmy like . . . well . . . a fish, a bunch of flashbangs went off, disorienting the combatants. A hole was blown through the ceiling, and a shadowy figure dropped through, landing smoothly next to the knife-wielding dolphin.

"You've made quite the mess of things, Jimmy."

"Mr. Stranger! What're you doing here?"

"I was about to ask you the same thing," Tom Stranger said as he used a sweet judo throw to toss the dolphin on its snout. "But there is no time for chitchat."

A big crew of dolphins was heading their way. Jimmy's army had gotten trounced fairly quickly and were in full retreat. Tom Stranger took up a fighting stance.

"Kick their ass, Mr. Stranger!"

"There is no need for violence, my dolphin friends. I merely seek information pertaining to the whereabouts of my client. Let us resolve this peacefully, then I will force these hooligans to leave your establishment, and I will arrange for this young man to pay for all the damages and any emotional distress he has caused."

"Wait . . . What?"

"Silence, Jimmy. Grownups are talking. Now, please, let us be reasonable."

The biggest dolphin ever swaggered up. He was wearing a bunch of gold chains and had prison tats from SeaWorld. "INSERT DOLPHIN NOISE HERE"

"That is a terribly cruel thing to say about my mother."

The dolphins charged. Having been left with no choice, Tom Stranger responded. It was flipper against fist. Only Interdimensional Insurance Agents fight like watching a Jet Li movie on fast forward, so the dolphins never had a chance. He clothes-lined one, body-slammed another, and when they inevitably threw a chair at him, Mr. Stranger caught it and flung it right back, knocking that jerky dolphin right out the front window and into the street.

There was a *cha-chunk* noise as the dolphin behind the bar racked a shotgun. Only before it could fire, Muffy appeared and stuck a giant plasma cannon against its nose.

"Drop it, you cetacean son of a bitch, before I blast you into chum."

"Ms. Wappler, please! Remember we are trying not to be so culturally insensitive."

"Sorry, Mr. Stranger."

Inappropriate or not, the dolphin put the shotgun down. The techno music had stopped. The floor was covered in moaning, semiconscious dolphins and humans. The knock-down, drag-out fight was over.

"I swept the place, Mr. Stranger. They've got a money laundering operation, and a meth lab in the basement, but no sign of Wendell anywhere."

"Drat." He looked over at Jimmy, who was busy picking splinters out of his hair. "I know your world is remarkably odd, but are you unfamiliar with the concept of how employment works?"

"I know I got fired, but I was going to prove those evaluations wrong and take care of this claim."

"Strange . . . As statistically improbable as it sounds, even deprived of the firm's resources you still somehow figured out that this pod of criminal dolphins hired out some of their cartel assassins to a secret cabal of shady businessmen to thwart a hostile takeover, in the same amount of time it took me to come to the same conclusion."

"Uh, yeah, that's like totally what I was thinking happened."

Mr. Stranger seemed confused. He looked at Muffy, who was blowing a bubble. She shrugged.

"So do I get my job back?"

"Hmmm . . . We will revisit the accuracy of our employee evaluations later." He went over to the big boss dolphin and picked him up by his dorsal fin. "We know Wendell was taken by members of your pod. Now talk."

The prison-hardened dolphin made an extremely rude gesture. Which was saying something since it was kind of limited, not having fingers and all.

Jimmy realized that they'd been joined by some of the Junior Associates. They were all taller than he was and super buffed. Plus they were like smart and good at stuff. To be honest, they made Jimmy feel a little dumpy and inadequate.

Face-Punch went over to the Alpha Dolphin. "A tough guy, huh? Back on my planet we had a way of making dolphins talk. I'll need a hair dryer and a ShamWow."

"*Nyet*," said McSpetsnaz. "There is no time for reverse waterboarding. There is deep fryer in kitchen. We should see how much dolphin can fit."

"I respect your enthusiasm, Junior Associates, but inserting sentient beings into deep fat fryers is against company policy. Such barbarity is better suited for firms like Conundrum and Company or United Airlines. " Tom Stranger sighed and released the dolphin. "Besides, if we engage in atrocities, we will be plagued with negative dolphin reviews forever."

Jimmy thought back to the profound bartender wisdom of that Danny Trejo guy. "We could just try asking him nicely."

Tom Stranger didn't seemed convinced, but Jimmy *was* on a roll. "Very well."

"Cool. I got this. Okay, Mr. Dolphin Mob Boss dude. I'm really sorry about the bus crash. With all due respect and stuff, we really need to get this manatee back, so could you like do us a solid and help us out?"

The dolphin studied Jimmy with his beady, shifty, little black eyes, and slowly nodded in agreement.

"See?" Jimmy turned around and grinned. "Told you guys—"

Then the dolphin grabbed yet another chair and broke that one over Jimmy's head, too.

"Enough of this foolishness and carrying on." Tom Stranger put the evil dolphin in a headlock and squeezed. "I tried being polite, but if I am to receive a one-star review in pursuit of my duties, so be it. Where is the manatee?"

From Jimmy's new position on the floor, he had a good view out the big hole in the wall. At first he thought he was hallucinating from all those traumatic brain injuries, but the big thing outside seemed pretty real. It looked like a gigantic spaceship was rising out of the ocean. "Uh, Mr. Stranger?"

"Where, curse you, where?" Mr. Stranger shouted as the dolphin's face turned from grey to purple. Jimmy reached over and started tugging on his pant leg. "What?"

Jimmy pointed at the big warship that was rising into the sky until it blotted out the sun. It was like a sleek, manatee version of the Space Battleship Yamato. It began blaring a warning through loudspeakers as it hovered over the beach.

"*FLOOOOOO.*"

Tom Stranger dropped the obstinate dolphin. "For those of you who do not speak the language, the manatees have dispatched ships like this to a hundred worlds as part of a *punitive expedition.* They just declared the land mammals have one hour to return Wendell which, all things considered, is a remarkably merciful time frame, or the perpetuators will taste their righteous vengeance."

"That doesn't sound too bad," Jimmy said hopefully. "For everybody other than the perps obviously."

"Except historically, manatees aren't very good at target identification," said Face-Punch. "Back on my home world, off the coast of Innsmouth, a manatee strike team mistook King Triton for Dagon. It was the worst friendly fire incident of the Deep War."

"Oh, man, not Ariel's dad!"

"The claims paperwork still haunts my nightmares. Dead flounders and talking crabs everywhere . . . Sorry, Jimmy. Where I'm from *The Little Mermaid* is considered a very tragic movie. We've got to do something, Mr. Stranger."

"You are correct, Junior Associate." He began dragging the evil dolphin over toward the hole. "I'll start by turning this miscreant over to the manatees."

The dolphin thrashed in terror. "INSERT DOLPHIN NOISE HERE"

"Begging for mercy will do you no good. Manatees laugh at the Geneva Convention. Now do you want to talk?"

"INSERT DOLPHIN NOISE HERE"

"See? That wasn't so hard. Thank you for your cooperation." He karate-chopped the dolphin and knocked it unconscious.

"What just happened?"

"Now I know where the kidnappers are. Sadly, I was just in that reality. Come, Junior Associates, we need to get back to Jimmy's home dimension." Scowling, he looked at the battleship looming overhead. "And we must hurry."

"Yeah, man. It's like high noon out there."

"Worse. It's *nigh hoon.*"

❖ CHAPTER SIX ❖
Tom Networks on the Golf Course

Somewhere over Florida
Earth #169-J-00561

THE STRANGER & Stranger battlemech blasted through the dimensional rift and tore across the sky at Mach 3. Tom, Muffy, Jimmy, and the three Junior Associates were all crowded into the cockpit, making Tom glad that he had purchased a battlemech with a roomy interior.

After the dolphin crime lord had admitted that it was his crew who had been hired to kidnap Wendell, Tom had quickly figured out the entire complicated plot. Someone was trying to stop the CorreiaTech merger by pitting two of Tom's clients against each other. The damages would be astronomical. The paperwork never-ending.

Muffy was looking at a spreadsheet. "Mr. Stranger, if this incident causes an interdimensional war, we insure *both* sides! Whoever is found at fault, the payout would ruin our third quarter numbers."

"And millions of innocents would die."

"Oh, yeah, that too. Total bummer."

"I shudder to think of all the customer dissatisfaction that could cause." Tom pounded one fist against the control panel. "*Not on my watch*! Prepare yourselves, Junior Associates. We will be over the drop zone shortly. Somewhere inside that compound the dolphins have hidden Wendell. The humans there are unaware that they are being set up, but they will attempt to defend themselves, as will the manatee raiders. We will split into teams to cover more ground. You must find Wendell, secure him, and avoid harming any of our clients, human or manatee. Stun weapons only."

"What about dolphins?" asked McSpetsnaz.

"For them you may set your Wombats to *mulch*. There is our destination, the Mar-a-Lago Resort and Presidential Golf Retreat."

"All signals are being jammed," Hardsack shouted. "I can't make contact with the clients."

There was a huge manatee battleship floating ahead of them. It began firing its particle beam cannons.

"Taking evasive maneuvers." Tom's super-quick reflexes saved the day as he pulled the stick and rolled the mech between the death rays. Of course, Jimmy had unbuckled his seat belt in order to get a drumstick from the Kentucky Fried Velociraptor to-go bucket and wound up smashed against the ceiling by centrifugal force. One of the manatee's rail guns got lucky and blew a hole through their shields and shattered the window.

Muffy reached out with her robot hand and snagged Jimmy by the sleeve right before he would have gotten sucked out the hole. "Seat belts are company policy for a reason, Jimmy! Why do I even write all those safety briefings if you dipsticks never bother to read them?"

Jimmy screamed incoherently in response.

"Well I, for one, appreciate your timely emails, Ms. Wappler." Tom grimaced as one of the mech's arms was torn off. Manatees were incredibly lethal marksmen, and despite Tom's *Top Gun*-like piloting skills, the mech took several more hits.

"We are going down. Now remember, team, this America is a new client. Prior to my saving their previous vice president from Ball Sharks, they were insured with Conundrum and Company. Let's show them what proper customer service looks like."

As the flaming mech hurtled toward the ground, the Junior Associates began bailing out. Since each of them was rated fairly high on the Grylls Survivability Scale, they didn't even bother with parachutes. An impact at this velocity was only sufficient to kill four or five Bear Grylls, tops. Unfortunately, not all of his team were up for such strenuous activity. "By the way, Ms. Wappler, would you kindly stick a jet pack on Jimmy or something? I would hate for him to explode on impact."

"So does this mean that Jimmy is rehired, sir?"

Tom glanced over at the screaming intern as he flailed back and forth in the thousand-mile-an-hour fire wind over the hull breach, through which could be seen the ground rushing up to violently meet them.

"Well, it was rather sloppy, but he did provide some quality customer service to our client today. I think that perhaps Jimmy, coming from such an outlandish and silly universe, may actually turn out to be a benefit. At times it's as if his very presence alters the laws of probability. Let's give him another chance."

"*Aaaaaaaaahhhhaaaaaaahhhhaaaaaaaa!*"

"You are most welcome, Jimmy."

"Aw, that was really nice of you." Muffy shoved an anti-gravity belt into Jimmy's arms, and then let him career wildly into the atmosphere. "Let's face it, Mr. Stranger, you're really a big softie." Then Muffy unbuckled, tucked her arms to her sides, and smoothly flew through the hole.

Needing to draw the manatees' fire, Tom stayed in his crippled mech, wrestling with the controls as missiles exploded all around. He activated his personal energy shield as the cabin was engulfed in flames. He'd already gotten feathers all over this suit today; getting charred to a crisp would make him look completely unprofessional.

The mech was headed right for the golf course. Trying to minimize casualties and maximize customer satisfaction, Tom aimed for a water feature on the fourth hole. Except a manatee photon cannon blasted his stabilizers into shrapnel and the controls seized up. The mech went into an out-of-control spin and slammed into the green at several times terminal velocity, erupting in a huge fireball.

Miles above, the manatee gunners high-flippered. Which is sort of like a high five, but you get the idea. They hadn't even known what they were shooting at, but manatees simply loved to blow shit up.

Jimmy the Intern somehow managed not to die. Luckily for him, he got the anti-gravity thingy figured out right before he would have been turned into sidewalk pizza. According to the help menu, the device created a *repellant force field*, not that Jimmy understood what those words meant. Unfortunately, he cranked it up a little too high, and ended up bouncing on impact like he was riding a giant hamster ball, through a bunch of trees, a flock of very startled ducks, and directly into a big glass window, which shattered, and then the stupid belt shorted out as he skidded through a luncheon on his face.

"Whoa." He groaned as he sat up. If it wasn't for all the bruises and the sick carpet burn on his forehead, that landing would have been *Die Hard*-level cool. Then Jimmy realized he was being stared at by a whole bunch of old guys in tuxedos and rich ladies with furs and little dogs in their purses. This place was *really* fancy. They had like monocles and stuff. He looked up and saw that he had crashed through a big banner that read WELCOME WORLD LEADERS.

They were staring at him in shocked silence. Jimmy waved. "Hey, everybody. Don't mind me."

"Where did you come from, young man?"

"He fell out of the sky!"

"Well, we started in outer space, but no biggie. I'm just your friendly neighborhood insurance guy."

"It's like the commercials!" cried Chancellor Angela Merkel. "If you say the incantation, insurance agents will suddenly materialize."

"*Like a good neighbor, State Farm is there,*" sang the president of China. He looked around expectantly, but then got disappointed when nobody else appeared out of thin air.

"Wrong company, dudes. I'm not like Beetlejuice or something." Jimmy got up and brushed the broken glass off his clothes. He was feeling pretty awesome. Nothing builds confidence like a near-death experience and getting your job back. Super smooth, he whipped out a business card. "Stranger & Stranger, for all your interdimensional insurance needs. Call us for a free rate quote."

"This is all so very exciting!" declared the kid from *High School Musical*, or maybe it was the Prime Minister of Canada Jimmy always got those two mixed up. "These summits have been such a drag since my real da—uh . . . I mean, Fidel Castro died. He was the life of the party."

"But anyways, we're all going to get blown up by that big floating battleship outside, unless any of you guys has seen a manatee around here?"

The world leaders all simultaneously pointed toward the buffet.

Jimmy followed all the fingers, and there, in the middle of the table, past the organic kale gold-leaf truffles, was Wendell T. Manatee, frozen just like Han Solo in carbonite, serving as the decorative centerpiece.

"Friggin' sweet!" He'd done it! *Boom. Evaluate this performance, Muffy!* "Alright, anybody here know how to safely thaw a manatee?" But nobody did, because they were politicians, which meant they were basically useless.

"Some suspicious caterers left that there. We all just assumed the frozen sea cow was an artistic statement about the catastrophic dangers of man-made climate change."

"Okay, I got to ask, is that like actually a real thing or just something you guys made up to mess with people?"

The world leaders all had a good laugh.

There were a few golfers near the impact zone. The mech had plowed a giant crater in the green. Munitions were cooking off, creating a chain of secondary explosions. Fire leapt hundreds of feet into the sky.

"You all saw that. That thing fell right on my ball."

"Yes, Mr. Defense Secretary Mad Dog, sir," said the Secret Service agent serving as the caddy. "You get a mulligan."

"Damned right I do," the SecDef muttered as fiery debris rained down around him.

The President of the United States was sitting in the golf cart, tweeting: *Giant robots falling out of sky. SAD. Probably made in China. BUY AMERICAN!*

Tom Stranger walked out of the pillar of fire, carrying his Doomsday Briefcase, and dusting off his suit. "Pardon my interruption, gentle clients, but there are shenanigans afoot."

The SecDef gave him a polite nod. "Tom."

Tom returned the nod. "Chaos."

"Freeze, scumbag!" shouted the Secret Service agent as he pulled his pistol and aimed it at Tom.

"Damn, you kids are high strung. Relax, Carl. This is just our

Interdimensional Insurance Agent." SecDef pointed his golf club at Tom's chest. "I'm assuming this has something to do with that big grey spaceship up there ruining my view."

"Correct. Did you not receive the manatees' list of demands?"

"That's what that was?" The Secretary of Defense shrugged. "Nobody speaks manatee on this planet."

Carl the Secret Service Agent was putting away his gun. "We ran *floo* through Google Translate for a threat assessment. It came back saying it was about how they *wanted to ravish our porcupines.*"

"Sadly, you typed it incorrectly. The message was *floooooo* with six o's. It is a very nuanced language."

"So majestic," agreed the SecDef.

The President had not looked up from his phone and was still busy tweeting: *Sea Cows come here. Should learn to speak English. Bigly good like we do! BAD.*

"Their message actually said you must turn over their leader or they would declare war."

The Secret Service agent didn't seem impressed. "They're just gassy herbivores. Who cares?"

But SecDef just shook his head. "You know how manatees get all those scars, Carl?"

"Sure, they just float along until they get wacked by speed boats."

"That's what they want you to think. The scarred-up ones are really veterans of the Deep War. You ever been menaced by Fish Men, Carl?"

"No."

"Then thank a manatee . . . and read a friggin' history book once in a while." SecDef turned back to Tom. "I didn't realize that was a manatee vessel. I thought it was just more of those damned obnoxious Space Vegans. But all right, I could use a good fight. Golf is dumb." He chucked his nine iron into the fire. "Waste of a good rifle range. I just snuck out here with the boss because we were sick of listening to those namby-pamby Euro-weenies. How do we best proceed, Tom?"

"They gave you a one-hour ultimatum." A laser beam lanced out of the sky and blasted a nearby tree into splinters. "And it would appear that was about an hour ago . . . Run!"

Explosions rocked the golf course as the manatees began their bombardment. The three of them piled into the golf cart next to the

President, who was still tweeting: *They say manatees don't ruin golf. FAKE NEWS. BUILD A WALL!*

The golf cart took off with a fierce electric hum.

Tom looked up to see that a swarm of fighters had launched from the battleship and were headed their way. "We have incoming."

"Put the hammer down, Carl!" SecDef ordered.

"I'm going as fast as I can, sir!" he cried as they bounced wildly across the green.

The targeting implant in Tom's eye zeroed in on the fighters' weak spots. He drew his Combat Wombat. "Aim for the intakes."

"Roger that." Surprisingly, SecDef had hidden a Stinger missile in his golf bag. "What? I told you I hate this sport. I only ever used the one club for everything. Might as well put something useful in this stupid bag."

"Personally, I find golf to be rather relaxing," Tom said as he began to rapidly blast the oncoming fighters out of the sky, forcing the pilots to eject. Even floating toward the ground, suspended beneath parachutes, the manatees still managed to appear relaxed about the whole thing. As Jimmy would say, they were *pretty chill.*

There were explosions all around them. Tom threw down smoke bombs and nanite swarms for cover. Carl managed to get some serious air by jumping the golf cart over a sand trap. Fighters flashed by, billowing smoke. Chaos downed another fighter with a shrieking surface-to-air missile as tracers zipped back and forth. The President continued tweeting furiously.

Tom activated his communications uplink. "Come in, Junior Associates. Does anyone have eyes on Wendell?"

"*I found him, Mr. Stranger!*"

"Jimmy?" That was certainly improbable, but the intern had a gift, like an idiot savant of insurance. "Well done. We are on the way. Everyone converge on Jimmy's position."

"*I'm just getting him thawed out and . . . Hey. What's that? Oh, crap—*"

Then there was a *thud* noise over the line and Jimmy was suddenly silenced.

"Jimmy? Come in, Jimmy."

But Tom received a bone-chilling answer instead. "INSERT DOLPHIN NOISE HERE"

The line went dead.

"To the clubhouse! And hurry, Agent Carl. Dolphin assassins have assaulted my intern."

"I am *so* confused right now!"

"Serpentine! Serpentine!" bellowed Chaos.

The golf cart zipped wildly across the blasted golf course, narrowly dodging explosions, until they smashed through the convention center's fence and up the stairs. The wild jostling caused the President to make a typo: *Despite the constant negative press covfefe*

But it was too late. He's already hit submit. POTUS narrowed his eyes dangerously and scowled at Carl. The poor Secret Service agent gulped in fear.

"Don't worry. This should all be covered. I'll be back with the claim paperwork shortly." Tom Stranger bailed out of the golf cart and ran into Mar-a-Lago.

Inside, the resort was pandemonium. Desperate now that their plot had been exposed, the remaining dolphins had attacked to keep Jimmy from thawing Wendell. Most of the world leaders had run away or were hiding under tables, except for Bibi Netanyahu who had gleefully Krav Maga'd one dolphin unconscious. Unfortunately, Jimmy had been taken hostage by one of the others. It was hiding behind him, one flipper around Jimmy's neck, while the other flipper held a gun to Jimmy's head.

"Sorry, Mr. Stranger. I tried my best but this *stupid fish* got the drop on me."

Jimmy's use of species slurs were the least of their problems at this point. "Remain calm, Jimmy."

"Don't worry. Do what you've got to do. I've moved way up on the Grylls Survivability Scale since I started. I could probably survive getting shot in the brain. The GSS says I'm as tough as a ficus now."

"Hmmm . . . that comparison would imply you are still vulnerable to things like low humidity, drafts, and overwatering."

"So not even a teensy bit bulletproof?"

Tom shook his head in the negative. "Not even a little bit."

"Well, crap." Jimmy suddenly looked a lot less confident. "Never mind then."

Two more dolphins uncloaked next to the buffet table and leveled their weapons at Tom. He would be able to take them easily, but not in time to save Jimmy. The lead dolphin was gibbering threats about how if Tom didn't surrender, it would blow Jimmy's head off. Tom slowly placed his Combat Wombat and Doomsday Briefcase on the carpet and then raised his hands to show he was now unarmed.

"You might as well surrender. I figured out your scheme. The only thing I do not know is who hired you mercenary scum to start this war."

The dolphin activated its infolink, and a hologram appeared between them. It was the head of a wild-haired, grinning, fat man— sort of like a low-rent Guy Fieri only with blue hair. Tom groaned when he saw his rival Interdimensional Insurance Agent, nemesis, and all around jerk face, Jeff Conundrum, appear. "Not you again."

"Heya, Stranger Things."

"You can't be behind this. I left you trapped in Hell."

"Yeah, and that place really sucked! Thanks a lot for ditching me there, by the way. It was all nightmare suffering, grumpy torture demons, and it's really humid so everybody always has swamp butt. Only Hell couldn't hold me, Tommy boy. I escaped! But while I was there, in between painful fiery pitchfork pokings, I came up with this nefarious master plan. Pretty cool, huh?"

"Why would you do all this, Jeff?"

"Easy. Conundrum and Company insures a bunch of those evil companies. If the merger went through, they'd fall under your Premium Platinum Plan and I'd lose all that business. Wendell the financial wizard had to go. So I hired these fanatical dolphin separatists to do my dirty work, knowing you'd be too PC to risk hurting their feelings after your last snafu. Then I started dropping clues that the bums on this loser planet were the guilty party. That's what they get for dumping my coverage and switching to you!"

"But why go through all the effort to rile up the manatees and frame this universe for the crime?"

"That was the best part, Strange Brew. *Revenge!* No matter how it turned out, one of your clients was going to be dissatisfied. You've won Number One in Customer Satisfaction for three years running. I was going to break your winning streak!" Jeff laughed maniacally.

"You would cause an interdimensional war just to keep me from being voted Number One in Customer Service for a fourth year in a row?" Tom whistled. Jeff Conundrum hadn't been quite right in the head for a long time, and apparently a stay in Hell hadn't improved him any. "That's evil even by your standards, Jeff."

"Yeah, psycho," Jimmy chimed in. "That's all sorts of messed up." But then the dolphin thumped Jimmy over the head with the pistol so he quit talking.

"Well, I for one thought it sounded like a perfectly clever plan," squeaked one of the world leaders from beneath a table.

"Shut up, Trudeau! Nobody ever cares what Canada thinks about anything!" Jeff Conundrum roared. "Any second now, Tom, manatee commandos will kick in the door, and when they see their hero looking like a big freeze pop next to the hors d'oeuvres, they'll be so mad they'll bust a cap on this whole planet. I'll keep my business. You'll not win Number One in Customer Satisfaction *and* you'll be dead. So I win! I win big this time, Tom!"

But Tom's keenly-honed Insurance Agent instincts had noticed something the dolphins had not. Before they had appeared, Jimmy had been chipping away at Wendell's block of ice, and a crack had formed. The crack had continued spreading while Jeff had been monologing. *Villains never learn.*

"You'll never get away with this, Jeff."

"What're you going to do, Tom? Make a move and your intern gets it!"

"I personally do not need to do anything. Company policy says that a Level Ten claim requires a team of agents in order to render maximum customer service . . . Face-Punch, are you in position?"

"*I'm only five thousand meters away, sir,*" the Junior Associate answered over their comlink. "*Piece of cake.*"

"What does cake have to do with anything?"

Jeff Conundrum was confused, but he was only hearing half the conversation. "Who is getting punched with cake now, huh?"

"*Sorry, Mr. Stranger. Jimmy's use of slang is contagious. I meant I am ready to dispense this claim with extreme prejudice.*"

"Then let us *earn* those one-star dolphin reviews. Fire."

BOOM!

A bullet hole appeared in the wall. The shot was so close that it cut off Jimmy's man bun before striking its intended target. The hostage-taking dolphin was sent hurtling across the buffet.

"Oh, man!" Jimmy had been drenched in dolphin puree. "Right in the blowhole!"

The other dolphins reacted, but not quickly enough.

Tom had known the sonic crack of the Junior Associate's Sniper Wombat would further weaken the block of ice. It shattered and Wendell T. Manatee fell out. The dolphins looked up in terror as they were engulfed in shadow, but it was too late. "*HOOOOON!*" And they were crushed beneath Wendell's sleek blubber.

The smoke was clearing. The dolphin terrorists were down. "Are you unharmed, Wendell and Jimmy?"

Wendell, always calm under pressure, nodded at Tom in the affirmative, but he was already busy contacting his people on his comlink to call off their armada.

"Kinda." Jimmy held up the sad ball of hair that had once been his glorious hipster topknot.

"I'm okay, too!"

"No one asked you, Justin Trudeau." Tom's home world hadn't even had a Canada. They'd just had North Idaho and French Idaho. He turned his attention back to the hologram of Jeff, who was looking rather flustered at the sudden carnage.

"Okay, I'll admit I wasn't expecting you to mulch my dolphins that hard-core."

"That is the difference between us, Jeff. I understand that being a good agent isn't about the customer satisfaction surveys or the awards. It's about doing what you know in your hearts is the best thing for your clients." He turned toward Jimmy and gave him a nod of approval. "And sometimes superior customer service requires following your instincts, no matter how stunningly bad those instincts may seem."

"Thanks, I think?" Jimmy said.

"That's touching, Walker, Texas Stranger."

"That one doesn't even make sense, Jeff."

"I'm running out of things with Strange in the title. So sue me! You may have foiled my plans this time, Tom and Jimmy, but I'll be back. You've not seen the last of Jeff Conundrum!"

"Not this time. The Multiverse has had enough of your bad attitude and lackluster customer service." Tom reached down and picked up his Doomsday Briefcase. "You have gone too far and must be stopped for good."

"What're you going to do about it, smart guy? Huh? You're talking to a hologram of my big awesome head. I'm safely like a billion miles and ten realities away in an armored bunker riding a comet made of Kryptonite."

Tom opened the briefcase. An eerie green glow and a banshee wail gushed out.

"Oooh, scary," Jeff mocked.

"Is this going to be like that part in *Indiana Jones* where ghosts come out and melt our faces off?" Jimmy asked nervously.

"Possible, but unlikely. I had the Ark of the Covenant stacked way in the back." Tom reached inside the briefcase and rummaged around for a bit. He stuck his arm in all the way up to his shoulder, revealing that the briefcase was far bigger on the inside than on the outside. It was also very cluttered with various powerful technologies and artifacts, so it took him a moment to find what he was looking for. Luckily Tom didn't have to use this thing very often. "Ah, here we go." He pulled out a tiny, struggling man, dressed all in green, with a four-leaf clover in his hat.

"Is that a friggin' leprechaun?" Jimmy asked.

"Oh no," squeaked the hologram of Jeff Conundrum, suddenly afraid.

"Which feckin' gobshites dare summon me! Oh, heya, Tom. Ye got two wishes left, then I'm free. Back to me cereal empire!"

"I am aware, Fergus." Leprechauns were a cross-dimensional menace and all-around pain in the butt, but sometimes agents had to make sacrifices.

"Who do ye want me to implode now? I still feel a wee bit badly about what I did to yer carpet and yer HR department from last time."

Wendell covered his eyes with his flippers.

"No implosions. I merely wish for you to bring Jeff Conundrum here."

"I know that Conudrum, the sap. I called his help line once. Spent two hours getting the runaround from a See 'n Say. *Dog goes woof*, me arse. This wish is on the house."

"Whoa, Tom, buddy, let's talk this out like reasonable insurance—"

The leprechaun snapped his tiny fingers and the real Jeff

magically appeared in the room with them. "—professionals." Jeff looked around. "Oh, crap."

The president of China clapped his hands in delight. "It works! I did not even have to sing the song this time!"

"Now, Tom, boyo, let me tell ye of me magically delicious Lucky Charms. Ye skip the milk and soak 'em direct in whiskey—" Tom shoved the leprechaun roughly back into the briefcase. He had better things to do than listen to the crazed ramblings of a cereal-addicted marshmallow junkie.

Some manatee commandos hovered into the resort in their power armor, led by Muffy "Sparkles" Wappler, who was chewing her bubble gum in a loud and most satisfied manner. "Just like I told you guys, here's your culprit." She gestured at Jeff Conundrum. "He's all yours."

"No! Not manatee justice. Please, send me back to Hell instead."

Wendell's roughnecks grabbed Conundrum by his neon glowing suspenders and dragged him away as he kicked and struggled. "You'll still lose, Tom! Nobody's customer service is good enough to fix this mess! Mu-wha-ha-ha-ha—" but manatees have no patience for gloating super villain laughs, so they "accidentally" banged Jeff's head against the door frame on the way out.

Tom looked around. Past the cowering world leaders and flattened dolphins, through the broken window, the golf course still burned. The President had wandered in and was composing a snarky tweet. It would be all over social media. Sadly, Jeff was right. This claim was a big mess, and it would take a lot of work to satisfy these customers.

But it was moments like this which separated outstanding insurance agents from the merely great.

"It's time to roll up our sleeves, team."

❖ EPILOGUE ❖
Mandatory Overtime

SEVERAL GRUELING HOURS LATER, Tom was alone on Home Office World, putting the finishing touches on the settlement paperwork and thinking about his productive workday.

Since they were so fiscally responsible, the manatees had accepted full responsibility for all the damages they had caused against all non-dolphin actors. So they'd not even needed to go to Arbitration. Because of the exchange rate between Wendell's ultra high-tech home world and Jimmy's relatively backward Earth, it didn't even cost them much. The manatees repaired the Mar-a-Lago golf course for less than their daily lettuce budget.

But then it had gotten personal. The negotiations had almost broken down over the pain and suffering payouts. Both sides were proud, hard-headed negotiators, and both had been wronged. A respected neutral statesman had to be brought in from off world to mediate. Adam Baldwin was paid handsomely for his time.

Eventually, it was decided that the President of Earth #169-J-00561 would be compensated for the pain and suffering caused by his infamous typo with a one-year supply of Kentucky Fried Velociraptor Extra Crispy Taco Bowls. A settlement which Tom had to admit he was a little envious of. Carl the Secret Service Agent was able to keep his job. The Secretary of Defense declared today to have been the finest round of golf he'd ever played.

Tom had no idea what happened to Justin Trudeau, but he usually did not concern himself with world leaders from any country which did not at least have its own aircraft carrier.

Harambe the Gorilla from Earth #984-A-3256 had, in fact, been fired from his bouncer job due to the bus incident, but Tom recognized talent when he saw it. After interviewing with Muffy, it was decided the gorilla would start on Monday as their new HR manager.

The dolphin home worlds disavowed the fanatical dolphin separatists hired as mercenaries by Jeff Conundrum. They also said they had no idea what Tom was talking about when he brought up all those "offended" one-star reviews. Tom remained suspicious of their denials.

Even though his evil company merger deal had fallen apart, overall CorreiaTech Prime had been very pleased with the outcome of his Level Ten claim. He ended up making a great deal of money that afternoon selling anti-human weapon systems to the manatees and anti-manatee weapon systems to the humans, in preparation for potential future conflicts. Then he'd secretly made even more money under the table selling both types of weapons to some really vengeful dolphins. The Interdimensional Lord of Hate was kind of a dick like that.

As for rogue insurance agent Jeff Conundrum, he had been taken to the dreaded manatee black-site prison known only as *Under-Gitmo*. Which, despite the name, was actually beneath a lake in Minnesota.

In order to thank his rescuers and to apologize for his followers' overly enthusiastic vigilante behavior, Wendell the Manatee had thrown a pool party and invited all the humans who had been so terribly wronged. All of the supermodels and rock stars who followed Wendell on Twitter also attended. Tom was not a fan of such frivolity, but he had excused his exhausted team to go to the celebration. *What the heck*? They had earned it, and it was the weekend.

Everyone had a fine time. Despite Conundrum's best efforts, it appeared that customer satisfaction had been brought to the Multiverse once more.

Tom had briefly joined them at the Mar-a-Lago Presidential Water Slide Park. However, he was too preoccupied with work to partake in the festivities. Jimmy, on the other hand, did not have that issue. He had already declared himself Beer Pong Champion of the Multiverse, and then gotten into a drunken slap fight when he'd accused one of Wendell's posse of "manateesplaining." (In his defense, Jimmy had been in a bad mood because it turned out all the contestants in the wet T-shirt contest were lady sea cows). Luckily the fight had been broken up by the Swedish Bikini Team before anyone had been hurt.

Frankly, Jimmy was totally unsuited for Interdimensional Insurance. Yet, somehow, he had still managed to save the day. There was no rational or logical explanation for that. It was enough to make Tom question his earlier decision to rehire Jimmy as his intern.

But then there had been a glimmer of hope. Tom had been having a coworker-appropriate conversation with Muffy, when someone had tossed a head of cabbage to the hungry manatees loafing in the pool. Jimmy had seen this and, without hesitation, sprung into action.

"Ambassador Cabgar! NOOOO!" Jimmy leapt into the pool and begun fighting to save what he'd wrongfully assumed was a potential client. "Get your filthy snouts off him!" He tore a leaf from a manatee's mouth. "You monsters! Spit him out." He grabbed that manatee by the jowls and shook him. "Spit! Give it! Bad water cow! Bad!"

It was in that moment that Tom understood. Though Jimmy may have only had one heart, it was in the right place. He was terrible at quite literally everything else, but Jimmy really did care about their customers. So Tom decided then and there that he would do everything in his power to help Jimmy achieve his true insurance potential. Of course, the manatee commandos did not like having their dinner interrupted by a drunken human, so they began to kick the living crap out of poor Jimmy.

"You think maybe we should step in before they drown him, Mr. Stranger?"

"No. I think we shall consider this a *teachable moment*. Have a pleasant weekend, Ms. Wappler."

"See ya Monday!" Muffy said as she wandered off to try to get Adam Baldwin's autograph.

Then Tom had returned to Home Office World to wrap up their paperwork. Late that night, as he made an addendum to subsection 14, paragraph 4, appendix J of the claim, Tom Stranger smiled, because he knew he had the best job in the Multiverse.

I told the story about how Tom Stranger *came to be in the last Target Rich Environment, but it is kind of fun how Mike Kupari gave me an idea for some really silly blog posts, and those somehow turned into a bestselling series of audiobooks narrated by a famous actor. I recently completed Tom Stranger 3, Apocalypse Cow.*

One fun note, on all those bits where it said INSERT DOLPHIN NOISE HERE, *we used the same exact dolphin sounds for all of those dialog bits with wildly different meanings. It's a very nuanced language.*

❖ ❖ ❖